ZE[illegible]

PHILOSOPH[illegible]NE

RELIGION OF THE SAMURAI

KAITEN NUKARIYA

Edited by Robert Buratti

SUB ROSA PUBLISHING

ISBN: 978-0-9872078-8-3

CONTENTS

INTRODUCTION

Buddhism is geographically divided into two schools[1] —the Southern, the older and simpler, and the Northern, the later and more developed faith. The former, based mainly on the Pali texts[2] is known as Hinayana[3] (small vehicle), or the inferior doctrine; while the latter, based on the various Sanskrit texts,[4] is known as Mahayana (large vehicle), or superior doctrine. The chief tenets of the Southern School are so well known to occidental scholars that they almost always mean the Southern School by the word Buddhism. But with regard to the Northern School very little is known to the West, owing to the fact that most of its original texts were lost, and that

---

[1] The Southern School has its adherents in Ceylon, Burma, Siam, Anan, etc.; while the Northern School is found in Nepal, China, Japan, Tibet, etc.

[2] They chiefly consist of the Four Nikayas: (1) Digha Nikaya (Dirghagamas, translated into Chinese by Buddhaya?as, A.D. 412-413); (2) Majjhima Nikaya (Madhyamagamas, translated into Chinese by Gautama Sanghadeva, A.D. 397-398); (3) Sanyutta Nikaya (Samyuktagamas, translated into Chinese by Gunabhadra, of the earlier Sung dynasty, A.D. 420 479); (4) Anguttara Nikaya (Ekottaragamas, translated into Chinese by Dharmanandi, A.D. 384-385). Out of these Hinayana books, the English translation of twenty-three suttas by Rhys Davids exist in 'Sacred Books of Buddhist,' vols. ii.-iii., and of seven suttas by the same author in 'Sacred Books of the East,' vol. xi.

[3] The Southern Buddhists never call their faith Hinayana, the name being an invention of later Buddhists, who call their doctrine Mahayana in contradistinction to the earlier form of Buddhism. We have to notice that the word Hinayana frequently occurs in Mahayana books, while it does not in Hinayana books.

[4] A catalogue of the Buddhist Canon, K'-yuen-luh, gives the titles of 897 Mahayana sutras, yet the most important books often quoted by Northern Buddhist teachers amount to little more than twenty. There exist the English translation of Larger Sukhavati-vyuha-sutra, Smaller Sukhavati-vyuha-sutra, Vajracchedika-sutra, Larger Prajna-paramita-hradya-sutra, Smaller Prajna-paramita-hrdaya-sutra, by Max M?ller, and Amitayur-dhyana-sutra, by J. Takakusu, in 'Sacred Books of the East,' vol. xlix. An English translation of Saddharma-pundarika-sutra, by Kern, is given in 'Sacred Books of the East,' Vol. xxi. Compare these books with 'Outlines of Mahayana Buddhism,' by D. Suzuki.

the teachings based on these texts are written in Chinese, or Tibetan, or Japanese languages unfamiliar to non-Buddhist investigators.

It is hardly justifiable to cover the whole system of Buddhism with a single epithet[5] 'pessimistic' or 'nihilistic,' because Buddhism, having been adopted by savage tribes as well as civilized nations, by quiet, enervated people as well as by warlike, sturdy hordes, during some twenty-five hundred years, has developed itself into beliefs widely divergent and even diametrically opposed. Even in Japan alone it has differentiated itself into thirteen main sects and forty-four sub-sects[6] and is still in full vigour, though in other countries it has already passed its prime. Thus Japan seems to be the best representative of the Buddhist countries where the majority of people abides by the guiding principle of the Northern School. To study her religion, therefore, is to penetrate into Mahayanism, which still lies an unexplored land for the Western minds. And to investigate her faith is not to dig out the remains of Buddhist faith that existed twenty centuries ago, but to touch the heart and soul of Mahayanism that enlivens its devotees at the present moment.

The object of this little book is to show how the Mahayanistic view of life and of the world differs markedly from that of Hinayanism, which is generally taken as Buddhism by occidentals, to explain how the religion of Buddha has adapted itself to its environment in the Far East, and also to throw light on the existing state of the spiritual life of modern Japan.
For this purpose we have singled out of thirteen Japanese sects the Zen

---

[5] Hinayanism is, generally speaking, inclined to be pessimistic, but Mahayanism in the main holds the optimistic view of life. Nihilism is advocated in some Mahayana sutras, but others set forth idealism or realism.

[6] (1) The Ten Dai Sect, including three sub-sects; (2) The Shin Gon Sect, including eleven sub-sects; (3) The Ritsu Sect; (4) The Rin Zai Sect, including fourteen sub-sects; (5) The So To Sect; (6) The O Baku Sect; (7) The Jo Do Sect, including two sub-sects; (8) The Shin Sect, including ten sub-sects; (9) The Nichi Ren Sect, including nine sub-sects; (10) The Yu Zu Nen Butsu Sect; (11) The Hosso Sect; (12) The Ke Gon Sect; (13) The Ji Sect. Out of these thirteen Buddhist sects, Rin Zai, So To, and O Baku belong to Zen. For further information, see 'A Short History of the Twelve Japanese Buddhist Sects,' by Dr. B. Nanjo.

Sect, [7] not only because of the great influence it has exercised on the nation, but because of the unique position it holds among the established religious systems of the world. In the first place, it is as old as Buddhism itself, or even older, for its mode of practising Meditation has been handed down without much alteration from pre-Buddhistic recluses of India; and it may, on that account, provide the student of comparative religion with an interesting subject for his research.[8]

There exists a society formed by men who have broken with the old creeds of Buddhism, and who call themselves the New Buddhists. It has for its organ 'The New Buddhism,' and is one of the influential religious societies in Japan. We mean by the New Buddhists, however, numerous educated young men who still adhere to Buddhist sects, and are carrying out a reformation.

Thirdly, Buddhist denominations, like non-Buddhist religions, lay stress on scriptural authority; but Zen denounces it on the ground that words or characters can never adequately express religious truth, which can only be realized by mind; consequently it claims that the religious truth attained by Shakya Muni in his Enlightenment has been handed down neither by word of mouth nor by the letters of scriptures, but from teacher's mind to disciple's through the line of transmission until the present day. It is an isolated instance in the whole history of the world's religions that holy scriptures are declared to be 'no more than waste[9] paper by religionists, as done by Zen masters.

Fourthly, Buddhist as well as non-Buddhist religions regard, without

[7] The word Zen is the Sinico-Japanese abbreviation of the Sanskrit Dhyana, or Meditation. It implies the whole body of teachings and discipline peculiar to a Buddhist sect now popularly known as the Zen Sect.

In the second place, in spite of its historical antiquity, ideas entertained by its advocates are so new that they are in harmony with those of the New Buddhists;

[8] Accordingly the statement of these ideas may serve as an explanation of the present movement conducted by young and able reformers of Japanese Buddhism.

[9] Lin Tsi Luh (Rin-zai-roku).

exception, their founders as superhuman beings, but the practisers of Zen hold the Buddha as their predecessor, whose spiritual level they confidently aim to attain. Furthermore, they liken one who remains in the exalted position of Buddhaship to a man bound by a gold chain, and pity his state of bondage. Some of them went even so far as to declare Buddhas and Bodhisattvas to be their servants and slaves.[10] Such an attitude of religionists can hardly be found in any other religion.

Fifthly, although non-Buddhist people are used to call Buddhism idolatry, yet Zen can never be called so in the accepted sense of the term, because it, having a grand conception of Deity, is far from being a form of idol-worship; nay, it sometimes even took an iconoclastic attitude as is exemplified by Tan Hia,[11] who warmed himself on a cold morning by making a fire of wooden statues. Therefore our exposition on this point will show the real state of existing Buddhism, and serve to remove religious prejudices entertained against it.

Sixthly, there is another characteristic of Zen, which cannot be found in any other religion-that is to say, its peculiar mode of expressing profound religious insight by such actions as the lifting up of a hair-brush, or by the tapping of the chair with a staff, or by a loud outcry, and so forth. This will give the student of religion a striking illustration of differentiated forms of religion in its scale of evolution.
Besides these characteristics, Zen is noted for its physical and mental training. That the daily practice of Zazen[12] and the breathing exercise remarkably improves one's physical condition is an established fact. And history proves that most Zen masters enjoyed a long life in spite of their extremely simple mode of living. Its mental discipline, however, is by far more fruitful, and keeps one's mind in equipoise, making one neither passionate nor dispassionate, neither sentimental nor unintelligent, neither

---

10 "Shakya and Maitreya," says Go So, "are servants to the other person. Who is that other person?" (Zen-rin-rui-ju, Vol. i., p. 28).

11 A Chinese Zen teacher, well known for his peculiarities, who died in A.D. 824. For the details of this anecdote, see Zen-rin-rui-ju, Vol. i., P. 39.

12 The sitting-in-meditation, for the full explanation of which see Chapter VIII.

nervous nor senseless. It is well known as a cure to all sorts of mental disease, occasioned by nervous disturbance, as a nourishment to the fatigued brain, and also as a stimulus to torpor and sloth. It is self-control, as it is the subduing of such pernicious passions as anger, jealousy, hatred, and the like, and the awakening of noble emotions such as sympathy, mercy, generosity, and what not. It is a mode of Enlightenment, as it is the dispelling of illusion and of doubt, and at the same time it is the overcoming of egoism, the destroying of mean desires, the uplifting of the moral ideal, and the disclosing of inborn wisdom.

The historical importance of Zen can hardly be exaggerated. After its introduction into China in the sixth century, A.D., it grew ascendant through the Sui (598-617) and the Tang dynasty (618-906), and enjoyed greater popularity than any other sect of Buddhism during the whole period of the Sung (976-1126) and the Southern Sung dynasty (1127-1367). In these times its commanding influence became so irresistible that Confucianism, assimilating the Buddhist teachings, especially those of Zen, into itself and changing its entire aspect, brought forth the so-called Speculative philosophy.[13] And in the Ming dynasty (1368-1659) the principal doctrines of Zen were adopted by a celebrated Confucian scholar, Wang Yang Ming,[14] who thereby founded a school, through which Zen exercised profound influence on Chinese and Japanese men of letters, statesmen, and soldiers.

As regards Japan, it was first introduced into the island as the faith first for the Samurai or the military class, and moulded the characters of many distinguished soldiers whose lives adorn the pages of her history. Afterwards it gradually found its way to palaces as well as to cottages through literature and art, and at last permeated through every fibre of the national life. It is Zen that modern Japan, especially after the Russo-Japanese War, has acknowledged as an ideal doctrine for her rising generation.

---

[13] See 'A History of Chinese Philosophy,' by Ryukichi Endo, and A History of Chinese Philosophy,' by Giichi Nakauchi.

[14] For the life of this distinguished scholar and soldier (1472-1529), see 'A Detailed Life of O Yo Mei' by Takejiro Takase, and also 'O-yo-mei-shutsu-shin-sei-ran-roku.'

CHAPTER I

HISTORY OF ZEN IN CHINA

To-day Zen as a living faith can be found in its pure form only among the Japanese Buddhists. You cannot find it in the so-called Gospel of Buddha anymore than you can find Unitarianism in the Pentateuch, nor can you find it in China and India any more than you can find life in fossils of bygone ages. It is beyond all doubt that it can be traced back to Shakya Muni himself, nay, even to pre-Buddhistic times, because Brahmanic teachers practised Dhyana, or Meditation,[15] from earliest times.

"Compressing his breathings let him, who has subdued all motions, breathe forth through the nose with the gentle breath. Let the wise man without fail restrain his mind, that chariot yoked with vicious horses.

"Let him perform his exercises in a place level, pure, free from pebbles, fire, and dust, delightful by its sounds, its water, and bowers; not painful to the eye, and full of shelters and eaves.

"When Yoga, is being performed, the forms which come first, producing apparitions in Brahman, are those of misty smoke, sun, fire, wind, fire-flies, lightnings, and a crystal moon.

"When, as earth, water, light, heat, and ether arises, the fivefold quality of Yoga takes place, then there is no longer illness, old age, or pain for him who has obtained a body produced by the fire of Yoga.

The first results of Yoga they call lightness, healthiness, steadiness, a good complexion, an easy pronunciation, a sweet odour, and slight excretions "(Cvet. Upanisad, ii. 8-13).

"When the five instruments of knowledge stand still together with the mind, and when the intellect does not move, that is called the highest state.

"This, the firm holding back of the senses, is what is called Yoga.

---

15 "If a wise man hold his body with its three parts (chest, neck, and head) erect, and turn his senses with the mind towards the heart, he will then in the boat of Brahman cross all the torrents which cause fear.

He must be free from thoughtlessness then, for Yoga comes and goes" (Katha Upanisad, ii. 10, 11).

"This is the rule for achieving it (viz., concentration of the mind on the object of meditation): restraint of the breath, restraint of the senses, meditation, fixed attention, investigation, absorption-these are called the sixfold Yoga. When beholding by this Yoga, be beholds the gold-coloured maker, the lord, the person, Brahman, the cause; then the sage, leaving behind good and evil, makes everything (breath, organs of sense, body, etc.) to be one in the Highest Indestructible (in the pratyagatman or Brahman) " (Maitr. Upanisad, vi. 18).

"And thus it has been elsewhere: There is the superior fixed attention (dharana) for him-viz., if he presses the tip of the tongue down the palate, and restrain the voice, mind, and breath, he sees Brahman by discrimination (taraka). And when, after the cessation of mind, he sees his own Self, smaller than small, and shining as thc Highest Self, then, having seen his Self as the Self, he becomes Self-less, and because he is Self-less, he is without limit, without cause, absorbed in thought. This is the highest mystery—viz., final liberation " (Maitr. Upanisad, vi. 20).

Amrtab. Upanisad, 18, describes three modes of sitting-namely, the Lotus-seat (Padmasana), the sitting with legs bent underneath; the mystic diagram seat (Svastika); and the auspicious-seat (Bhadrasana);—while Yogacikha directs the choice of the Lotus-posture, with attention concentrated on the tip of the nose, hands and feet closely joined.

But Brahmanic Zen was carefully distinguished even by early Buddhists[16] as the heterodox Zen from that taught by the Buddha. Our Zen originated in the Enlightenment of Shakya Muni, which took place in his thirtieth year, when he was sitting absorbed in profound meditation under the Bodhi Tree.

The sutra is believed by many Buddhists, not without reason, to be the exposition of that Mahayana doctrine which Acvaghosa restated in his Craddhotpada-castra. The sutra was translated, first, into Chinese by Gunabbadra, in A.D. 443; secondly, by Bodhiruci in A.D. 513; and, thirdly,

---

[16] The anonymous author of Lankavatara-sutra distinguishes the heterodox Zen from the Hinayana Zen, the Hinayana Zen from the Mahayana Zen, and calls the last by the name of the Buddha's Holy Zen.

by Ciksanada in A.D. 700-704. The book is famous for its prophecy about Nagdrajuna, which (according to Dr. Nanjo's translation) is as follows:

"After the Nirvana of the Tathagata,
There will be a man in the future,
Listen to me carefully, O Mahatma,
A man who will hold my law.
In the great country of South,
There will be a venerable Bhiksu
The Bodhisattva Nagarjuna by name,
Who will destroy the views of Astikas and Nastikas,
Who will preach unto men my Yana,
The highest Law of the Mahayana,
And will attain to the Pramudita-bhumi."

It is said that then he awoke to the perfect truth and declared: "All animated and inanimate beings are Enlightened at the same time." According to the tradition[17] of this sect Shakya Muni transmitted his mysterious doctrine from mind to mind to his oldest disciple Mahakacyapa at the assembly hold on the Mount of Holy Vulture, and the latter was acknowledged as the first patriarch, who, in turn, transmitted the doctrine to Ananda, the second

---

[17] The incident is related as follows: When the Buddha was at the assembly on the Mount of Holy Vulture, there came a Brahmaraja who offered the Teacher a golden flower, and asked him to preach the Dharma. The Buddha took the flower and held it aloft in his hand, gazing at it in perfect silence. None in the assembly could understand what he meant, except the venerable Mahakacyapa, who smiled at the Teacher. Then the Buddha said: "I have the Eye and Treasury of Good Dharma, Nirvana, the Wonderful Spirit, which I now hand over to Mahakacyapa." The book in which this incident is described is entitled 'Sutra on the Great Brahman King's Questioning Buddha to Dispel a Doubt,' but there exists no original text nor any Chinese translation in the Tripitaka. It is highly probable that some early Chinese Zen scholar of the Sung dynasty (A.D. 960-1126) fabricated the tradition, because Wang Ngan Shih (O-an-seki), a powerful Minister under the Emperor Shan Tsung (Shin-so, A.D. 1068-1085), is said to have seen the book in the Imperial Library. There is, however, no evidence, as far as we know, pointing to the existence of the Sutra in China. In Japan there exists, in a form of manuscript, two different translations of that book, kept in secret veneration by some Zen masters, which have been proved to be fictitious by the present writer after his close examination of the contents. See the Appendix to his Zen-gaku-hi-han-ron.

patriarch, and so till Bodhidharma, the twenty-eighth[18] patriarch. We have little to say about the historical value of this tradition, but it is worth while to note that the list of the names of these twenty-eight patriarchs contains many eminent scholars of Mahayanism, or the later developed school of Buddhism, such as Acvaghosa,[19] Nagarjuna,[20] Kanadeva,[21] and Vasubhandhu.[22]

The first twenty-three patriarchs are exactly the same as those given in 'The Sutra on the Nidana of transmitting Dharmapitaka,' translated in A.D. 472. King Teh Chwen Tang Iuh (Kei-toku-den-to-roku), a famous Zen history of China, gives two elaborate narratives about the transmission of Right Dharma from teacher to disciple through these twenty-eight patriarchs, to be trusted without hesitation. It would not be difficult for any scholar of

---

[18] The following is the list of the names of the twenty-eight patriarchs:
1. Mahakacyapa. 2. Ananda. 3. Canavasu. 4. Upagupta. 5. Dhrtaka. 6. Micchaka. 7. Vasumitra. 8. Buddhanandi. 9. Buddhamitra. 10. Parcva. 11. Punyayacas. 12. Acvaghosa. 13. Kapimala. 14. Nagarjuna. 15. Kanadeva. 16. Rahulata. 17. Samghanandi. 18. Samghayacas. 19. Kumarata. 20. Jayata. 21. Vasubandhu. 22. Manura. 23. Haklanayacas. 24. Simha. 25. Vacasuta. 26. Punyamitra. 27. Prajnyatara. 28. Bodhidharma.

[19] One of the founders of Mahayana Buddhism, who flourished in the first century A.D. There exists a life of his translated into Chinese by Kumarajiva in A.D. 401-409. The most important of his works are: Mahayanacraddhotpada-castra, Mahalankara-sutra-castra, Buddha-caritakavya.

[20] The founder of the Madhyamika school of Mahayana Buddhism, who lived in the second century A.D. A life of his was translated into Chinese by Kumarajiva in A.D. 401-409. Twenty-four books are ascribed to him, of which Mahaprajñaparamita-castra, Madhyamika-castra, Prajnyadipa-castra, Dvadacanikaya-castra, Astadacakaca-castra, are well known.

[21] Sometimes called Aryadeva, a successor of Nagarjuna. A life of his was translated into Chinese by Kumarajiva in A.D. 401-409. The following are his important works: Cata-castra, 'Castra by the Bodhisattva Deva on the refutation of four heretical Hinayana schools mentioned in the Lankatvatara-sutra'; 'Castra by the Bodhisattva Deva on the explanation of the Nirvana by twenty Hinayana teachers mentioned in the Lankavatara-sutra.'

[22] A younger brother of Asamga, a famous Mahayanist of the fifth century A.D. There are thirty-six works ascribed to Vasubandhu, of which Dacabhumika-castra, Aparimitayus-sutra-castra, Mahapari-nirvana-sutra-castra, Mahayana-catadharmavidyadvara-castra, Vidya-matrasiddhi-tridaca-castra, Bodhicittopadana-castra, Buddha-gotra-castra, Vidyamatrasiddhivincatigatha-castra, Madhyantavibhaga-castra, Abhidharma-koca-castra, Tarka-castra, etc., are well known.

sense to find these statements were made from the same motive as that of the anonymous author who gives a short life, in Dirghagama-sutra, of each of the six Buddhas, the predecessors of Shakya Muni, if he carefully compare the list given above with the lists of the patriarchs of the Sarvastivada school given by San Yin (So-yu died A.D. 518) in his Chuh San Tsung Ki (Shutsu-san zo-ki).

Introduction of Zen into China by Bodhidharma

An epoch-making event took place in the Buddhist history of China by Bodhidharma's coming over from Southern India to that country in about A.D. 520.[23] It was the introduction, not of the dead scriptures, as was repeatedly done before him, but of a living faith, not of any theoretical doctrine, but of practical Enlightenment, not of the relies of Buddha, but of the Spirit of Shakya Muni; so that Bodhidharma's position as a representative of Zen was unique. He was, however, not a missionary to be favourably received by the public. He seems to have behaved in a way quite opposite to that in which a modern pastor treats his flock. We imagine him to have been a religious teacher entirely different in every point from a popular Christian missionary of our age. The latter would smile or try to smile at every face he happens to see and would talk sociably; while the former would not smile at any face, but would stare at it with the large glaring eyes that penetrated to the innermost soul. The latter would keep himself scrupulously clean, shaving, combing, brushing, polishing, oiling, perfuming, while the former would be entirely indifferent to his apparel, being always clad in a faded yellow robe. The latter would compose his sermon with a great care, making use of rhetorical art, and speak with force and elegance; while the former would sit as absolutely silent as the bear, and kick one off, if one should approach him with idle questions.

[23] Buddhist historians differ in opinion respecting the date of Bodhidharma's appearance in China. Compare Chwen Fah Chan Tsung Lun (Den bo sho ju ron) and Hwui Yuen (E-gen).

Bodhidharma and the Emperor Wu

No sooner had Bodhidharma landed at Kwang Cheu in Southern China than he was invited by the Emperor[24] Wu, who was an enthusiastic Buddhist and good scholar, to proceed to his capital of Chin Liang. When he was received in audience, His Majesty asked him: "We have built temples, copied holy scriptures, ordered monks and nuns to be converted. Is there any merit, Reverend Sir, in our conduct?" The royal host, in all probability, expected a smooth, flattering answer from the lips of his new guest, extolling his virtues, and promising him heavenly rewards, but the Blue-eyed Brahmin bluntly answered: "No merit at all." This unexpected reply must have put the Emperor to shame and doubt in no small degree, who was informed simply of the doctrines of the orthodox Buddhist sects. 'Why not,' he might have thought within himself, 'why all this is futile? By what authority does he declare all this meritless? What holy text can be quoted to justify his assertion? What is his view in reference to the different doctrines taught by Shakya Muni? What does he hold as the first principle of Buddhism?' Thus thinking, he inquired: "What is the holy truth, or the first principle?" The answer was no less astonishing: "That principle transcends all. There is nothing holy."

The crowned creature was completely at a loss to see what the teacher meant. Perhaps he might have thought: 'Why is nothing holy? Are there not holy men, Holy Truths, Holy Paths stated in the scriptures? Is he himself not one of the holy men?' "Then who is that confronts us?" asked the monarch again. "I know not, your majesty," was the laconic reply of Bodhidharma, who now saw that his new faith was beyond the understanding of the Emperor.

The elephant can hardly keep company with rabbits. The petty orthodoxy can by no means keep pace with the elephantine stride of Zen. No wonder that Bodhidharma left not only the palace of the Emperor Wu, but also the State of Liang, and went to the State of Northern Wei.[25] There he spent

[24] The Emperor Wu (Bu-Tei) of the Liang dynasty, whose reign was A.D. 502-549.]

[25] Northern Gi dynasty (A.D. 386-534).

nine years in the Shao Lin[26] Monastery, mostly sitting silent in meditation with his face to the wall, and earned for himself the appellation of 'the wall-gazing Brahmin.' This name itself suggests that the significance of his mission was not appreciated by his contemporaries. But neither he was nor they were to blame, because the lion's importance is appreciated only by the lion. A great personage is no less great because of his unpopularity among his fellow men, just as the great Pang[27] is no less great because of his unpopularity among the winged creatures. Bodhidharma was not popular to the degree that he was envied by his contemporary Buddhists, who, as we are told by his biographers, attempted to poison him three times,[28] but without success.

Bodhidharma and his Successor the Second Patriarch

China was not, however, an uncultivated[29] land for the seed of Zen—nay, there had been many practisers of Zen before Bodhidharma. Fourteen Zen sutras, including such important books as Mahanapanadhyana-sutra, Dhyanacarya-dharmasanyjnya-sutra, Dhyanacarya-saptatrimcadvarga-sutra, were translated by Ngan Shi Kao (An-sei-ko) as early as A.D. 148-170. Cullamargabhumi-sutra was translated by K' Yao (Shi-yo) in A.D. 185; Dharmatara-dhyana-sutra by Buddhabhadra in A.D. 398-421; Dhyananisthitasamadhi-dharma-parygya-sutra by Kumarajiva in A.D. 402; 'An Abridged Law on the Importance of Meditation' by Kumarajiva in A.D. 405; Pancadvara-dhyanasutra-maharthadharma by Dharmamitra in A.D. 424-441. Furthermore, Mahayana books closely related to the doctrine of Zen were not unknown to China before Bodhidharma. Pratyutpanna-buddhasammukhavasthita-samadhi was translated by K' Leu Cia Chan (Shi-ru-ga-sen) in A.D. 164-186;

---

[26] Sho-rin-ji, erected by the Emperor Hiao Ming of Northern Wei A.D. 497.

[27] Chwang-tsz in his famous parable compares a great sage with the Pang, an imaginary bird of enormous size, with its wings of ninety thousand miles. The bird is laughed at by wrens and sparrows because of its excessive size.

[28] This reminds us of Nan Yoh Hwui Sz (Nan-gaku-e-shi, died A.D. 577), who is said to have learned Zen under Bodhidharma. He says in his statement of a vow that he was poisoned three times by those who envied him.

[29] The translation of Hinayana Zen sutras first paved the way for our faith.

Vimalakirttinirdeca-sutra, which is much used in Zen, by Kumarajiva in A.D. 384-412; Lankavatara-sutra, which is said to have been pointed out by Bodhidharma as the best explanation of Zen, by Gunabhadra in A.D. 433; Saddharma-pundarika-sutra, in its complete form, by Kumarajiva in A.D. 406; Avatamsaka-sutra by Buddhabhadra in A.D. 418; Mahaparinirvana-sutra by Dharmaraksa in A.D. 423.

If we are not mistaken, Kumarajiva, who came to China A.D. 384, made a valuable contribution towards the foundation of Zen in that country, not merely through his translation of Zen sutras above mentioned, but by the education of his disciples, such as Sang Chao (So-jo, died A.D. 414), Sang Shang (So-sho, whose writings undoubtedly influenced later Zen teachers. A more important personage in the history of Zen previous to the Blue-eyed Brahmin is Buddhabhadra, a well-known Zen master, who came over to China A.D. 406. His translation of Dharmatara-dhyana-sutra (which is said to have been preached by Bodhidharma himself when he was in India) and that of Avatamsaka-sutra may be said without exaggeration to have laid the corner-stone for Zen. He gave a course of lectures on the Zen sutra for the first time in China in A.D. 413, and it was through his instruction that many native practisers of Zen were produced, of whom Chi Yen (Chi-gon) and Huen Kao (Gen-ko) are well known. In these days Zen should have been in the ascendant in India, because almost all Indian scholars-at least those known to us-were called Zen teachers-for instance, Buddhabhadra, Buddhasena, Dharmadhi, and some others were all Zen scholars.

Chinese Buddhist scholars did no less than Indian teachers toward the uprising of Zen. The foremost among them is Hwui Yuen (E-on, died A.D. 414), who practised Zen by the instruction of Buddhabhadra. He founded the Society of the White Lotus, which comprised eighteen eminent scholars of the age among its members, for the purpose of practising Meditation and of adoring Buddha Amitabha. We must not forget that during the Western and the Eastern Tsin (Shin) dynasties (A.D. 265-420) both Taoism and Buddhism grew prosperous to no small extent. And China produced, on the one hand, Taoists of an eccentric type, such as the Seven Wise Men of the Bamboo Forest, while she gave birth to many recluse-like men of letters, such as Tao Yuen Ming (To-yen-mei, died A.D. 427) and some others on the other. Besides there were some scholars who studied

Buddhism in connection with Taoism and Confucianism, and led a secluded life. To the last class of scholars belonged Chwen Hih (Hu dai shi), known as Chwen the Great. He is said to have been accustomed to wear a Confucianist hat, a Buddhist robe, and Taoist shoes. It was in A.D. 534 that he presented a memorial to the Emperor Wu, in which he explained the three grades of good. "The Highest Good consists," says he, "in the emptiness of mind and non-attachment. Transcendence is its cause, and Nirvana is its result. The Middle Good consists in morality and good administration. It results in a peaceful and happy life in Heaven and in Earth. The Lowest Good consists in love and protection of sentient beings." Thus his idea of good, as the reader will see without difficulty, is the result of a compromise of Taoism and Buddhism. Sin Wang Ming (Sin-o-mei, On the Mind-King), one of his masterpieces, together with other minor poems, are still used as a textbook of Zen. This fact unmistakably proves that Taoist element found its way into the constituents of Zen from its very outset in China.

All that he had to do was to wait for an earnest seeker after the spirit of Shakya Muni. Therefore he waited, and waited not in vain, for at last there came a learned Confucianist, Shang Kwang (Shin-ko) by name, for the purpose of finding the final solution of a problem which troubled him so much that he had become dissatisfied with Confucianism, as it had no proper diet for his now spiritual hunger. Thus Shang Kwang was far from being one of those half-hearted visitors who knocked the door of Bodhidharma only for the sake of curiosity. But the silent master was cautious enough to try the sincerity of a new visitor before admitting him to the Meditation Hall. According to a biography[30] of his, Shang Kwang was not allowed to enter the temple, and had to stand in the courtyard covered deep with snow. His firm resolution and earnest desire, however, kept him standing continually on one spot for seven days and nights with beads of the frozen drops of tears on his breast. At last he cut off his left arm with a sharp knife, and presented it before the inflexible teacher to show his resolution to follow the master even at the risk of his life.

[30] King Teh Chwen Tang Luh (Kei-toku-den-to-roku), published by Tao Yuen (Do-gen) A.D. 1004, gives a detailed narrative concerning this incident as stated here, but earlier historians tell us a different story about the mutilation of Shang Kwang's arm. Compare Suh Kas San Chwen (Zoku-ko-so-den) and Hwui Yuen (E-gen).

Thereupon Bodhidharma admitted him into the order as a disciple fully qualified to be instructed in the highest doctrine of Mahayanism.

Our master's method of instruction was entirely different from that of ordinary instructors of learning. He would not explain any problem to the learner, but simply help him to get enlightened by putting him an abrupt but telling question. Shang Kwang, for instance, said to Bodhidharma, perhaps with a sigh: "I have no peace of mind. Might I ask you, sir, to pacify my mind?" "Bring out your mind (that troubles you so much)," replied the master, "here before me! I shall pacify it." "It is impossible for me," said the disciple, after a little consideration, "to seek out my mind (that troubles me so much)." "Then," exclaimed Bodhidharma, "I have pacified your mind." Hereon Shang Kwang was instantly Enlightened. This event is worthy of our notice, because such a mode of instruction was adopted by all Zen teachers after the first patriarch, and it became one of the characteristics of Zen.

Bodhidharma's Disciples and the Transmission of the Law[31]

Bodhidharma's labour of nine years in China resulted in the initiation of a number of disciples, whom some time before his death he addressed as follows: "Now the time (of my departure from this world) is at hand. Say, one and all, how do you understand the Law?" Tao Fu (Do-fuku) said in response to this: "The Law does not lie in the letters (of the Scriptures), according to my view, nor is it separated from them, but it works." The Master said: "Then you have obtained my skin." Next Tsung Chi (So-ji), a nun, replied: "As Ananda[32] saw the kingdom of Aksobhya[33] only once but not twice, so I understand the Law". The master said: "Then you have attained to my flesh." Then Tao Yuh (Do-iku) replied: "The four elements[34]

---

[31] For details, see Chwen Tang Luh and Den Ka Roku, by Kei Zan.
As for the life of Bodhidharma, Dr. B. Matsumoto's 'A Life of Bodhidharma' may well be recommended to the reader.

[32] A favourite disciple of Shakya Muni, and the Third Patriarch of Zen.

[33] The: name means I Immovable,' and represents the firmness of thought.

[34] Earth, water, fire, and air.

are unreal from the first, nor are the five aggregates[35] really existent. All is emptiness according to my view." The master said: "Then you have acquired my bone." Lastly, Hwui Ko (E-ka), which was the Buddhist name given by Bodhidharma, to Shang Kwang, made a polite bow to the teacher and stood in his place without a word. "You have attained to my marrow." So saying, Bodhidharma handed over the sacred Kachaya, [36] which he had brought from India to Hwui Ko, as a symbol of the transmission of the Law, and created him the Second Patriarch.

The Second and the Third Patriarchs

After the death of the First Patriarch, in A.D. 528, Hwui Ko did his best to propagate the new faith over sixty years. On one occasion a man suffering from some chronic disease called on him, and requested him in earnest: "Pray, Reverend Sir, be my confessor and grant me absolution, for I suffer long from an incurable disease." "Bring out your sin (if there be such a thing as sin)," replied the Second Patriarch, "here before me. I shall grant you absolution." "It is impossible," said the man after a short consideration, "to seek out my sin." "Then," exclaimed the master, "I have absolved you. Henceforth live up to Buddha, Dharma, and Samgha."[37] "I know, your reverence," said the man, "that you belong to Samgha; but what are Buddha and Dharma?" "Buddha is Mind itself. Mind itself is Dharma. Buddha is identical with Dharma. So is Samgha." "Then I understand," replied the man, "there is no such thing as sin within my body nor without it, nor anywhere else. Mind is beyond and above sin. It is no other than Buddha and Dharma." Thereupon the Second Patriarch saw the man was well qualified to be taught in the new faith, and converted him, giving him the name of Sang Tsung (So-san). After two years' instruction and discipline,

---

[35] (1) Rupa, or form; (2) Vedana, or perception; (3) Samjnya, or consciousness; (4) Karman (or Samskara), or action; (5) Vijnyana, or knowledge.

[36] The clerical cloak, which is said to have been dark green. It became an object of great veneration after the Sixth Patriarch, who abolished the patriarchal system and did not hand the symbol over to successors.

[37] The so-called Three Treasures of the Buddha, the Law, and the Order.

he[38] bestowed on Sang Tsung the Kachaya handed down from Bodhidharma, and authorized him as the Third Patriarch. It is by Sang Tsung that the doctrine of Zen was first reduced to writing by his composition of Sin Sin[39] Ming (Sin zin-mei, On Faith and Mind), a metrical exposition of the faith.

The Fourth Patriarch and the Emperor Tai Tsung (Tai-so)

The Third[40] Patriarch was succeeded by Tao Sin (Do-shin), who being initiated at the age of fourteen, was created the Fourth Patriarch after nine years' study and discipline. Tao Sin is said never to have gone to bed for more than forty years of his patriarchal career.[41] In A.D. 643 the Emperor Tai Tsung (627-649), knowing of his virtues, sent him a special messenger, requesting him to call on His Majesty at the palace. But he declined the invitation by a memorial, saying that be was too aged and infirm to visit the august personage. The Emperor, desirous of seeing the reputed patriarch, sent for him thrice, but in vain. Then the enraged monarch ordered the messenger to behead the inflexible monk, and bring the head before the throne, in case he should disobey the order for the fourth time. As Tao Sin was told of the order of the Emperor, he stretched out his neck ready to be decapitated. The Emperor, learning from the messenger what had happened, admired all the more the imperturbable patriarch, and bestowed rich gifts upon him. This example of his was followed by later Zen masters, who would not condescend to bend their knees before temporal power, and it became one of the characteristics of Zen monks that they would never approach rulers and statesmen for the sake of worldly fame and profit, which they set at naught.

---

38 The Second Patriarch died in A.D. 593—that is, sixty-five years after the departure of the First Patriarch.

39 A good many commentaries were written on the book, and it is considered as one of the best books on Zen.

40 He died in A.D. 606, after his labour of thirteen years as the teacher.

41 He died in A.D. 651-that is, forty-five years after the death of the Third Patriarch.

The Fifth and the Sixth Patriarchs

Tao Sin transmitted the Law to Hung Jan (Ko-nin), who being educated from infancy, distinguished himself as the Abbot of the Hwang Mei Monastery at Ki Cheu. The Fifth Patriarch, according to his biographer, gathered about him seven hundred pupils, who came from all quarters. Of these seven hundred pupils the venerable Shang Sin (Jin-shu) was most noted for his learning and virtues, and he might have become the legitimate successor of Hung Jan, had not the Kachaya of Bodhidharma been carried away by a poor farmer's son of Sin Cheu. Hwui Nang, the Sixth Patriarch, seems to have been born a Zen teacher. The spiritual light of Buddha first flashed in his mind when he happened to hear a monk reciting a sutra. On questioning the monk, be learned that the book was Vajracchedika-prajnya-paramita-sutra,[42] and that Hung Jan, the Abbot of the Hwang Mei Monastery, was used to make his disciples recite the book that it might help them in their spiritual discipline. Hereupon he made up his mind to practise Zen, and called on Hung Jan at the Monastery. "Who are you," demanded the Fifth Patriarch, "and whence have you come?" "I am a son of the farmer," replied the man, "of Sin Cheu in the South of Ta Yu Ling." "What has brought you here?" asked the master again. "I have no other purpose than to attain to Buddhahood," answered the man. "O, you, people of the South," exclaimed the patriarch, "you are not endowed with the nature of Buddha." "There may be some difference between the Southern and the Northern people," objected the man, "but how could you distinguish one from the other as to the nature of Buddha?" The teacher recognized a genius in the man, but he did not admit the promising newcomer into the order, so Hwui Nang had to stay in the Monastery for eight months as a pounder of rice in order to qualify himself to be a Zen teacher.

[42] The book was translated into Chinese by Kumarajiva in A.D. 384. 417; also by Bodhiruci in A.D. 509, and by Paramartha in A.D. 592; then by Hiuen Tsang in A.D. 648. Many commentaries have been written on it by the prominent Buddhist authors of China and Japan.

The Spiritual Attainment of the Sixth Patriarch

Some time before his death (in 675 A.D.) the Fifth Patriarch announced to all disciples that the Spirit of Shakya Muni is hard to realize, that they should express their own views on it, on condition that anyone who could prove his right realization should be given with the Kachaya and created the Sixth Patriarch. Then the venerable Sung Siu, the head of the seven hundred disciples, who was considered by his brothers to be the man entitled to the honour, composed the following verses:

"The body is the Bodhi-tree.[43]
The mind is like a mirror bright on its stand.
Dust it and wipe it from time to time,
Lest it be dimmed by dust and dirt."

All who read these lines thought that the writer was worthy of the expected reward, and the Fifth Patriarch also, appreciating the significance of the verses, said: "If men in the future would practise Zen according to this view, they would acquire an excellent result." Hwui Nang, the rice-pounder, hearing of them, however, secretly remarked that they are beautiful, but hardly expressive of the Spirit of Shakya Muni, and wrote his own verses, which ran as follows:

"There is no Bodhi-tree,[44]
Nor is there a mirror stand.
Nothing exists from the first
What can be dimmed by dust and dirt?"

---

[43] The idea expressed by these lines is clear enough. Body is likened to the Bodhi-tree, under which Shakya Muni attained to his supreme enlightenment; for it is not in another body in the future existence, but in this very body that one had to get enlightened. And mind is pure and bright in its nature like a mirror, but the dirt and dust of passions and of low desires often pollute and dim it. Therefore one should dust and wipe it from time to time in order to keep it bright.

[44] These verses have often been misunderstood as expressive of a nihilistic view, but the real meaning is anything but nihilistic. Mind is pure and bright in its essence. It is always free from passions and mean desires, just as the sun is always bright, despite of cloud and mist that cover its face. Therefore one must get an insight into this essential nature of Mind, and realize that one has no mean desires and passions from the first, and also that there is no tree of Bodhi nor the mirror of Enlightenment without him, but they are within him.

Perhaps nobody ever dreamed such an insignificant fellow as the rice-pounder could surpass the venerable scholar in a religious insight, but the Fifth Patriarch saw at once an Enlightened Soul expressed in those lines; therefore he made up his mind to give the Kachaya to the writer, in whom he found a great spiritual leader of future generations. But he did it secretly at midnight, lest some of the disciples from envy do violence to Hwui Nang. He was, moreover, cautious enough to advise his successor to leave the Monastery at once, and go back to the South, that the latter might conceal his Enlightenment until a time would come for his missionary activities.

Flight of the Sixth Patriarch

On the following morning the news of what had happened during the night flew from mouth to mouth, and some of the enraged brothers attempted to pursue the worthy fugitive. The foremost among them, Hwui Ming (E-myo), overtook the Sixth Patriarch at a mountain pass not very far from the Monastery. Then Hwui Nang, laying down the Kachaya on a rock by the road, addressed the pursuer: "This is a mere symbol of the patriarchal authority, and it is not a thing to be obtained by force. Take it along with you, if you long for it." Upon this Hwui Ming, who began to be ashamed of his base act, tried to lift the Kachaya, but in vain, for it was, as he felt, as heavy as the rock itself. At last he said to the Sixth Patriarch: "I have come here, my brother, not for the sake of this robe, but for the sake of the Law. Grant my hearty desire of getting Enlightened." "If you have come for the Law," replied Hwui Nang, "you must put an end to all your struggles and longings. Think neither of good nor of evil (make your mind pure from all idle thoughts), then see how is, Hwui Ming, your original (mental) physiognomy!" Being thus questioned, Ming found in an instant the Divine Light of Buddha within himself, and became a disciple of the Sixth Patriarch.

The Development of the Southern and of the Northern School of Zen

After the death of the Fifth Patriarch the venerable Shang Siu, though not the legitimate successor of his master, was not inactive in the propagation of the faith, and gathered about him a number of enthusiastic admirers. This led to the foundation of the Northern school of Zen in opposition to the Southern school led by the Sixth Patriarch. The Empress Tseh Tien Wa Heu,[45] the real ruler of China at that time, was an admirer of Shang Siu, and patronized his school, which nevertheless made no further development.

In the meanwhile the Sixth Patriarch, who had gone to the South, arrived at the Fah Sing Monastery in Kwang Cheu, where Yin Tsung (In-shu), the abbot, was giving lectures on the Mahayana sutras to a number of student monks. It was towards evening that he happened to overhear two monks of the Monastery discussing about the flag floating in air. One of them said: "It is the wind that moves in reality, but not the flag." "No," objected the other, "it is the flag that moves in reality, but not the wind." Thus each of them insisted on his own one-sided view, and came to no proper conclusion. Then the Sixth Patriarch introduced himself and said to them: "It is neither the wind nor the flag, but your mind that moves in reality." Yin Tsung, having heard these words of the stranger, was greatly astonished, and thought the latter should have been an extraordinary personage. And when he found the man to be the Sixth Patriarch of Zen, he and all his disciples decided to follow Zen under the master. Consequently Hwui Nang, still clad like a layman, changed his clothes, and began his patriarchal career at that Monastery. This is the starting-point of the great development of Zen in China.

Missionary Activity of the Sixth Patriarch

As we have seen above, the Sixth Patriarch was a great genius, and may be justly called a born Zen teacher. He was a man of no erudition, being a

[45] The Emperor Chung Tsung (Chu-so, A.D. 684-704) was a nominal sovereign, and the Empress was the real ruler from A.D. 684 to 705.

poor farmer, who had served under the Fifth Patriarch as a rice-pounder only for eight months, but he could find a new meaning in Buddhist terms, and show how to apply it to practical life. On one occasion, for instance, Fah Tah (Ho-tatsu), a monk who had read over the Saddharma-pundarika-sutra[46] three thousand times, visited him to be instructed in Zen. "Even if you read the sutra ten thousand times," said the Sixth Patriarch, who could never read the text, "it will do you no good, if you cannot grasp the spirit of the sutra." "I have simply recited the book," confessed the monk, "as it is written in characters. How could such a dull fellow as I grasp its spirit?" "Then recite it once," responded the master; "I shall explain its spirit." Hereupon Fah Tah began to recite the sutra, and when he read it until the end of the second chapter the teacher stopped him, saying: "You may stop there. Now I know that this sutra was preached to show the so-called greatest object of Shakya Muni's appearing on earth. That greatest object was to have all sentient beings Enlightened just as He Himself." In this way the Sixth Patriarch grasped the essentials of the Mahayana sutras, and freely made use of them as the explanation of the practical questions about Zen.

The Disciples under the Sixth Patriarch

Some time after this the Sixth Patriarch settled himself down at the Pao Lin Monastery, better known as Tsao Ki Shan (So-kei-zan), in Shao Cheu, and it grow into a great centre of Zen in the Southern States. Under his instruction many eminent Zen masters qualified themselves as Leaders of the Three Worlds. He did not give the patriarchal symbol, the Kachaya, to his successors, lest it might cause needless quarrels among the brethren, as was experienced by himself. He only gave sanction to his disciples who attained to Enlightenment, and allowed them to teach Zen in a manner best suited to their own personalities. For instance, Huen Kioh (Gen-kaku), a

[46] One of the most noted Mahayana sutras, translated by Dharmaraksa (A.D. 286) and by Kumarajiva (A.D. 406). The reader has to note that the author states the essential doctrine in the second chapter. See " Sacred Books of the East," vol. xxi., pp. 30-59.

scholar of the Tien Tai doctrine,[47] well known as the Teacher of Yung Kia[48] (Yo-ka), received a sanction for his spiritual attainment after exchanging a few words with the master in their first interview, and was at once acknowledged as a Zen teacher. When he reached the zenith of his fame, he was presented with a crystal bowl together with rich gifts by the Empress Tseh Tien; and it was in A.D. 705 that the Emperor Chung Tsung invited him in vain to proceed to the palace, since the latter followed the example of the Fourth Patriarch.

After the death[49] of the Sixth Patriarch (A.D. 713), the Southern Zen was divided into two schools, one being represented by Tsing Yuen (Sei-gen), the other by Nan Yoh (Nan-gaku.) Out of these two main schools soon developed the five[50] branches of Zen, and the faith made a splendid progress. After Tsing Yuen and Nan Yoh, one of the junior disciples of the Sixth Patriarch, Hwui Chung (E-chu), held an honourable position for sixteen years as the spiritual adviser to the Emperor Suh Tsung (A.D. 756762) and to the Emperor Tai Tsung (A.D. 763-779). These two Emperors were enthusiastic admirers of Zen, and ordered several times the Kachaya of Bodhidharma to be brought into the palace from the Pao Lin Monastery that they might do proper homage to it. Within some one hundred and thirty years after the Sixth Patriarch, Zen gained so great

---

[47] The Teacher of Tien Tai (Ten-dai, A.D. 538-597), the founder of the Buddhist sect of the same name, was a great scholar of originality. His doctrine and criticism on the Tripitaka greatly influenced the whole of Buddhism after him. His doctrine is briefly given in the second chapter.

[48] His Ching Tao Ko (Sho-do-ka), a beautiful metrical exposition of Zen, is still read by most students of Zen.

[49] There exists Luh Tan Fah Pao Tan King (Roku-so-ho-bo-dan-kyo), a collection of his sermons. It is full of bold statements of Zen in its purest form, and is entirely free from ambiguous and enigmatical words that encumber later Zen books. In consequence it is widely read by non-Buddhist scholars in China and Japan. Both Hwui Chung (E-chu), a famous disciple of the Sixth Patriarch, and Do-gen, the founder of the Soto Sect in Japan, deny the authority of the book, and declare it to be misleading, because of errors and prejudices of the compilers. Still, we believe it to be a collection of genuine sections given by the Sixth Patriarch, though there are some mistakes in its historical narratives.

[50] (1) The Tsao Tung (So-to) Sect, founded by Tsing Yuen (died in A.D. 740) and his successors; (2) the Lin Tsi (Rin-Zai) Sect, founded by Nan Yoh (died in 744) and his successors; (3) the Wei Yan (Yi-gyo) Sect, founded by Wei Shan (Yi-san, died in 853) and his disciple Yen Shan (Kyo-zan, died in 890); (4) the Yun Man (Un-mon) Sect, founded by Yun Man (died in 949); (5) the Pao Yen (Ho-gen) Sect, founded by Pao Yen (died in 958).

influence among higher classes that at the time of the Emperor Suen Tsung (A.D. 847-859) both the Emperor and his Prime Minister, Pei Hiu, were noted for the practice of Zen. It may be said that Zen had its golden age, beginning with the reign of the Emperor Suh Tsung, of the Tang dynasty, until the reign of the Emperor Hiao Tsung (1163-1189), who was the greatest patron of Buddhism in the Southern Sung dynasty. To this age belong almost all the greatest Zen scholars[51] of China.

---

51 During the Tang dynasty (A.D. 618-906) China produced, besides the Sixth Patriarch and his prominent disciples, such great Zen teachers as Ma Tsu (Ba-so, died in 788), who is probably the originator of the Zen Activity; Shih Teu (Seki-to, died in 790), the reputed author of Tsan Tung Ki (San-do-kai), a metrical writing on Zen; Poh Chang (Hyaku-jo, died 814), who first laid down regulations for the Zen Monastery; Wei Shan (Yi-san), Yang Shan (Kyo-zan), the founders of the Wei Yang Sect; Hwang Pah (O-baku, died in 850), one of the founders of the Lin Tsi Sect, and the author of Chwen Sin Pao Yao, (Den-sin-ho-yo), one of the best works on Zen; Lin Tsi (Rin-zai, died in 866), the real founder of the Lin Tsi Sect; Tung Shan (To-zan, died in 869), the real founder of the Tsao Tung Sect; Tsao Shan (So-zan, died in 901), a famous disciple of Tung Shan; Teh Shan (Toku-san, died in 865), who was used to strike every questioner with his staff; Chang Sha (Cho-sha, died in 823); Chao Cheu (Jo-shu, died in 897); Nan Tsuen (Nan-sen, died in 834); Wu Yeh (Mu-go, died in 823); who is said to have replied, 'Away with your idle thoughts,' to every questioner; Yun Yen (Un-gan, died in 829); Yoh Shan (Yaku-san, died in 834); Ta Mei (Tai-bai, died in 839), a noted recluse; Ta Tsz (Dai-ji, died in 862); Kwei Fung (Kei-ho, died in 841), the author of 'The Origin of Man,' and other numerous works; and Yun Ku (Un-go, died in 902).

To the period of the Five Dynasties (A.D. 907-959) belong such teachers as Sueh Fung (Set-po, died in. 908); Huen Sha (Gen-sha, died in 908); Yun Man (Un-mon, died in 949), the founder of the Yun Man Sect; Shen Yueh (Zen-getsu, died in 912), a renowned Zen poet; Pu Tai (Ho-tei, died in 916), well known for his peculiarities; Chang King (Cho-kei, died in 932); Nan Yuen (Nan-in, died in 952); Pao Yen (Ho-gen, died in 958), the founder of the Pao Yen Sect. During the Sung dynasty (A.D. 960-1126) appeared such teachers as Yang Ki (Yo-gi, died in 1049), the founder of the Yang Ki School of Zen; Sueh Teu (Set-cho, died in 1052), noted for poetical works; Hwang Lung (O ryu, died in 1069), the founder of the Hwang Lung School of Zen; Hwang Lin (Ko-rin, died in 987); Tsz Ming (Ji-myo, died in 1040); Teu Tsy (To-shi, died in 1083); Fu Yun (Fu-yo, died in 1118); Wu Tsu (Go-so, died in 1104); Yung Ming (Yo-myo, died in 975), the author of Tsung King Luh (Shu-kyo-roku); Ki Sung (Kai-su, died in 1071), a great Zen historian and author. In the Southern Sung dynasty (A.D. 1127-1279) flourished such masters as Yuen Wu (En-go, died in 1135), the author of Pik Yen Tsih (Heki-gan-shu); Chan Hieh (Shin-ketsu, flourished in 1151); Hung Chi (Wan-shi, died in 1157), famous for his poetical works; Ta Hwui (Dai-e, died in 1163), a noted disciple of Yuen Wu; Wan Sung (Ban-sho), flourished in 1193-1197), the author of Tsung Yun Luh (Sho-yo-roku); Ju Tsing (Nyo-jo), died in 1228), the teacher to Do-gen, or the founder of the So-to Sect in Japan.

To this age belong almost all the eminent men of letters,[52] statesmen, warriors, and artists who were known as the practisers of Zen. To this age belongs the production of almost all Zen books,[53] doctrinal and historical.

Three Important Elements of Zen

To understand how Zen developed during some four hundred years after the Sixth Patriarch, we should know that there are three important elements in Zen. The first of these is technically called the Zen Number—the method of practising Meditation by sitting cross-legged, of which we shall

---

[52] Among the great names of Zen believers the following are most important: Pang Yun (Ho-on, flourished in 785-804), whose whole family was proficient in Zen; Tsui Kiun (Sai-gun, flourished in 806-824); Luh Kang (Rik-ko), a lay disciple to Nan Tsun; Poh Loh Tien (Haku-raku-ten, died in 847), one of the greatest Chinese literary men; Pei Hiu (Hai-kyu, flourished 827-856), the Prime Minister under the Emperor Suen Tsung, a lay disciple to Hwang Pah; Li Ngao (Ri-ko, lived about 806), an author and scholar who practised Zen under Yoh Shan; Yu Chuh (U-teki, flourished 785-804), a local governor, a friend of Pang Yun; Yang Yih (Yo-oku, flourished in 976), one of the greatest writers of his age; Fan Chung Ngan (Han-chu an, flourished 1008-1052), an able statesman and scholar; Fu Pih (Fu shitsu, flourished 1041-1083), a minister under the Emperor Jan Tsung; Chang Shang Ying (Cho-sho-yei, 1086-1122), a Buddhist scholar and a statesman; Hwang Ting Kien (Ko-tei-ken, 1064-1094), a great poet; Su Shih (So-shoku, died in 1101), a great man of letters, well known as So-to-ba; Su Cheh (So-tetsu, died in 1112), a younger brother of So-to-ba, a scholar and minister under the Emperor Cheh Tsung; Chang Kiu Ching (Cho-Kyu-sei, flourished about 1131), a scholar and lay disciple of Ta Hwui; Yang Kieh (Yo-ketsu, flourished 1078-1086), a scholar and statesman.

[53] Of doctrinal Zen books, besides Sin Sin Ming by the Third Patriarch, and Fah Pao Tan King by the Sixth Patriarch, the following are of great importance:
(1) Ching Tao Ko (Sho-do-ka), by Huen Kioh (Gen-kaku). (2) Tsan Tung Ki (San-do-kai), by Shih Ten (Seki-to). (3) Pao King San Mei (Ho-kyo-san-mai), by Tung Shan (To-zan). (4) Chwen Sin Pao Yao (Den-sin-ho-yo), by Hwang Pah (O-baku). (5) Pih Yen Tsih (Heki-gan-shu), by Yuen Wu (En-go). (6) Lin Tsi Luh (Rin-zai-roku), by Lin Tsi (Rin-zai). (7) Tsung Yun Luh (Sho-yo-roku), by Wan Sung (Ban-sho).
Of historical Zen books the following are of importance:
(1) King teh Chwen Tan-Luh (Kei-toku-den-to-roku), published in 1004 by Tao Yuen (Do-gen). (2) Kwan Tang Luh (Ko-to roku), published in 1036 by Li Tsun Suh (Ri-jun-kyoku). (3) Suh Tang Luh (Zoku-O-roku), published in 1101 by Wei Poh (I-haku). (4) Lien Tang Luh (Ren-O-roku), published in 1183 by Hwui Wang (Mai-o). (5) Ching Tsung Ki (Sho-ju-ki), published in 1058 by Ki Sung (Kwai-su). (6) Pu Tang Luh (Fu-O-roku), published in 1201 by Ching Sheu (Sho-ju). (7) Hwui Yuen (E-gen), published in 1252 by Ta Chwen (Dai-sen). (8) Sin Tang Luh (Sin-W-roku), published in 1280-1294 by Sui (Zui). (9) Suh Chwen Tang Luh (Zoku-den-to-roku), by Wang Siu (Bun-shu). (10) Hwui Yuen Suh Lioh (E-gen-zoku-ryaku), by Tsing Chu (Jo-chu). (11) Ki Tang Luh (Kei-to-roku), by Yung Kioh (Yo-kaku).

treat later.[54] This method is fully developed by Indian teachers before Bodhidharma's introduction of Zen into China, therefore it underwent little change during this period. The second is the Zen Doctrine, which mainly consists of Idealistic and Pantheistic ideas of Mahayana Buddhism, but which undoubtedly embraces some tenets of Taoism. Therefore, Zen is not a pure Indian faith, but rather of Chinese origin. The third is the Zen Activity, or the mode of expression of Zen in action, which is entirely absent in any other faith.

It was for the sake of this Zen Activity that Hwang Pah gave a slap three times to the Emperor Suen Tsung; that Lin Tsi so often burst out into a loud outcry of Hoh (Katsu); that Nan Tsuen killed a cat at a single stroke of his knife in the presence of his disciples; and that Teh Shan so frequently struck questioners with his staff.[55] The Zen Activity was displayed by the Chinese teachers making use of diverse things such as the staff, the brush[56]of long hair, the mirror, the rosary, the cup, the pitcher, the flag, the moon, the sickle, the plough, the bow and arrow, the ball, the bell, the drum, the cat, the dog, the duck, the earthworm—in short, any and everything that was fit for the occasion and convenient for the purpose. Thus Zen Activity was of pure Chinese origin, and it was developed after the Sixth Patriarch.[57] For this reason the period previous to the Sixth Patriarch may be called the Age of the Zen Doctrine, while that posterior to the same master, the Age of the Zen Activity.

---

[54] See Chapter VII.

[55] A long official staff (Shu-jo) like the crosier carried by the abbot of the monastery.

[56] An ornamental brush (Hos-su) often carried by Zen teachers.

[57] The giving of a slap was first tried by the Sixth Patriarch, who struck one of his disciples, known as Ho Tseh (Ka-taku), and it was very frequently resorted to by the later masters. The lifting up of the brush was first tried by Tsing Yuen in an interview with his eldest disciple, Shih Ten, and it became a fashion among other teachers. The loud outcry of Hoh was first made use of by Ma Tsu, the successor of Nan Yoh. In this way the origin of the Zen Activity can easily be traced to the Sixth Patriarch and his direct disciples. After the Sung dynasty Chinese Zen masters seem to have given undue weight to the Activity, and neglected the serious study of the doctrine. This brought out the degeneration severely reproached by some of the Japanese Zen teachers.

Decline of Zen

The blooming prosperity of Zen was over towards the end of the Southern Sung dynasty (1127-1279), when it began to fade, not being bitten by the frost of oppression from without, but being weakened by rottenness within. As early as the Sung dynasty (960-1126) the worship of Buddha Amitabha[58] stealthily found its way among Zen believers, who could not fully realize the Spirit of Shakya Muni, and to satisfy these people the amalgamation of the two faiths was attempted by some Zen masters.[59]

---

[58] The faith is based on Larger Sukhavati-vyuha, Smaller Sukhavati-vyuha, and Amitayus-dhyana-sutra. It was taught in India by Acvaghosa, Nagariuna, and Vasubandhu. In China Hwui Yuen (E-on, died in A.D. 416), Tan Lwan (Don-ran, died in 542), Tao Choh (Do-shaku), and Shen Tao (Zen-do) (both of whom lived about 600-650), chiefly taught the doctrine. It made an extraordinary progress in Japan, and differentiated itself into several sects, of which Jodo Shu and Shin Shu are the strongest.

[59] It is beyond all doubt that Poh Loh Tien (Haku-raku-ten) practised Zen, but at the same time believed in Amitabha; so also Su Shih (So-shoku), a most noted Zen practiser, worshipped the same Buddha, Yang Kieh (Yo-keteu), who carried a picture of Amitabha wherever he went and worshipped it, seems to have thought there is nothing incompatible between Zen and his faith. The foremost of those Zen masters of the Sung dynasty that attempted the amalgamation is Yung Ming (Yo-myo, died in 975), who reconciled Zen with the worship of Amitabha in his Wan Shen Tung Kwei Tsih (Man-zen-do-ki-shu) and Si Ngan Yan Shan Fu (Sei-an-yo-sin-fu). He was followed by Tsing Tsz (Jo-ji) and Chan Hieh (Shin-ketsu, lived about 1151), the former of whom wrote Kwei Yuen Chih Chi (Ki-gen-jiki-shi), and the latter Tsing Tu Sin Yao (Jo-do-sin-yo), in order to further the tendency. In the Yuen dynasty Chung Fung (Chu-ho, died in 1323) encouraged the adoration of Amitabha, together with the practice of Zen, in his poetical composition (Kwan-shu-jo-go). In the Ming dynasty Yun Si (Un-sei, died in 1615), the author of Shen Kwan Tseh Tsin (Zen-kwan-saku-shin) and other numerous works, writing a commentary on Sukhavati-vyuha-sutra, brought the amalgamation to its height. Ku Shan (Ku-zan, died in 1657), a Zen historian and author, and his prominent disciple Wei Lin (E-rin), axe well known as the amalgamators. Yun Ming declared that those who practise Zen, but have no faith in Amitabha, go astray in nine cases out of ten; that those who do not practise Zen, but believe in Amitabha, are saved, one and all; that those who practise Zen, and have the faith in Amitabha, are like the tiger provided with wings; and that for those who have no faith in Amitabha, nor practise Zen, there exist the iron floor and the copper pillars in Hell. Ku Shan said that some practise Zen in order to attain Enlightenment, while others pray Amitabha for salvation; that if they were sincere and diligent, both will obtain the final beatitude. Wei Lin also observed: "Theoretically I embrace Zen, and practically I worship Amitabha." E-chu, the author of Zen-to-nenbutsu ('On Zen and the Worship of Amitabha'), points out that one of the direct disciples of the Sixth Patriarch favoured the faith of Amitabha, but there is no trustworthy evidence, as far as we know, that proves the existence of the amalgamation in the Tang dynasty.

This tendency steadily increasing with time brought out at length the period of amalgamation which covered the Yuen (1280-1367) and the Ming dynasties (1368-1659), when the prayer for Amitabha was in every mouth of Zen monks sitting in Meditation. The patrons of Zen were not wanting in the Yuen dynasty, for such a warlike monarch as the Emperor Shi Tsu (Sei-so), 1280-1294) is known to have practised Zen under the instruction of Miao Kao, and his successor Ching Tsung (1295-1307) to have trusted in Yih Shan,[60] a Zen teacher of reputation at that time. Moreover, Lin Ping Chung (Rin-hei-cha, died in 1274), a powerful minister under Shi Tsu, who did much toward the establishment of the administrative system in that dynasty, had been a Zen monk, and never failed to patronize his faith. And in the Ming dynasty the first Emperor Tai Tsu (1368-1398), having been a Zen monk, protected the sect with enthusiasm, and his example was followed by Tai Tsung (1403-1424), whose spiritual as well as political adviser was Tao Yen, a Zen monk of distinction. Thus Zen exercised an influence unparalleled by any other faith throughout these ages. The life and energy of Zen, however, was gone by the ignoble amalgamation, and even such great scholars as Chung Fung,[61]Yung Si,[62] Yung Kioh,[63] were not free from the overwhelming influence of the age.

We are not, however, doing justice to the tendency of amalgamation in these times simply to blame it for its obnoxious results, because it is beyond doubt that it brought forth wholesome fruits to the Chinese literature and

---

60 The Emperor sent him to Japan in 1299 with some secret order, but he did nothing political, and stayed as a Zen teacher until his death.

61 A most renowned Zen master in the Yuen dynasty, whom the Emperor Jan Tsung invited to visit the palace, but in vain.

62 An author noted for his learning and virtues, who was rather a worshipper of Amitabha than a Zen monk.

63 An author of voluminous books, of which Tung Shang Ku Cheh (To-jo-ko-tetsu) is well known.

philosophy. Who can deny that this tendency brought the Speculative[64] philosophy of the Sung dynasty to its consummation by the amalgamation of Confucianism with Buddhism especially with Zen, to enable it to exercise long-standing influence on society, and that this tendency also produced Wang Yang Ming,[65] one of the greatest generals and scholars that the world has ever seen, whose philosophy of Conscience[66] still holds a unique position in the history of human thought? Who can deny furthermore that Wang's philosophy is Zen in the Confucian terminology?

---

[64] This well-known philosophy was first taught by Cheu Men Shuh (Shu-mo-shiku, died in 1073) in its definite form. He is said to have been enlightened by the instruction of Hwui Tang, a contemporary Zen master. He was succeeded by Chang Ming Tao (Tei-mei-do, died in 1085) and Chang I Chwen (Tei-i-sen, died in 1107), two brothers, who developed the philosophy in no small degree. And it was completed by Chu Tsz (Shu-shi, died in 1200), a celebrated commentator of the Confucian classics. It is worthy to note that these scholars practised Meditation just as Zen monks. See 'History of Chinese Philosophy' (pp. 215-269), by G. Nakauchi, and 'History of Development of Chinese Thought,' by R. Endo.

[65] He was born in 1472, and died in 1529. His doctrine exercised a most fruitful influence on many of the great Japanese minds, and undoubtedly has done much to the progress of New Japan.

[66] See Den-shu-roku and O-ya-mei-zen-sho.

CHAPTER II

HISTORY OF ZEN IN JAPAN

The Establishment of the Rin Zai[67] School of Zen in Japan.

The introduction of Zen into the island empire is dated as early as the seventh century;[[68] but it was in 1191 that it was first established by Ei-sai, a man of bold, energetic nature. He crossed the sea for China at the age of twenty-eight in 1168, after his profound study of the whole Tripitaka[69] for eight years in the Hi-yei Monastery[70] the then centre of Japanese Buddhism.

---

[67] The Lin Tsi school was started by Nan Yoh, a prominent disciple of the Sixth Patriarch, and completed by Lin Tsi or Rin Zai.

[68] Zen was first introduced into Japan by Do sha (629-700) as early as 653-656, at the time when the Fifth Patriarch just entered his patriarchal career. Do-sho went over to China in 653, and met with Huen Tsang, the celebrated and great scholar, who taught him the doctrine of the Dharma-laksana. It was Huen Tsang who advised Do-sho to study Zen under Hwui Man (E-man). After returning home, he built a Meditation Hall for the purpose of practising Zen in the Gan-go monastery, Nara. Thus Zen was first transplanted into Japan by Do-sho, but it took no root in the soil at that time.
Next a Chinese Zen teacher, I Kung (Gi-ku), came over to Japan in about 810, and under his instruction the Empress Danrin, a most enthusiastic Buddhist, was enlightened. She erected a monastery named Dan-rin-ji, and appointed I Kung the abbot of it for the sake of propagating the faith. It being of no purpose, however, I Kung went back to China after some years.
Thirdly, Kaku-a in 1171 went over to China, where he studied Zen under Fuh Hai (Buk-kai), who belonged to the Yang Ki (Yo-gi) school, and came home after three years. Being questioned by the Emperor Taka-kura (1169-1180) about the doctrine of Zen, he uttered no word, but took up a flute and played on it. But his first note was too high to be caught by the ordinary ear, and was gone without producing any echo in the court nor in society at large.

[69] The three divisions of the Buddhist canon, viz.:
(1) Sutra-pitaka, or a collection of doctrinal books. (2) Vinaya-pitaka, or a collection of works on discipline. (3) Abhidharma-pitaka, or a collection of philosophical and expository works.

[70] The great monastery erected in 788 by Sai-cho (767-822), the founder of the Japanese Ten Dai Sect, known as Den Gyo Dai Shi.

After visiting holy places and great monasteries, he came home, bringing with him over thirty different books on the doctrine of the Ten-Dai Sect.[71]This, instead of quenching, added fuel to his burning desire for adventurous travel abroad. So he crossed the sea over again in 1187, this time intending to make pilgrimage to India; and no one can tell what might have been the result if the Chinese authorities did not forbid him to cross the border. Thereon he turned his attention to the study of Zen, and after five years' discipline succeeded in getting sanction for his spiritual attainment by the Hu Ngan (Kio-an), a noted master of the Rin Zai school, the then abbot of the monastery of Tien Tung Shan (Ten-do-san). His active propaganda of Zen was commenced soon after his return in 1191 with splendid success at a newly built temple[72] in the province of Chiku-zen. In 1202 Yori-iye, the Shogun, or the real governor of the State at that time, erected the monastery of Ken-nin-ji in the city of Kyo-to, and invited him to proceed to the metropolis. Accordingly he settled himself down in that temple, and taught Zen with his characteristic activity.

This provoked the envy and wrath of the Ten Dai and the Shin Gon[73] teachers, who presented memorials to the Imperial court to protest against his propagandism of the new faith. Taking advantage of the protests, Ei-sai wrote a book entitled Ko-zen-go-koku-ron ('The Protection of the State by the Propagation of Zen'), and not only explained his own position, but

---

[71] The sect was named after its founder in China, Chi I (538-597), who lived in the monastery of Tien Tai Shan (Ten-dai-san), and was called the Great Teacher of Tien Tai. In 804 Den-gyo went over to China by the Imperial order, and received the transmission of the doctrine from Tao Sui (Do-sui), a patriarch of the sect. After his return he erected a monastery on Mount Hi-yei, which became the centre of Buddhistic learning.

[72] He erected the monastery of Sho-fuku-ji in 1195, which is still prospering.

[73] The Shin Gon or Mantra Sect is based on Mahavairocanabhi-sambodhi-sutra, Vajracekhara-sutra, and other Mantra-sutras. It was established in China by Vajrabodhi and his disciple Amoahavajra, who came from India in 720. Ku kai (774-835), well known as Ko Bo Dai Shi, went to China in 804, and received the transmission of the doctrine from Hwui Kwo (Kei-ka), a, disciple of Amoghavajra. In 806 he came back and propagated the faith almost all over the country. For the detail see 'A Short History of the Twelve Japanese Buddhist Sects' (chap. viii.), by Dr. Nanjo.

exposed the ignorance[74] of the protestants. Thus at last his merit was appreciated by the Emperor Tsuchi-mikado (1199-1210), and he was promoted to So Jo, the highest rank in the Buddhist priesthood, together with the gift of a purple robe in 1206. Some time after this he went to the city of Kama-kura, the political centre, being invited by Sane-tomo, the Shogun, and laid the foundation of the so-called Kama-kura Zen, still prospering at the present moment.

The Introduction of the So-To School[75] of Zen

Although the Rin Zai school was, as mentioned above, established by Ei-sai, yet he himself was not a pure Zen teacher, being a Ten Dai scholar as well as an experienced practiser of Mantra. The first establishment of Zen in its purest form was done by Do-gen, now known as Jo Yo Dai Shi. Like Ei-sai, he was admitted into the Hi-yei Monastery at an early age, and devoted himself to the study of the Canon. As his scriptural knowledge increased, he was troubled by inexpressible doubts and fears, as is usual with great religious teachers. Consequently, one day he consulted his uncle, Ko-in, a distinguished Ten Dai scholar, about his troubles. The latter, being unable to satisfy him, recommended him Ei-sai, the founder of the new faith. But as Ei-sai died soon afterwards, he felt that he had no competent teacher left, and crossed the sea for China, at the age of twenty-four, in 1223. There he was admitted into the monastery of Tien Tung Shan (Ten-do-san), and assigned the lowest seat in the hall, simply because be was a foreigner. Against this affront he strongly protested. In the Buddhist community, he said, all were brothers, and there was no difference of nationality. The only way to rank the brethren was by seniority, and he therefore claimed to occupy his proper rank. Nobody, however, lent an ear to the poor new-comer's protest, so he appealed twice to the Chinese Emperor Ning Tsung (1195-1224), and by the Imperial order he gained his object.

---

[74] Sai-cho, the founder of the Japanese Ten Dai Sect, first learned the doctrine of the Northern School of Zen under Gyo-hyo (died in 797), and afterwards he pursued the study of the same faith under Siao Jan in China. Therefore to oppose the propagation of Zen is, for Ten Dai priests, as much as to oppose the founder of their own sect.

[75] This school was started by Tsing-Yuen (Sei-gen), an eminent disciple of the Sixth Patriarch, and completed by Tsing Shan (To-zan).

After four years' study and discipline, he was Enlightened and acknowledged as the successor by his master Ju Tsing (Nyo-jo died in 1228), who belonged to the Tsao Tung (So To) school. He came home in 1227, bringing with him three important Zen books.[76] Some three years he did what Bodhidharma, the Wall-gazing Brahmin, had done seven hundred years before him, retiring to a hermitage at Fuka-kusa, not very far from Kyo-to. Just like Bodhidharma, denouncing all worldly fame and gain, his attitude toward the world was diametrically opposed to that of Ei-sai. As we have seen above, Ei-sai never shunned, but rather sought the society of the powerful and the rich, and made for his goal by every means. But to the Sage of Fuka-kusa, as Do-gen was called at that time, pomp and power was the most disgusting thing in the world. Judging from his poems, be seems to have spent these years chiefly in meditation; dwelling now on the transitoriness of life, now on the eternal peace of Nirvana; now on the vanities and miseries of the world; now listening to the voices of Nature amongst the hills; now gazing into the brooklet that was, as he thought, carrying away his image reflected on it into the world.

The Characteristics of Do-gen, the Founder of the Japanese So To Sect

In the meantime seekers after a new truth gradually began to knock at his door, and his hermitage was turned into a monastery, now known as the Temple of Ko-sho-ji.[77]It was at this time that many Buddhist scholars and men of quality gathered about him but the more popular he became the

---

[76] (1) Pao King San Mei (Ho-kyo-san-mai, 'Precious Mirror Samadhi'), a metrical exposition of Zen, by Tung Shan (To-zan, 806-869), one of the founders of the So To school. (2) Wu Wei Hien Hueh (Go-i-ken-ketsu. 'Explanation of the Five Categories'), by Tung Shan and his disciple Tsao Shan (So-zan). This book shows us how Zen was systematically taught by the authors. (3) Pih Yen Tsih (Heki-gan-shu, 'A Collection and Critical Treatment of Dialogues'), by Yuen Wu.

[77] It was in this monastery (built in 1236) that Zen was first taught as an independent sect, and that the Meditation Hall was first opened in Japan. Do-gen lived in the monastery for eleven years, and wrote some of the important books. Za-zen-gi ('The Method of Practising the Cross-legged Meditation') was written soon after his return from China, and Ben-do-wa and other essays followed, which are included in his great work, entitled Sho-bo-gen-zo) ('The Eye and Treasury of the Right Law').

more disgusting the place became to him. His hearty desire was to live in a solitude among mountains, far distant from human abodes, where none but falling waters and singing birds could disturb his delightful meditation. Therefore he gladly accepted the invitation of a feudal lord, and went to the province of Echi-zen, where his ideal monastery was built, now known as Ei-hei-ji.[78]

In 1247, being requested by Toki-yori, the Regent General (1247-1263), he came down to Kama-kura, where he stayed half a year and went back to Ei-hei-ji. After some time Toki-yori, to show his gratitude for the master, drew up a certificate granting a large tract of land as the property of Ei-hei-ji, and handed it over to Gen-myo, a disciple of Do-gen. The carrier of the certificate was so pleased with the donation that he displayed it to all his brethren and produced it before the master, who severely reproached him saying: "O, shame on thee, wretch! Thou art -defiled by the desire of worldly riches even to thy inmost soul, just as noodle is stained with oil. Thou canst not be purified from it to all eternity. I am afraid thou wilt bring shame on the Right Law." On the spot Gen-myo was deprived of his holy robe and excommunicated. Furthermore, the master ordered the 'polluted' seat in the Meditation Hall, where Gen-myo was wont to sit, to be removed, and the 'polluted' earth under the seat to be dug out to the depth of seven feet.

In 1250 the ex-Emperor Go-sa-ga (1243-1246) sent a special messenger twice to the Ei-hei monastery to do honour to the master with the donation of a purple robe, but he declined to accept it. And when the mark of distinction was offered for the third time, he accepted it, expressing his feelings by the following verses:
"Although in Ei-hei's vale the shallow waters leap,
Yet thrice it came, Imperial favour deep.
The Ape may smile and laugh the Crane
At aged Monk in purple as insane."

---

[78] The monastery was built in 1244 by Yoshi-shige (Hatano), the feudal lord who invited Do-gen. He lived in Ei-hei-ji until his death, which took place in 1253. It is still flourishing as the head temple of the So To Sect.

He was never seen putting on the purple robe, being always clad in black, that was better suited to his secluded life.

The Social State of Japan when Zen was established by Ei-sai and Do-gen

Now we have to observe the condition of the country when Zen was introduced into Japan by Ei-sai and Do-gen. Nobilities that had so long governed the island were nobilities no more. Enervated by their luxuries, effeminated by their ease, made insipient by their debauchery, they were entirely powerless. All that they possessed in reality was the nominal rank and hereditary birth. On the contrary, despised as the ignorant, sneered at as the upstart, put in contempt as the vulgar, the Samurai or military class had everything in their hands. It was the time when Yori-tomo[79](1148-1199) conquered all over the empire, and established the Samurai Government at Kama-kura. It was the time when even the emperors were dethroned or exiled at will by the Samurai. It was the time when even the Buddhist monks[80] frequently took up arms to force their will. It was the time when Japan's independence was endangered by Kublai, the terror of the world. It was the time when the whole nation was full of martial spirit. It is beyond doubt that to these rising Samurais, rude and simple, the philosophical doctrines of Buddhism, represented by Ten Dai and Shin Gon, were too complicated and too alien to their nature. But in Zen they could find something congenial to their nature, something that touched their chord of sympathy, because Zen was the doctrine of chivalry in a certain sense.

The Resemblance of the Zen Monk to the Samurai

Let us point out in brief the similarities between Zen and Japanese chivalry. First, both the Samurai and the Zen monk have to undergo a strict discipline and endure privation without complaint. Even such a prominent

---

79 The Samurai Government was first established by Yoritomo, of the Minamoto family, in 1186, and Japan was under the control of the military class until 1867, when the political power was finally restored to the Imperial house.

80 They were degenerated monks (who were called monk-soldiers), belonging to great monasteries such as En-ryaku-ji (Hi-yei), Ko-fuku-ji (at Nara), Mi-i-dera, etc.

teacher as Ei-sai, for example, lived contentedly in such needy circumstances that on one occasion[81] he and his disciples had nothing to eat for several days. Fortunately, they were requested by a believer to recite the Scriptures, and presented with two rolls of silk. The hungry young monks, whose mouths watered already at the expectation of a long-looked-for dinner, were disappointed when that silk was given to a poor man, who called on Ei-sai to obtain some help. Fast continued for a whole week, when another poor follow came in and asked Ei-sai to give something. At this time, having nothing to show his substantial mark of sympathy towards the poor, Ei-sai tore off the gilt glory of the image of Buddha Bhecajya and gave it. The young monks, bitten both by hunger and by anger at this outrageous act to the object of worship, questioned Ei-sai by way of reproach: "Is it, sir, right for us Buddhists to demolish the image of a Buddha?" "Well," replied Ei-sai promptly, "Buddha would give even his own life for the sake of suffering people. How could he be reluctant to give his halo?" This anecdote clearly shows us self-sacrifice is of first importance in the Zen discipline.

The Honest Poverty of the Zen Monk and the Samurai

Secondly, the so-called honest poverty is a characteristic of both the Zen monk and the Samurai. To get rich by an ignoble means is against the rules of Japanese chivalry or Bushido. The Samurai would rather starve than to live by some expedient unworthy of his dignity. There are many instances, in the Japanese history, of Samurais who were really starved to death in spite of their having a hundred pieces of gold carefully preserved to meet the expenses at the time of an emergency; hence the proverb: "The falcon would not feed on the ear of corn, even if he should starve." Similarly, we know of no case of Zen monks, ancient and modern, who got rich by any ignoble means. They would rather face poverty with gladness of heart. Fu-gai, one of the most distinguished Zen masters just before the Restoration, supported many student monks in his monastery. They were often too numerous to be supported by his scant means. This troubled his disciple much whose duty it was to look after the food-supply, as there was no other

---

[81] The incident is told by Do-gen in his Zui-mon-ki.

means to meet the increased demand than to supply with worse stuff. Accordingly, one day the disciple advised Fu-gai not to admit new students any more into the monastery. Then the master, making no reply, lolled out his tongue and said: "Now look into my mouth, and tell if there be any tongue in it." The perplexed disciple answered affirmatively. "Then don't bother yourself about it. If there be any tongue, I can taste any sort of food." Honest poverty may, without exaggeration, be called one of the characteristics of the Samurais and of the Zen monks; hence a proverb: "The Zen monk has no money, moneyed Monto[82] knows nothing."

The Manliness of the Zen Monk and of the Samurai

Thirdly, both the Zen monk and the Samurai were distinguished by their manliness and dignity in manner, sometimes amounting to rudeness. This is due partly to the hard discipline that they underwent, and partly to the mode of instruction. The following story,[83] translated by Mr. D. Suzuki, a friend of mine, may well exemplify our statement:

When Rin-zai[84] was assiduously applying himself to Zen discipline under Obak (Huang Po in Chinese, who died 850), the head monk recognized his genius. One day the monk asked him how long he had been in the monastery, to which Rin-zai replied: 'Three years.' The elder said: 'Have you ever approached the master and asked his instruction in Buddhism?' Rin-zai said: 'I have never done this, for I did not know what to ask.' 'Why, you might go to the master and ask him what is the essence of Buddhism?'

"Rin-zai, according to this advice, approached Obak and repeated the question, but before he finished the master gave him a slap.

"When Rin-zai came back, the elder asked how the interview went. Said Rin-zai: 'Before I could finish my question the master slapped me, but I fail to grasp its meaning.' The elder said: 'You go to him again and ask the same question.' When he did so, he received the same response from the master. But Rin-zai was urged again to try it for the third time, but the outcome did not improve.

---

82 The priest belonging to Shin Shu, who are generally rich.

83 The Journal of the Pali Text Society, 1906-1907.

84 Lin Tsi, the founder of the Lin Tsi school.

"At last he went to the elder, and said 'In obedience to your kind suggestion, I have repeated my question three times, and been slapped three times. I deeply regret that, owing to my stupidity, I am unable to comprehend the hidden meaning of all this. I shall leave this place and go somewhere else.' Said the elder: 'If you wish to depart, do not fail to go and see the master to say him farewell.'

"Immediately after this the elder saw the master, and said: 'That young novice, who asked about Buddhism three times, is a remarkable fellow. When he comes to take leave of you, be so gracious as to direct him properly. After a hard training, he will prove to be a great master, and, like a huge tree, he will give a refreshing shelter to the world.'

"When Rin-zai came to see the master, the latter advised him not to go anywhere else, but to Dai-gu (Tai-yu) of Kaoan, for he would be able to instruct him in the faith.

"Rin-zai went to Dai-gu, who asked him whence he came. Being informed that he was from Obak, Dai-gu further inquired what instruction he had under the master. Rin-zai answered: 'I asked him three times about the essence of Buddhism, and he slapped me three times. But I am yet unable to see whether I had any fault or not.' Dai-gu said: 'Obak was tender-hearted even as a dotard, and you are not warranted at all to come over here and ask me whether anything was faulty with you.'

"Being thus reprimanded, the signification of the whole affair suddenly dawned upon the mind of Rin-zai, and he exclaimed: 'There is not much, after all, in the Buddhism of Obak.' Whereupon Dai-gu took hold of him, and said: 'This ghostly good-for-nothing creature! A few minutes ago you came to me and complainingly asked what was wrong with you, and now boldly declare that there is not much in the Buddhism of Obak. What is the reason of all this? Speak out quick! speak out quick!' In response to this, Rin-zai softly struck three times his fist at the ribs of Dai-gu. The latter then released him, saying: 'Your teacher is Obak, and I will have nothing to do with you.'

"Rin-zai took leave of Dai-gu and came back to Obak, who, on seeing him come, exclaimed: 'Foolish fellow! what does it avail you to come and go all the time like this?' Rin-zai said: 'It is all due to your doting kindness.'

"When, after the usual salutation, Rin-zai stood by the side of Obak, the latter asked him whence he had come this time. Rin-zai answered: "In obedience to your kind instruction, I was with Dai-gu. Thence am I come.'

And he related, being asked for further information, all that had happened there.

"Obak said: 'As soon as that fellow shows himself up here, I shall have to give him a good thrashing.' 'You need not wait for him to come; have it right this moment,' was the reply; and with this Rin-zai gave his master a slap on the back.

"Obak said: 'How dares this lunatic come into my presence and play with a tiger's whiskers?' Rin-zai then burst out into a Ho,[85] and Obak said: 'Attendant, come and carry this lunatic away to his cell.'"

The Courage and the Composure of Mind of the Zen Monk and of the Samurai

Fourthly, our Samurai encountered death, as is well known, with unflinching courage. He would never turn back from, but fight till his last with his enemy. To be called a coward was for him the dishonour worse than death itself. An incident about Tsu Yuen (So-gen), who came over to Japan in 1280, being invited by Toki-mune[86] (Ho-jo), the Regent General, well illustrates how much Zen monks resembled our Samurais. The event happened when he was in China, where the invading army of Yuen spread terror all over the country. Some of the barbarians, who crossed the border of the State of Wan, broke into the monastery of Tsu Yuen, and threatened to behead him. Then calmly sitting down, ready to meet his fate, he composed the following verses:

"The heaven and earth afford me no shelter at all;
I'm glad, unreal are body and soul.
Welcome thy weapon, O warrior of Yuen! Thy trusty steel,
That flashes lightning, cuts the wind of Spring, I feel."

---

85 A loud outcry, frequently made use of by Zen teachers, after Rin-zai. Its Chinese pronunciation is 'Hoh,' and pronounced 'Katsu' in Japanese, but 'tsu' is not audible.

86 A bold statesman and soldier, who was the real ruler of Japan 1264-1283.

This reminds us of Sang Chao[87] (So-jo), who, on the verge of death by the vagabond's sword, expressed his feelings in the follow lines:

"In body there exists no soul.
The mind is not real at all.
Now try on me thy flashing steel,
As if it cuts the wind of Spring, I feel."

Zen and the Regent Generals of the Ho-Jo Period

No wonder, then, that the representatives of the Samurai class, the Regent Generals, especially such able rulers as Toki-yori, Toki-mune, and others noted for their good administration, of the Ho-jo period (1205-1332) greatly favoured Zen. They not only patronized the faith, building great temples[88] and inviting best Chinese Zen teachers[89] but also lived just as Zen monks, having the head shaven, wearing a holy robe, and practising cross-legged Meditation.

---

[87] The man was not a pure Zen master, being a disciple of Kumarajiva, the founder of the San Ron Sect. This is a most remarkable evidence that Zen, especially the Rin Zan school, was influenced by Kumarajiva and his disciples. For the details of the anecdote, see E-gen.

The barbarians, moved by this calm resolution and dignified air of Tsu Yuen, rightly supposed him to be no ordinary personage, and left the monastery, doing no harm to him.

[88] To-fuku-ji, the head temple of a sub-sect of the Rin Zai under the same name, was built in 1243. Ken-cho-ji, the head temple of a subsect of the Rin Zai under the same name, was built in 1253. En-gaku ji, the head temple of a sub-sect of the Rin Zai under the same name, was built in 1282. Nan-zen-ji, the head temple of a sub-sect of the Rin Zai under the same name, was erected in 1326.

[89] Tao Lung (Do-ryu), known as Dai-kaku Zen-ji, invited by Tokiyori, came over to Japan in 1246. He became the founder of Ken-cho-ji-ha, a sub-sect of the Rin Zai, and died in 1278. Of his disciples, Yaku-o was most noted, and Yaku-o's disciple, Jaku-shitsu, became the founder of Yo-genji-ha, another sub-sect of the Rin Zai. Tsu Yuen (So-gen), known as Buk-ko-koku-shi, invited by Toki-mune, crossed the sea in 1280, became the founder of En-gaku-ji-ha (a sub-sect of the Rin Zai), and died in 1286. Tsing Choh (Sei-setsu), invited by Taka-toki, came in 1327, and died in 1339. Chu Tsun (So-shun) came in 1331, and died in 1336. Fan Sien (Bon-sen) came together with Chu Tsun, and died in 1348. These were the prominent Chinese teachers of that time.

Toki-yori (1247-1263), for instance, who entered the monastic life while be was still the real governor of the country, led as simple a life, as is shown in his verse, which ran as follows:

"Higher than its bank the rivulet flows;
Greener than moss tiny grass grows.
No one call at my humble cottage on the rock,
But the gate by itself opens to the Wind's knock."

Toki-yori attained to Enlightenment by the instruction of Do-gen and Do-ryu, and breathed his last calmly sitting cross-legged, and expressing his feelings in the following lines:

"Thirty-seven of years,
Karma mirror stood high;
Now I break it to pieces,
Path of Great is then nigh."

His successor, Toki-mune (1264-1283), a bold statesman and soldier, was no less of a devoted believer in Zen. Twice he beheaded the envoys sent by the great Chinese conqueror, Kublai, who demanded Japan should either surrender or be trodden under his foot. And when the alarming news of the Chinese Armada's approaching the land reached him, be is said to have called on his tutor, Tsu Yuen, to receive the last instruction. "Now, reverend sir," said. he, "an imminent peril threatens the land." "How art thou going to encounter it?" asked the master. Then Toki-mune burst into a thundering Ka with all his might to show his undaunted spirit in encountering the approaching enemy. "O, the lion's roar!" said Tsu Yuen.
"Thou art a genuine lion. Go, and never turn back." Thus encouraged by the teacher, the Regent General sent out the defending army, and successfully rescued the state from the mouth of destruction, gaining a splendid victory over the invaders, almost all of whom perished in the western seas.

Zen after the Downfall of the Ho-Jo Regency

Towards the end of the Ho-Jo period,[90] and after the downfall of the Regency in 1333, sanguinary battles were fought between the Imperialists and the rebels. The former, brave and faithful as they were, being outnumbered by the latter, perished in the field one after another for the sake of the ill-starred Emperor Go-dai-go (1319-1338), whose eventful life ended in anxiety and despair.

Another teacher who gained lasting influence on the Court is Nan-po, known as Dai-O-Koku-Shi (1235-1308), who was appointed the abbot of the monastery of Man-ju-ji in Kyo to by the Emperor Fushi-mi. One of his disciples, Tsu-o, was the spiritual adviser to both the Emperor Hana-zono (1308-1318) and the Emperor Go-dai-go. And another disciple, Myo-cho, known as Dai-To-Koku-Shi (1282-1337), also was admired by the two Emperors, and created the abbot of Dai-toku-ji, as the founder of a sub-sect of the Rin Zai under the same name. It was for Myo-cho's disciple, Kan-zan (1277 1360), that the Emperor Hana-zono turned his detached palace into a monastery, named Myo-shin-ji, the head temple of a sub-sect of the Rin Zai under the same name.

It was at this time that Japan gave birth to Masa-shige (Kusu-noki), an able general and tactician of the Imperialists, who for the sake of the Emperor not only sacrificed himself and his brother, but by his will his son and his son's successor died for the same cause, boldly attacking the enemy whose number was overwhelmingly great. Masa-shige's loyalty, wisdom, bravery, and prudence are not merely unique in the history of Japan, but perhaps in the history of man. The tragic tale about his parting with his beloved son, and his bravery shown at his last battle, never fail to inspire the Japanese

---

[90] Although Zen was first favoured by the Ho-jo Regency and chiefly prospered at Kamakura, yet it rapidly began to exercise its influence on nobles and Emperors at Kyo-to. This is mainly due to the activity of En-ni, known as Sho-Ichi-Koku-Shi (1202-1280), who first earned Zen under Gyo-yu, a disciple of Ei-sai, and afterwards went to China, where he was Enlightened under the instruction of Wu Chun, of the monastery of King Shan. After his return, Michi-iye (Fuji-wara), a powerful nobleman, erected for him To-fuku-ji in 1243, and he became the founder of a sub-sect of the Rin Zai, named after that monastery. The Emperor Go-saga (1243-1246), an admirer of his, received the Moral Precepts from him. One of his disciples, To-zan, became the spiritual adviser of the Emperor Fushi-mi (1288-1298), and another disciple, Mu kwan, was created the abbot of the monastery of Nan-zen-ji by the Emperor Kame-yama (1260-1274), as the founder of a sub-sect of the Rin Zai under the same name.

with heroism. He is the best specimen of the Samurai class. According to an old document,[91] this Masa-shige was the practiser of Zen, and just before his last battle he called on Chu Tsun (So-shun) to receive the final instruction. "What have I to do when death takes the place of life?" asked Masa-shige. The teacher replied:
"Be bold, at once cut off both ties,
The drawn sword gleams against the skies."

Thus becoming, as it were, an indispensable discipline for the Samurai, Zen never came to an end with the Ho-jo period, but grew more prosperous than before during the reign[92] of the Emperor Go-dai-go, one of the most enthusiastic patrons of the faith.

The Shoguns of the Ashi-kaga period (1338-1573) were not less devoted to the faith than the Emperors who succeeded the Emperor Go-dai-go. And even Taka-uji (1338-1357), the notorious founder of the Shogunate, built a monastery and invited So-seki,[93] better known as Mu-So-Koku-Shi, who was respected as the tutor by the three successive Emperors after Go-dai-

---

[91] The event is detailed at length in a life of So-shun, but some historians suspect it to be fictitious. This awaits a further research.

[92] As we have already mentioned, Do-gen, the founder of the Japanese So To Sect, shunned the society of the rich and the powerful, and led a secluded life. In consequence his sect did not make any rapid progress until the Fourth Patriarch of his line, Kei-zan (1268-1325) who, being of energetic spirit, spread his faith with remarkable activity, building many large monasteries, of which Yo-ko-ji, in the province of No-to, So-ji-ji (near Yokohama), one of the head temples of the sect, are well known. One of his disciples, Mei ho (1277-1350), propagated the faith in the northern provinces; while another disciple, Ga-san (1275-1365), being a greater character, brought up more than thirty distinguished disciples, of whom Tai-gen, Tsu-gen, Mu-tan, Dai-tetsu, and Jip-po, are best known. Tai-gen (died 1370) and big successors propagated the faith over the middle provinces, while Tsu-gen (1332-1391) and his successors spread the sect all over the north-eastern and south-western provinces. Thus it is worthy of our notice that most of the Rin Zai teachers confined their activities within Kamakura and Kyo-to, while the So To masters spread the faith all over the country.

[93] So-seki (1276-1351) was perhaps the greatest Zen master of the period. Of numerous monasteries built for him, E-rin-ji, in the province of Kae, and Ten-ryu-ji, the head temple of a sub-sect of the Rin Zai under the same name, are of importance. Out of over seventy eminent disciples of his, Gi-do (1365-1388), the author of Ku-ge-shu; Shun-oku (1331-1338), the founder of the monastery of So-koku-ji, the head temple of a sub-sect of the Rin Zai under the same name; and Zek-kai (1337-1405), author of Sho-ken-shu, are best known.

go. Taka-uji's example was followed by all succeeding Shoguns, and Shogun's example was followed by the feudal lords and their vassals. This resulted in the propagation of Zen throughout the country. We can easily imagine how Zen was prosperous in these days from the splendid monasteries[94] built at this period, such as the Golden Hall Temple and the Silver Hall Temple that still adorn the fair city of Kyo-to.

Zen in the Dark Age

The latter half of the Ashikaga period was the age of arms and bloodshed. Every day the sun shone on the glittering armour of marching soldiers. Every wind sighed over the lifeless remains of the brave. Everywhere the din of battle resounded. Out of these fighting feudal lords stood two champions. Each of them distinguished himself as a veteran soldier and tactician. Each of them was known as an experienced practiser of Zen. One was Haru-nobu[95] (Take-da, died in 1573), better known by his Buddhist name, Shin-gen. The other was Teru-tora[96] (Uye-sugi, died in 1578), better known by his Buddhist name, Ken-shin. The character of Shin-gen can be imagined from the fact that he never built any castle or citadel or fortress to guard himself against his enemy, but relied on his faithful vassals and people; while that of Ken-shin, from the fact that he provided his enemy, Shin-gen, with salt when the latter suffered from want of it, owing to the cowardly stratagem of a rival lord. The heroic battles waged by these two great generals against each other are the flowers of the Japanese war-history. Tradition has it that when Shin-gen's army was put to rout by the furious attacks of Ken-shin's troops, and a single warrior mounted on a huge charger rode swiftly as a sweeping wind into Shin-gen's head-quarters, down came a blow of the heavy sword aimed at Shin-gen's

---

[94] Myo-shin-ji was built in 1337 by the Emperor Hana-zono; Ten-ryu-ji was erected by Taka-uji, the first Shogun of the period, in 1344; So-koku-ji by Yosh-imitsu, the third Shogun, in 1385; Kin-Kaku-ji, or Golden Hall Temple, by the same Shogun, in 1397; Gin-kaku-ji, or Silver Hall Temple, by Yoshi-masa, the eighth Shogun, in 1480.

[95] Shin-gen practised Zen under the instruction of Kwai-sen, who was burned to death by Nobu-naga (O-da) in 1582. See Hon-cho-ko-so-den.

[96] Ken-shin learned Zen under Shu-ken, a So Ta master. See To-jo-ren-to-roku.

forehead, with a question expressed in the technical terms of Zen: "What shalt thou do in such a state at such a moment?" Having no time to draw his sword, Shin-gen parried it with his war-fan, answering simultaneously in Zen words: "A flake of snow on the red-hot furnace!" Had not his attendants come to the rescue Shin-gen's life might have gone as 'a flake of snow on the red-hot furnace.' Afterwards the horseman was known to have been Ken-shin himself. This tradition shows us how Zen was practically lived by the Samurais of the Dark Age.

Although the priests of other Buddhist sects had their share in these bloody affairs, as was natural at such a time, yet Zen monks stood aloof and simply cultivated their literature. Consequently, when all the people grew entirely ignorant at the end of the Dark Age, the Zen monks were the only men of letters. None can deny this merit of their having preserved learning and prepared for its revival in the following period.[97]

Zen under the Toku-gana Shogunate

Peace was at last restored by Iye-yasu, the founder of the Toku-gana Shogunate (1603-1867). During this period the Shogunate gave countenance to Buddhism on one hand, acknowledging it as the state religion, bestowing rich property to large monasteries, making priests take rank over common people, ordering every householder to build a Buddhist altar in his house; while, on the other hand, it did everything to extirpate Christianity, introduced in the previous period (1544). All this paralyzed the missionary spirit of the Buddhists, and put all the sects in dormant state. As

---

[97] After the introduction of Zen into Japan many important books were written, and the following are chief doctrinal works: Ko-zen-go-koku-ron, by Ei-sai; Sho bo-gen-zo; Gaku-do-yo-zin-shu; Fu-kwan-za-zen-gi; Ei-hei-ko-roku, by Do-gen; Za-zen-yo-zin-ki; and Den-ko-roku, by Kei-zan.

for Zen[98] it was still favoured by feudal lords and their vassals, and almost all provincial lords embraced the faith.

It was about the middle of this period that the forty-seven vassals of Ako displayed the spirit of the Samurai by their perseverance, self-sacrifice, and loyalty, taking vengeance on the enemy of their deceased lord. The leader of these men, the tragic tales of whom can never be told or heard without tears, was Yoshi-o (O-ishi died 1702), a believer of Zen,[99] and his tomb in the cemetery of the temple of Sen-gaku-ji, Tokyo, is daily visited by hundreds of his admirers. Most of the professional swordsmen forming a class in these days practised Zen. Mune-nori[100] (Ya-gyu), for instance, established his reputation by the combination of Zen and the fencing art.

The following story about Boku-den (Tsuka-hara), a great swordsman, fully illustrates this tendency:
"On a certain occasion Boku-den took a ferry to cross over the Yabase in the province of Omi. There was among the passengers a Samurai, tall and square-shouldered, apparently an experienced fencer. He behaved rudely toward the fellow-passengers, and talked so much of his own dexterity in the art that Boku-den, provoked by his brag, broke silence. 'You seem, my friend, to practise the art in order to conquer the enemy, but I do it in order not to be conquered,' said Boku-den. 'O monk,' demanded the man, as Boku-den was clad like a Zen monk, 'what school of swordsmanship do

---

[98] The So To Sect was not wanting in competent teachers, for it might take pride in its Ten-kei (1648-1699), whose religious insight was unsurpassed by any other master of the age; in its Shi getsu, who was a commentator of various Zen books, and died 1764; in its Men-zan (1683-1769), whose indefatigable works on the exposition of So To Zen are invaluable indeed; and its Getsu-shu (1618-1696) and Man-zan (1635-1714), to whose labours the reformation of the faith is ascribed. Similarly, the Rin Zai Sect, in its Gu-do (1579-1661); in its Isshi (1608-1646); in its Taku-an (1573-1645), the favourite tutor of the third Shogun, Iye-mitsu; in its Haku-in (1667-1751), the greatest of the Rin Zai masters of the day, to whose extraordinary personality and labour the revival of the sect is due; and its To-rei (1721-1792), a learned disciple of Haku-in. Of the important Zen books written by these masters, Ro-ji-tan-kin, by Ten-kei; Men-zan-ko-roku, by Men-zan; Ya-sen-kwan-wa, Soku-ko-roku, Kwai-an-koku-go, Kei-so-doku-zui, by Haku-in; Shu-mon-mu-jin-to-ron, by To-rei, are well known.

[99] See "Zen Shu," No. 151.

[100] He is known as Ta-jima, who practised Zen under Taku-an.

you belong to?' Well, mine is the Conquering-enemy-without-fighting-school.' 'Don't tell a fib, old monk. If you could conquer the enemy without fighting, what then is your sword for?' 'My sword is not to kill, but to save,' said Boku-den, making use of Zen phrases; 'my art is transmitted from mind to mind.' 'Now then, come, monk,' challenged the man, 'let us see, right at this moment, who is the victor, you or I.' The gauntlet was picked up without hesitation. 'But we must not fight,' said Boku-den, 'in the ferry, lest the passengers should be hurt. Yonder a small island you see. There we shall decide the contest.' To this proposal the man agreed, and the boat was pulled to that island. No sooner had the boat reached the shore than the man jumped over to the land, and cried: 'Come on, monk, quick, quick!' Boku-den, however, slowly rising, said: 'Do not hasten to lose your head. It is a rule of my school to prepare slowly for fighting, keeping the soul in the abdomen.' So saying he snatched the oar from the boatman and rowed the boat back to some distance, leaving the man alone, who, stamping the ground madly, cried out: 'O, you fly, monk, you coward. Come, old monk!' 'Now listen,' said Boku-den, 'this is the secret art of the Conquering-enemy-without-fighting-school. Beware that you do not forget it, nor tell it to anybody else.' Thus, getting rid of the brawling fellow, Boku-den and his fellow-passengers safely landed on the opposite shore."[101] The O Baku School of Zen was introduced by Yin Yuen (In-gen) who crossed the sea in 1654, accompanied by many able disciples.[102] The Shogunate gave him a tract of land at Uji, near Kyo-to, and in 1659 he built there a monastery noted for its Chinese style of architecture, now known as O-baku-san. The teachers of the same school[103] came one after another from China, and Zen[104] peculiar to them, flourished a short while.

---

101 Shi-seki-shu-ran.

102 In-gen (1654-1673) came over with Ta-Mei (Dai-bi, died 1673), Hwui Lin (E-rin died 1681), Tuh Chan (Doku-tan, died 1706), and others. For the life of In-gen: see Zoku-ko-shu-den and Kaku-shu-ko-yo.

103 Tsih Fei (Soku-hi died 1671), Muh Ngan (Moku-an died 1684), Kao Tsuen (Ko-sen died 1695), the author of Fu-so-zen-rin-so-bo-den, To-koku-ko-so-den, and Sen-un-shu, are best known.

104 This is a sub-sect of the Rin Zai School, as shown in the following table:

TRANSMISSION OF ZEN FROM CHINA TO JAPAN

1. Bodhidharma.
2. Hwui Ko (E-ka).
3. San Tsang (So-san).
4. Tao Sin (Do-shin).
5. Hung Jan (Ko nin).

—-THE NORTHERN SECT
 6. Shang Siu (Jin-shu).

—-THE SOUTHERN SECT
6. Hwui Nang (E-no).

—-THE RIN ZAI SCHOOL.
7. Nan Yoh (Nan-gaku).

—-10. Gi-ku.
—-11. Lin Tsi (Rin-zai).
—-21. Yuen Wu (En-go).
—-22. Fuh Hai (Bukkai).
—-28. Kaku-a.

—-THE O BAKU SCHOOL.
42. In-gen.
—-25. Hti Ngan (Kyo-an).
—-26. Ei-sai.

—-THE SO TO SCHOOL.
7. Tsing Yuen (Sei-gen).
—-8. Shih Teu (Seki-to).
—-11. Tung Shan (To-zan).
—-23. Ju Tsing (Nyo-jo).
—-24. Do-gen.

The O Baku School is the amalgamation of Zen and the worship of Amitabha, and different from the other two schools. The statistics for 1911 give the following figures:

The Number of Temples:
The So To School 14,255
The Rin Zai School 6,128
The O Baku School 546

The Number of Teachers:
The So To School 9,576
The Rin Zai School 4,523
The O Baku School 349

It was also in this period that Zen gained a great influence on the popular literature characterized by the shortest form of poetical composition. This was done through the genius of Ba-sho,[105] a great literary man, recluse and traveller, who, as his writings show us, made no small progress in the study of Zen. Again, it was made use of by the teachers of popular[106] ethics, who did a great deal in the education of the lower classes. In this way Zen and its peculiar taste gradually found its way into the arts of peace, such as literature, fine art, tea-ceremony, cookery, gardening, architecture, and at last it has permeated through every fibre of Japanese life.

Zen after the Restoration

After the Restoration of the Mei-ji (1867) the popularity of Zen began to wane, and for some thirty years remained in inactivity; but since the Russo-Japanese War its revival has taken place. And now it is looked upon as an ideal faith, both for a nation full of hope and energy, and for a person who

---

[105] He (died 1694) learned Zen under a contemporary Zen master (Buccho), and is said to have been enlightened before his reformation of the popular literature.

[106] The teaching was called Shin-gaku, or the 'learning of mind.' It was first taught by Bai-gan (Ishi-da), and is the reconciliation of Shintoism and Buddhism with Confucianism. Bai-gan and his successors practised Meditation, and were enlightened in their own way. Do-ni (Naka-zawa, died 1803) made use of Zen more than any other teacher.

has to fight his own way in the strife of life. Bushido, or the code of chivalry, should be observed not only by the soldier in the battle-field, but by every citizen in the struggle for existence. If a person be a person and not a beast, then he must be a Samurai-brave, generous, upright, faithful, and manly, full of self-respect and self-confidence, at the same time full of the spirit of self-sacrifice. We can find an incarnation of Bushido in the late General Nogi, the hero of Port Arthur, who, after the sacrifice of his two sons for the country in the Russo-Japanese War, gave up his own and his wife's life for the sake of the deceased Emperor. He died not in vain, as some might think, because his simplicity, uprightness, loyalty, bravery, self-control, and self-sacrifice, all combined in his last act, surely inspire the rising generation with the spirit of the Samurai to give birth to hundreds of Nogis. Now let us see in the following chapters what Zen so closely connected with Bushido teaches us.

CHAPTER III

THE UNIVERSE IS THE SCRIPTURE[107] OF ZEN

Scripture is no More than Waste Paper

There are twofold Tripitakas (or the three collections of the Buddhist scriptures)-namely, the Mahayana-tripitaka and the Hinayana-tripitaka. The former are the basis of the Mahayana, or the higher and reformed Buddhism, full of profound metaphysical reasonings; while the latter form that of the Hinayana, or the lower and early Buddhism, which is simple and ethical teaching. These twofold Tripitakas are as follows:

THE MAHAYANA-TRIPITAKA

The Sutra Pitaka.-The Saddharma-pundarika-sutra, Samdhi-nirmocana-sutra, Avatamsaka-sutra, Prajnyaparamita-sutra, Amitayus-sutra, Mahaparinirvana-sutra, etc.

The Vinaya Pitaka.—Brahmajala-sutra, Bodhisattva-caryanirdeca, etc.
The Abhidharma Pitaka.—Mahaprajnyaparamita-sutra, Mahayana-craddhotpada-castra, Madhyamaka-castra, Yogacarya bhumi-castra, etc.

THE HINAYANA-TRIPITAKA

The Sutra Pitaka.—Dirghagama, Ekottaragama, Madhyamagama, Samyuktagama, etc.

The Vinaya Pitaka.—Dharmagupta-vinaya, Mahasamghika-vinaya, Sarvastivada-vinaya, etc.

The Abhidharma Pitaka.—Dharma-skandha-pada, Samgiti-paryaya-pada, Jnyanaprasthana-castra, Abhidharma-kosa-castra, etc.

---

[107] Zen is not based on any particular sutra, either of Mahayana or of Hinayana.

The term 'Tripitaka,' however, was not known at the time of Shakya Muni, and almost all of the northern Buddhist records agree in stating that the Tripitaka was rehearsed and settled in the same year in which the Muni died. Mahavansa also says: "The book called Abhidharma-pitaka was compiled, which was preached to god, and was arranged in due order by 500 Budhu priests." But we believe that Shakya Muni's teaching was known to the early Buddhists, not as Tripitaka, but as Vinaya and Dharma, and even at the time of King Acoka (who ascended the throne about 269 B.C.) it was not called Tripitaka, but Dharma, as we have it in his Edicts. Mahayanists unanimously assert the compilation of the Tripitaka in the first council of Rajagrha, but they differ in opinion as to the question who rehearsed the Abhidharma; notwithstanding, they agree as for the other respects, as you see in the following:

The Sutra Pitaka, compiled by Ananda; the Vinaya Pitaka, compiled by Upali; the Abhidharma Pitaka, compiled by Ananda—according to Nagarjuna (Mahaprajnyaparamita-castra).

The Sutra Pitaka, compiled by Ananda; the Vinaya Pitaka, compiled by Upali; the Abhidharma Pitaka, compiled by Kacyapa according to Huen Tsang (Ta-tan-si-yu-ki).

The Sutra Pitaka, compiled by Ananda; the Vinaya Pitaka, compiled by Upali; the Abhidharma Pitaka, compiled by Purna—according to Paramartha ('A Commentary on the History of the Hinayana Schools').

The above-mentioned discrepancy clearly betrays the uncertainty of their assertions, and gives us reason to discredit the compilation of Abhidharma Pitaka at the first council. Besides, judging from the Dharma-gupta-vinaya and other records, which states that Purna took no part in the first council, and that he had different opinions as to the application of the rules of discipline from that of Kacyapa, there should be some errors in Paramartha's assertion. Of these three collections of the Sacred Writings, the first two, or Sutra and Vinaya, of Mahayana, as well as of Himayana, are believed to be the direct teachings of Shakya Muni himself, because all the instructions are put in the mouth of the Master or sanctioned by him. The

Mahayanists, however, compare the Hinayana doctrine with a resting-place on the road for a traveller, while the Mahayana doctrine with his destination. All the denominations of Buddhism, with a single exception of Zen, are based on the authority of some particular sacred writings. The Ten Dai Sect, for instance, is based on Saddharma-pundarika-sutra; the Jo Do Sect on Larger Sukhavati-vyuha, Smaller Sukhavati-vyuha, and Amitayus-dhyana-sutra; the Ke Gon Sect on Avatamsaka-sutra; the Hosso Sect on Samdhi-nirmocana-sutra.

Zen is based on the highest spiritual plane attained by Shakya Muni himself. It can only be realized by one who has attained the same plane. To describe it in full by means of words is beyond the power even of Gotama himself. It is for this reason that the author of Lankavatara-sutra insists that Shakya Muni spoke no word through his long career of forty-nine years as a religious teacher, and that of Mahaprajnyaparamita-sutra[108] also express the same opinion. The Scripture is no more nor less than the finger pointing to the moon of Buddhahood. When we recognize the moon and enjoy its benign beauty, the finger is of no use. As the finger has no brightness whatever, so the Scripture has no holiness whatever. The Scripture is religious currency representing spiritual wealth. It does not matter whether money be gold, or sea-shells, or cows. It is a mere substitute. What it stands for is of paramount importance. Away with your stone-knife! Do not watch the stake against which a running hare once struck its head and died. Do not wait for another hare. Another may not come for ever. Do not cut the side of the boat out of which you dropped your sword to mark where it sunk. The boat is ever moving on. The Canon is the window through which we observe the grand scenery of spiritual nature. To hold communion directly with it we must get out of the window. It is a mere stray fly that is always buzzing within it, struggling to get out. Those who spend most of their lives in the study of the Scriptures, arguing and explaining with hair-splitting reasonings, and attain no higher plane in spirituality, are religious flies good for nothing but their buzzing about the nonsensical technicalities. It is on this account that Rin-zai declared:[109] 'The twelve divisions of the Buddhist Canon are nothing better than waste paper.'

---

[108] Mahaprajnyaparamita-sutra, vol. 425.

[109] Rin-zai-roku.

No Need of the Scriptural Authority for Zen

Some Occidental scholars erroneously identify Buddhism with the primitive faith of Hinayanism, and are inclined to call Mahayanism, a later developed faith, a degenerated one. If the primitive faith be called the genuine, as these scholars think, and the later developed faith be the degenerated one, then the child should be called the genuine man and the grown-up people be the degenerated ones; similarly, the primitive society must be the genuine and the modern civilization be the degenerated one. So also the earliest writings of the Old Testament should be genuine and the four Gospels be degenerated. Beyond all doubt Zen belongs to Mahayanism, yet this does not imply that it depends on the scriptural authority of that school, because it does not trouble itself about the Canon whether it be Hinayana or Mahayana, or whether it was directly spoken by Shakya Muni or written by some later Buddhists. Zen is completely free from the fetters of old dogmas, dead creeds, and conventions of stereotyped past, that check the development of a religious faith and prevent the discovery of a new truth. Zen needs no Inquisition. It never compelled nor will compel the compromise of a Galileo or a Descartes. No excommunication of a Spinoza or the burning of a Bruno is possible for Zen.

On a certain occasion Yoh Shan (Yaku-san) did not preach the doctrine for a long while, and was requested to give a sermon by his assistant teacher, saying: "Would your reverence preach the Dharma to your pupils, who long thirst after your merciful instruction?" "Then ring the bell," replied Yoh Shan. The bell rang, and all the monks assembled in the Hall eager to bear the sermon. Yoh Shan went up to the pulpit and descended immediately without saying a word. "You, reverend sir," asked the assistant, "promised to deliver a sermon a little while ago. Why do you not preach?" "Sutras are taught by the Sutra teachers," said the master; "Castras are taught by the Castra teachers. No wonder that I say nothing."[110] This little episode will show you that Zen is no fixed doctrine embodied in a Sutra or a Castra, but a conviction or realization within us.

---

[110] Zen-rin-rui-shu and E-gen.

To quote another example, an officer offered to Tung Shan (To-zan) plenty of alms, and requested him to recite the sacred Canon. Tung Shan, rising from his chair, made a bow respectfully to the officer, who did the same to the teacher. Then Tung Shan went round the chair, taking the officer with him, and making a bow again to the officer, asked: "Do you see what I mean?" "No, sir," replied the other. "I have been reciting the sacred Canon, why do you not see?"[111] Thus Zen does not regard Scriptures in black and white as its Canon, for it takes to-days and tomorrows of this actual life as its inspired pages.

The Usual Explanation of the Canon

An eminent Chinese Buddhist scholar, well known as Ten Dai Dai Shi (A.D. 538-597), arranged the whole preachings of Shakya Muni in a chronological order in accordance with his own religious theory, and observed that there were the Five Periods in the career of the Buddha as a religious teacher. He tried to explain away all the discrepancies and contradictions, with which the Sacred Books are encumbered, by arranging the Sutras in a line of development. His elucidation was so minute and clear, and his metaphysical reasonings so acute and captivating, that his opinion was universally accepted as an historical truth, not merely by the Chinese, but also by the Japanese Mahayanists. We shall briefly state here the so-called Five Periods.

Shakya Muni attained to Buddhaship in his thirtieth year, and sat motionless for seven days under the Bodhi tree, absorbed in deep meditation, enjoying the first bliss of his Enlightenment. In the second week he preached his Dharma to the innumerable multitude of Bodhisattvas,[112] celestial beings, and deities in the nine assemblies held at seven different places. This is the origin of a famous Mahayana book entitled Buddhavatamsaka-mahavaipulya-sutra. In this book the Buddha set forth his profound Law just as it was discovered by his highly Enlightened mind, without considering the mental states of his hearers. Consequently the ordinary

---

111 Zen-rin-rui-sha and To-zan-roku.

112 Bodhisattva is an imaginary personage, or ideal saint, superior to Arhat, or the highest saint of Hinayanism. The term 'Bodhisattva' was first applied to the Buddha before his Enlightenment, and afterwards was adopted by Mahayanists to mean the adherent of Mahayanism in contradistinction with the Cravaka or hearers of Hinayanism.

hearers (or the Buddha's immediate disciples) could not understand the doctrine, and sat stupefied as if they were 'deaf and dumb,' while the great Bodhisattvas fully understood and realized the doctrine. This is called the first period, which lasted only two or three[113] weeks.

Thereupon Shakya Muni, having discovered that ordinary bearers were too ignorant to believe in the Mahayana doctrine and appreciate the greatness of Buddhahood, thought it necessary to modify his teaching so as to adjust it to the capacity of ordinary people. So he went to Varanasi (or Benares) and preached his modified doctrine—that is, Hinayanism. The instruction given at that time has been handed down to us as the four Agamas,[114] or the four Nikayas. This is called the second period, which lasted about twelve years. It was at the beginning of this period that the Buddha converted the five ascetics,[115] who became his disciples. Most of the Çravakas or the adherents of Hinayanism were converted during this period. They trained their hearts in accordance with the modified Law, learned the four noble truths,[116] and worked out their own salvation.

The Buddha then having found his disciples firmly adhering to Hinayanism without knowing that it was a modified and imperfect doctrine, he had to lead them up to a higher and perfect doctrine that he might lead them up to Buddhahood. With this object in view Shakya Muni preached Vimalakirtti-

---

113 Bodhiruci says to the effect that the preachings in the first five assemblies were made in the first week, and the rest were delivered in the second week. Nagarjuna says that the Buddha spoke no word for fifty-seven days after his Enlightenment. It is said in Saddharma-pundarika-sutra that after three weeks the Buddha preached at Varanasi, and it says nothing respecting Avatamsaka-sutra. Though there are divers opinions about the Buddha's first sermon and its date, all traditions agree in this that he spent some time in meditation, and then delivered the first sermon to the five ascetics at Varanasi.

114 (1) Anguttara, (2) Majjhima, (3) Digha, (4) Samyutta.

115 Kondanynya, Vappa, Baddiya, Mahanana, Assaji.

116 The first is the sacred truth of suffering; the second the truth of the origin of suffering —that is, lust and desire; the third the sacred truth of the extinction of suffering; the fourth the sacred truth of the path that leads to the extinction of suffering. There are eight noble paths that lead to the extinction of suffering—that is, Right faith, Right resolve, Right speech, Right action, Right living, Right effort, Right thought, and Right meditation.

nirdeca-sutra[117], Lankavatara-sutra, and other sutras, in which he compared Hinayanism with Mahayanism, and described the latter in glowing terms as a deep and perfect Law, whilst he set forth the former at naught as a superficial and imperfect one. Thus he showed his disciples the inferiority of Hinayanism, and caused them to desire for Mahayanism. This is said to be the third period, which lasted some eight years.

The disciples of the Buddha now understood that Mahayanism was far superior to Hinayanism, but they thought the higher doctrine was only for Bodhisattvas and beyond their understanding. Therefore they still adhered to the modified doctrine, though they did no longer decry Mahayanism, which they had no mind to practise. Upon this Shakya Muni preached Prajnyaparamita-sutras[118] in the sixteen assemblies held at four different places, and taught them Mahayanism in detail in order to cause them to believe it and practise it. Thus they became aware that there was no definite demarcation between Mahayanism and Hinayanism, and that they might become Mahayanists. This is the fourth period, which lasted about twenty-two years. Now, the Buddha, aged seventy-two, thought it was high time to preach his long-cherished doctrine that all sentient beings can attain to Supreme Enlightenment; so he preached Saddharma-pundarika-sutra, in which he prophesied when and where his disciples should become Buddhas. It was his greatest object to cause all sentient beings to be Enlightened and enable them to enjoy the bliss of Nirvana. It was for this

---

117 This is one of the most noted Mahayana books, and is said to be the best specimen of the sutras belonging to this period. It is in this sutra that most of Shakya's eminent disciples, known as the adherents of Hinayanism, are astonished with the profound wisdom, the eloquent speech, and the supernatural power of Vimalakirtti, a Bodhisattva, and confess the inferiority of their faith. The author frequently introduces episodes in order to condemn Hinayanism, making use of miracles of his own invention.

118 Nagarjuna's doctrine depends mainly on these sutras.

These five periods above mentioned can scarcely be called historical in the proper sense of the term, yet they are ingeniously invented by Ten Dai Dai Shi to set the Buddhist Scriptures in the order of doctrinal development, and place Saddharma-pundarika in the highest rank among the Mahayana books. His argument, however dogmatic and anti-historical in no small degree, would be not a little valuable for our reader, who wants to know the general phase of the Buddhist Canon, consisting of thousands of fascicles.

that he had endured great pain and hardships through his previous existences. It was for this that he had left his heavenly abode to appear on earth. It was for this that he had preached from time to time through his long career of forty-seven years. Having thus realized his great aim, Shakya Muni had now to prepare for his final departure, and preached Mahaparinirvana-sutra in order to show that all the animated and inanimate things were endowed with the same nature as his. After this last instruction he passed to eternity. This is called the fifth period, which lasted some eight years.

Sutras used by Zen Masters

Ten Dai failed to explain away the discrepancies and contradictions of which the Canon is full, and often contradicted himself by the ignoring of historical[119] facts.

The foundation of Hinayanism consists in the four Nikayas, or four Agamas, the most important books of that school. Besides the four Agamas, there exist in the Chinese Tripitaka numerous books translated by various authors, some of which are extracts from Agamas, and some the lives of the Buddha, while others are entirely different sutras, apparently of later date. Judging from these sources, it seems to us that most of Shakya Muni's original teachings are embodied into the four Agamas. But it is still a matter of uncertainty that whether they are stated in Agamas now extant just as they were, for the Buddha's preachings were rehearsed immediately after the Buddha's death in the first council held at Rajagrha, yet not consigned to writing. They were handed down by memory about one hundred years. Then the monks at Vaisali committed the so-called Ten Indulgences, infringing the rules of the Order, and maintained that Shakya Muni had not condemned them in his preachings. As there were, however, no written sutras to disprove their assertion, the elders, such as Yaca, Revata, and others, who opposed the Indulgences, had to convoke the second council of 700 monks, in which they succeeded in getting the Indulgences condemned, and rehearsed the Buddha's instruction for the

[119] Let us state our own opinion on the subject in question.

second time. Even in this council of Vaisali we cannot find the fact that the Master's preachings were reduced to writing. The decisions of the 700 elders were not accepted by the party of opposition, who held a separate council, and settled their own rules and doctrine. Thus the same doctrine of the Teacher began to be differently stated and believed.

This being the first open schism, one disruption after another took place among the Buddhistic Order. There were many different schools of the Buddhists at the time when King Acoka ascended the throne (about 269 B.C.), and the patronage of the King drew a great number of pagan ascetics into the Order, who, though they dressed themselves in the yellow robes, yet still preserved their religious views in their original colour. This naturally led the Church into continual disturbances and moral corruption. In the eighteenth year of Acoka's reign the King summoned the council of 1,000 monks at Pataliputra (Patna), and settled the orthodox doctrine in order to keep the Dharma pure from heretical beliefs. We believe that about this time some of the Buddha's preachings were reduced to writing, for the missionaries despatched by the King in the year following the council seem to have set out with written sutras. In addition to this, some of the names of the passages of the Dharma are given in the Bharbra edict of the King, which was addressed to the monks in Magadha. We do not suppose, however, that all the sutras were written at once in these days, but that they were copied down from memory one after another at different times, because some of the sutras were put down in Ceylon 160 years after the Council of Patna.

In the introductory book of Ekottaragama (Anguttara Nikaya), now extant in the Chinese Tripitaka, we notice the following points: (1) It is written in a style quite different from that of the original Agama, but similar to that of the supplementary books of the Mahayana sutras; (2) it states Ananda's compilation of the Tripitaka after the death of the Master; (3) it refers to the past Buddhas, the future Buddha Maitreya, and innumerable Bodhisattvas; (4) it praises the profound doctrine of Mahayanism. From this we infer that the Agama was put in the present form after the rise of the Mahayana School, and handed down through the hand of Mahasanghika scholars, who were much in sympathy with Mahayanism.
Again, the first book of Dirghagama, (Digha Nikaya), that describes the

line of Buddhas who appeared before Shakya Muni, adopts the whole legend of Gotama's life as a common mode of all Buddhas appearing on earth; while the second book narrates the death of Gotama and the distribution of his relies, and refers to Pataliputra, the new capital of Acoka. This shows us that the present Agama is not of an earlier date than the third century B.C. Samyuktagama (Samyutta Nikaya) also gives a detailed account of Acoka's conversion, and of his father Bindusara. From these evidences we may safely infer that the Hinayana sutras were put in the present shape at different times between the third century B.C. and the first century A.D. With regard to the Mahayana sutras we have little doubt about their being the writings of the later Buddhist reformers, even if they are put in the mouth of Shakya Muni. They are entirely different from the sutras of Hinayanism, and cannot be taken as the preachings of one and the same person. The reader should notice the following points:

(1) Four councils were held for the rehearsal of the Tripitaka namely, the first at Rajagrha, in the year of Shakya Muni's death; the second at Vaisali, some 100 years after the Buddha; the third at the time of King Acoka, about 235 years after the Master; the fourth at the time of King Kanishka, the first century A.D. But all these councils were held to compile the Hinayana sutras, and nothing is known of the rehearsal of the Mahayana books. Some are of opinion that the first council was held within the Sattapanni cave, near Rajagrha, where the Hinayana Tripitaka was rehearsed by 500 monks, while outside the cave there assembled a greater number of monks, who were not admitted into the cave, and rehearsed the Mahayana Tripitaka. This opinion, however, is based on no reliable source.

(2) The Indian orthodox Buddhists of old declared that the Mahayana sutras were the fabrication of heretics or of the Evil One, and not the teachings of the Buddha. In reply to this, the Mahayanists had to prove that the Mahayana sutras were compiled by the direct disciples of the Master; but even Nagarjuna could not vindicate the compilation of the doubtful books, and said (in Mahaprajnyaparamita-castra) that they were compiled by Ananda and Manjucri, with myriads of Bodhisattvas at the outside of the Iron Mountain Range, which encloses the earth. Asanga also proved (in Mahayanalankara-sutra-castra) with little success that

Mahayanism was the Buddha's direct teachings. Some may quote Bodhisattva-garbhastha-sutra in favour of the Mahayana; but it is of no avail, as the sutra itself is the work of a later date.

(3) Although almost all of the Mahayana sutras, excepting Avatamsaka-sutra, treat of Hinayanism as the imperfect doctrine taught in the first part of the Master's career, yet not merely the whole life of Gotama, but also events which occurred after his death are narrated in the Hinayana sutras. This shows that the Mahayana sutras were composed after the establishment of early Buddhism.

(4) The narratives given in the Hinayana sutras in reference to Shakya Muni seem to be based on historical facts, but those in the Mahayana books are full of wonders and extravagant miracles far from facts.

(5) The Hinayana sutras retain the traces of their having been classified and compiled as we see in Ekottaragama, while Mahayana books appear to have been composed one after another by different authors at different times, because each of them strives to excel others, declaring itself to be the sutra of the highest doctrine, as we see in Saddharma-pundarika, Samdhinirmocana, Suvarnaprabhasottamaraja, etc.

(6) The dialogues in the Hinayana sutras are in general those between the Buddha and his disciples, while in the Mahayana books imaginary beings called Bodhisattvas take the place of disciples. Moreover, in some books no monks are mentioned.

(7) Most of the Mahayana sutras declare that they themselves possess those mystic powers that protect the reader or the owner from such evils as epidemic, famine, war, etc.; but the Hinayana sutras are pure from such beliefs.

(8) The Mahayana sutras extol not only the merits of the reading, but the copying of the sutras. This unfailingly shows the fact that they were not handed down by memory, as the Hinayana sutras, but written by their respective authors.

(9) The Hinayana sutras were written with a plain style in Pali, while the Mahayana books, with brilliant phraseology, in Sanskrit.

(10)The Buddha in the Hinayana sutras is little more than a human being, while Buddha or Tathagata in the Mahayana is a superhuman being or Great Deity.

(11)The moral precepts of the Hinayana were laid down by the Master every time when his disciples acted indecently, while those of the Mahayana books were spoken all at once by Tathagata.

(12)Some Mahayana sutras appear to be the exaggeration or modification of what was stated in the Hinayana books, as we see in Mahaparinirvana-sutra.

(13)If we take both the Hinayana and the Mahayana as spoken by one and the same person, we cannot understand why there are so many contradictory statements, as we see in the following:

(a) Historical Contradictions.—For instance, Hinayana sutras are held to be the first sermon of the Buddha by the author of Saddharma-pundarika, while Avatamsaka declares itself to be the first sermon. Nagarjuna holds that Prajnya sutras are the first.

(b) Contradictions as to the Person of the Master.—For instance, Agamas say the Buddha's body was marked with thirty-two peculiarities, while the Mahayana books enumerate ninety-seven peculiarities, or even innumerable marks.

(c) Doctrinal Contradictions.—For instance, the Hinayana sutras put forth the pessimistic, nihilistic view of life, while the Mahayana books, as a rule, express the optimistic, idealistic view.

(14) The Hinayana sutras say nothing of the Mahayana books, while the latter always compare their doctrine with that of the former, and speak of it in contempt. It is clear that the name 'Hinayana' was coined by the Mahayanists, as there is no sutra which calls itself 'Hinayana.' It is therefore

evident that when the Hinayana books took the present shape there appeared no Mahayana sutras.

(15) The authors of the Mahayana sutras should have expected the opposition of the Hinayanists, because they say not seldom that there might be some who would not believe in and oppose Mahayanism as not being the Buddha's teaching, but that of the Evil One. They say also that one who would venture to say the Mahayana books are fictitious should fall into Hell. For example, the author of Mahaparinirvana-sutra says: "Wicked Bhiksus would say all Vaipulya Mahayana sutras are not spoken by the Buddha, but by the Evil One."

(16) There are evidences showing that the Mahayana doctrine was developed out of the Hinayana one.

(a) The Mahayanists' grand conception of Tathagata is the natural development of that of those progressive Hinayanists who belonged to the Mahasamghika School, which was formed some one hundred years after the Master. These Hinayanists maintained that the Buddha had infinite power, endless life, and limitlessly great body. The author of Mahaparinirvana-sutra also says that Buddha is immortal, his Dharmakaya is infinite and eternal. The authors of Mahayana-mulagata-hrdayabhumi-dhyana-sutra and of Suvarnaprabha-sottamaraja-sutra enumerate the Three Bodies of Buddha, while the writer of Lankavatara-sutra describes the Four Bodies, and that of Avatamsaka-sutra the Ten Bodies of Tathagata.

(b) According to the Hinayana sutras, there are only four stages of saintship, but the Mahasamghika School increases the number and gives ten steps. Some Mahayana sutras also enumerate the ten stages of Bodhisattva, while others give forty-one or fifty two stages.

(c) The Himayana sutras name six past Buddhas and one future Buddha Maitreya, while the Mahayana sutras name thirty-five, fifty-three, or three thousand Buddhas.

(d) The Hinayana sutras give the names of six Vijnyanas, while the

Mahayana books seven, eight, or nine Vijnyanas.

(17) For a few centuries after the Buddha we hear only of Hinayanism, but not of Mahayanism, there being no Mahayana teacher.

(18) In some Mahayana sutras (Mahavairocanabhisambodhi-sutra, for example) Tathagata Vairocana takes the place of Gotama, and nothing is said of the latter.

(19) The contents of the Mahayana sutras often prove that they were, composed, or rewritten, or some additions were made, long after the Buddha. For instance, Mahamaya-sutra says that Acvaghosa would refute heretical doctrines 600 years after the Master, and Nagarjuna would advocate the Dharma 700 years after Gotama, while Lankavatara-sutra prophesies that Nagarjuna would appear in South India.

(20) The author of San-ron-gen-gi tells us Mahadeva, a leader of the Mahasamghika School, used Mahayana sutras, together with the orthodox Tripitaka 116 after the Buddha. It is, however, doubtful that they existed at so early a date.

(21) Mahaprajnyaparamita-castra, ascribed to Nagarjuna, refers to many Mahayana books, which include Saddharma-pundarika, Vimalakirtti-nirdeca, Sukhavati-vyuha, Mahaprajnyaparamita, Pratyutpanna-buddhasammukhavasthita-samadhi, etc. He quotes in his Dacabhumivibhasa-castra, Mahaparinirvana, Dacabhumi, etc.

(22) Sthiramati, whose date is said to be earlier than Nagarjuna and later than Acvaghosa, tries to prove that Mahayanism was directly taught by the Master in his Mahayanavataraka-castra. And Mahayanottaratantra-castra, which is ascribed by some scholars to him, refers to Avatamsaka, Vajracchedikka-prajnyaparamita, Saddharmapundarika, Crimala-devi-simhananda, etc.

(23) Chi-leu-cia-chin, who came to China in A.D. 147 or A.D. 164, translated some part of Mahayana books known as Maharatnakuta-sutra and Mahavaipulya-mahasannipata-sutra.

(24) An-shi-kao, who came to China in A.D. 148, translated such Mahayana books as Sukhavati-vyaha, Candra-dipa-samadhi, etc.

(25) Matanga, who came to China in A.D. 67, is said by his biographer to have been informed of both Mahayanism and Hinayanism to have given interpretations to a noted Mahayana book, entitled Suvarnaprabhasa.

(26) Sandhinirmocana-sutra is supposed to be a work of Asanga not without reason, because Asanga's doctrine is identical with that of the sutra, and the sutra itself is contained in the latter part of Yogacaryabhumi-castra. The author divides the whole preachings of the Master into the three periods that he might place the Idealistic doctrine in the highest rank of the Mahayana schools.

(27) We have every reason to believe that Mahayana sutras began to appear (perhaps Prajnya sutras being the first) early in the first century A.D., that most of the important books appeared before Nagarjuna, and that some of Mantra sutras were composed so late as the time of Vajrabodhi, who came to China in A.D. 719.

To say nothing of the strong opposition raised by the Japanese scholars,[120] such an assumption can be met with an assumption of entirely opposite nature, and the difficulties can never be overcome. For Zen masters, therefore, these assumptions and reasonings are mere quibbles unworthy of their attention.

To believe blindly in the Scriptures is one thing, and to be pious is another. How often the childish views of Creation and of God in the Scriptures concealed the light of scientific truths; how often the blind believers of them fettered the progress of civilization; how often religious men prevented us from the realizing of a new truth, simply because it is against the ancient folk-lore in the Bible. Nothing is more absurd than the constant dread in which religious men, declaring to worship God in truth and in spirit, are kept at the scientific discovery of new facts incompatible with the

---

[120] The foremost of them was Chuki Tominaga (1744), of whose life little is known. He is said to have been a nameless merchant at Osaka. His Shutsu-jo-ko-go is the first great work of higher criticism on the Buddhist Scriptures.

folk-lore. Nothing is more irreligious than to persecute the seekers of truth in order to keep up absurdities and superstitions of bygone ages. Nothing is more inhuman than the commission of 'devout cruelty' under the mask of love of God and man. Is it not the misfortune, not only of Christianity, but of whole mankind, to have the Bible encumbered with legendary histories, stories of miracles, and a crude cosmology, which from time to time come in conflict with science?

The Buddhist Scriptures are also overloaded with Indian superstitions and a crude cosmology, which pass under the name of Buddhism. Accordingly, Buddhist scholars have confused not seldom the doctrine of the Buddha with these absurdities, and thought it impious to abandon them. Kaiseki,[121] for instance, was at a loss to distinguish Buddhism from the Indian astronomy, which is utterly untenable in the face of the fact. He taxed his reason to the utmost to demonstrate the Indian theory and at the same time to refute the Copernican theory. One day he called on Yeki-do[122] a contemporary Zen master, and explained the construction of the Three Worlds as described in the Scriptures, saying that Buddhism would come to naught if the theory of the Three Worlds be overthrown by the Copernican. Then Yeki-do exclaimed: "Buddhism aims to destroy the Three Worlds and to establish Buddha's Holy Kingdom throughout the universe. Why do you waste your energy in the construction of the Three Worlds?"[123]

In this way Zen does not trouble itself about unessentials of the Scriptures, on which it never depends for its authority. Do-gen, the founder of the Japanese So To Sect, severely condemns (in his Sho-bo-gen-zo) the notions of the impurity of women inculcated in the Scriptures. He openly attacks those Chinese monks who swore that they would not see any woman, and ridicules those who laid down rules prohibiting women from getting access to monasteries. A Zen master was asked by a Samurai whether there was hell in sooth as taught in the Scriptures. "I must ask you," replied he,

---

[121] A learned Japanese Buddhist scholar, who died in 1882.

[122] A famous Zen master, the abbot of the So-ji-ji Monastery, who died in 1879.

[123] Kin-sei-zen-rin-gen-ko-roku.

"before I give you an answer. For what purpose is your question? What business have you, a Samurai, with a thing of that sort? Why do you bother yourself about such an idle question? Surely you neglect your duty and are engaged in such a fruitless research. Does this not amount to your stealing the annual salary from your lord?" The Samurai, offended not a little with these rebukes, stared at the master, ready to draw his sword at another insult. Then the teacher said smilingly: "Now you are in Hell. Don't you see?”

Does, then, Zen use no scripture? To this question we answer both affirmatively and negatively: negatively, because Zen regards all sutras as a sort of pictured food which has no power of appeasing spiritual hunger; affirmatively, because it freely makes use of them irrespective of Mahayana or Hinayana. Zen would not make a bonfire of the Scriptures as Caliph Omar did of the Alexandrian library. A Zen master, having seen a Confucianist burning his books on the thought that they were rather a hindrance to his spiritual growth, observed: "You had better burn your books in mind and heart, but not the books in black and white.”[124]

As even deadly poison proves to be medicine in the band of a good doctor, so a heterodox doctrine antagonistic to Buddhism is used by the Zen teachers as a finger pointing to the principle of Zen. But they as a rule resorted to Lankavatara-sutra,[[125] Vajracchedika-prajnya-paramita-

[124] Ukiyo-soshi.

[125] This book is the nearest approach to the doctrine of Zen, and is said to have been pointed out by Bodhidharma as the best book for the use of his followers. See Nanjo's Catalogue, Nos. 175, 1761 177.

sutra,[126]Vimalakirtti-nirdeca-sutra[127] Mahavaipulya-purnabuddha-sutra[128] Mababuddhosnisa-tathagata-guhyahetu-saksatkrta-prasannatha-sarvabhodhi sattvacarya-surangama-sutra,[129]Mahapari-nirvana-sutra,[130] Saddharma-pundarika-sutra, Avatamsaka-sutra, and so forth.

A Sutra Equal in Size to the Whole World

The holy writ that Zen masters admire is not one of parchment nor of palm-leaves, nor in black and white, but one written in heart and mind. On one occasion a King of Eastern India invited the venerable Prajnyatara, the teacher of Bodhidharma, and his disciples to dinner at his own palace.
Finding all the monks reciting the sacred sutras with the single exception of the master, the King questioned Prajnyatara: "Why do you not, reverend sir, recite the Scriptures as others do?" "My poor self, your majesty," replied he, "does not go out to the objects of sense in my expiration nor is it confined within body and mind in my inspiration. Thus I constantly recite hundreds, thousands, and millions of sacred sutras." In like manner the Emperor Wu, of the Liang dynasty, once requested Chwen Hih (Fu Dai-shi) to give a lecture on the Scriptures. Chwen went upon the platform, struck the desk

---

[126] The author of the sutra insists on the unreality of all things. The book was first used by the Fifth Patriarch, as we have seen in the first chapter. See Nanjo's Catalogue, Nos. 10, 11, 12, 13, 14, 15.

[127] The sutra agrees with Zen in many respects, especially in its maintaining that the highest truth can only be realized in mind, and cannot be expressed by word of mouth. See Nanjo's Catalogue, Nos. 144, 145, 146, 147, 148, 149.

[128] The sutra was translated into Chinese by Buddhatrata in the seventh century. The author treats at length of Samadhi, and sets forth a doctrine similar to Zen, so that the text was used by many Chinese Zenists. See Nanjo's Catalogue, Nos. 427 and 1629.

[129] The sutra was translated into Chinese by Paramiti and Mikacakya, of the Tang dynasty (618-907). The author conceives Reality as Mind or Spirit. The book belongs to the Mantra class, although it is much used by Zenists. See Nanjo's Catalogue, No. 446.

[130] The author of the book sets forth his own conception of Nirvana and of Buddha, and maintains that all beings are endowed with Buddha-nature. He also gives in detail an incredible account about Gotama's death.

with a block of wood, and came down. Pao Chi (Ho-shi), a Buddhist tutor to the Emperor, asked the perplexed monarch: "Does your Lordship understand him?" "No," answered His Majesty. "The lecture of the Great Teacher is over." As it is clear to you from these examples, Zen holds that the faith must be based not on the dead Scriptures, but on living facts, that one must turn over not the gilt pages of the holy writ, but read between the lines in the holy pages of daily life, that Buddha must be prayed not by word of mouth, but by actual deed and work, and that one must split open, as the author of Avatamsaka-sutra allegorically tells us, the smallest grain of dirt to find therein a sutra equal in size to the whole world. "The so-called sutra," says Do-gen, "covers the whole universe. It transcends time and space. It is written with the characters of heaven, of man, of beasts, of Asuras,[131] of hundreds of grass, and of thousands of trees. There are characters, some long, some short, some round, some square, some blue, some red, some yellow, and some white-in short, all the phenomena in the universe are the characters with which the sutra is written." Shakya Muni read that sutra through the bright star illuminating the broad expanse of the morning skies, when he sat in meditation under the Bodhi Tree.

Ling Yun (Rei-un) read it through the lovely flowers of a peach-tree in spring after some twenty years of his research for Light, and said:

"A score of years I looked for Light:
There came and went many a spring and fall.
E'er since the peach blossoms came in my sight,
I never doubt anything at all."

Hian Yen (Kyo-gen) read it through the noise of bamboo, at which he threw pebbles. Su Shih (So-shoku) read it through a waterfall, one evening, and said:

"The brook speaks forth the Tathagata's words divine,
The hills reveal His glorious forms that shine."

---

131 The name of a demon.

Great Men and Nature

All great men, whether they be poets or scientists or religious men or philosophers, are not mere readers of books, but the perusers of Nature. Men of erudition are often lexicons in flesh and blood, but men of genius read between the lines in the pages of life. Kant, a man of no great erudition, could accomplish in the theory of knowledge what Copernicus did in astronomy. Newton found the law of gravitation not in a written page, but in a falling apple. Unlettered Jesus realized truth beyond the comprehension of many learned doctors. Charles Darwin, whose theory changed the whole current of the world's thought, was not a great reader of books, but a careful observer of facts. Shakespeare, the greatest of poets, was the greatest reader of Nature and life. He could hear the music even of heavenly bodies, and said:

"There's not the smallest orb which thou beholdest,
But in his motion like an angel sings."

Chwang Tsz (So-shi), the greatest of Chinese philosophers, says: "Thou knowest the music of men, but not the music of the earth. Thou knowest the music of the earth, but not the music of the heaven."[132] Goethe, perceiving a profound meaning in Nature, says: "Flowers are the beautiful hieroglyphics of Nature with which she indicates how much she loves us."

Son-toku[133] (Ninomiya), a great economist, who, overcoming all difficulties and hardships by which he was beset from his childhood, educated himself, says: "The earth and the heaven utter no word, but they ceaselessly repeat the holy book unwritten."

---

[132] Chwang Tsz, vol. i., p. 10.

[133] One of the greatest self-made men in Japan, who lived 1787-1856.

The Absolute and Reality are but an Abstraction

A grain of sand you, trample upon has a deeper significance than a series of lectures by your verbal philosopher whom you respect. It contains within itself the whole history of the earth; it tells you what it has seen since the dawn of time; while your philosopher simply plays on abstract terms and empty words. What does his Absolute, or One, or Substance mean? What does his Reality or Truth imply? Do they denote or connote anything? Mere name! mere abstraction! One school of philosophy after another has been established on logical subtleties; thousands of books have been written on these grand names and fair mirages, which vanish the moment that your hand of experience reaches after them.

"Duke Hwan," says Chwang Tsz,[134] "seated above in his hall, was" (once) reading a book, and a wheelwright, Phien, was making a wheel below it. Laying aside his hammer and chisel, Phien went up the steps and said: 'I venture to ask your Grace what words you are reading?' The duke said: 'The words of sages.' 'Are these sages alive?' Phien continued. 'They are dead,' was the reply. 'Then,' said the other, 'what you, my Ruler, are reading is only the dregs and sediments of those old men.' The duke said:

'How should you, a wheelwright, have anything to say about the book which I am reading? If you can explain yourself, very well; if you cannot, you shall die.' The wheelwright said: 'Your servant will look at the thing from the point of view of his own art. In making a wheel, if I proceed gently, that is pleasant enough, but the workmanship is not strong; if I proceed violently, that is toilsome and the joinings do not fit. If the movements of my hand are neither (too) gentle nor (too) violent, the idea in my mind is realized. But I cannot tell (how to do this) by word of mouth; there is a knack in it. I cannot teach the knack to my son, nor can my son learn it from me. Thus it is that I am in my seventieth year, and am (still) making wheels in my old age. But these ancients, and what it was not possible for them to convey, are dead and gone. So then what you, my Ruler, are reading is but their dregs and sediments." Zen has no business with the dregs and sediments of sages of yore.

---

[134] Chwang Tsz, vol. ii., p. 24.

The Sermon of the Inanimate

The Scripture of Zen is written with facts simple and familiar, so simple and familiar with everyday life that they escape observation on that very account. The sun rises in the east. The moon sets in the west. High is the mountain. Deep is the sea. Spring comes with flowers; summer with the cool breeze; autumn with the bright moon; winter with the fakes of snow. These things, perhaps too simple and too familiar for ordinary observers to pay attention to, have had profound significance for Zen. Li Ngao (Ri-ko) one day asked Yoh Shan (Yaku-san): "What is the way to truth?" Yoh Shan, pointing to the sky and then to the pitcher beside him, said: "You see?" "No, sir," replied Li Ngao. "The cloud is in the sky," said Yoh Shan, "and the water in the pitcher." Huen Sha (Gen-sha) one day went upon the platform and was ready to deliver a sermon when he heard a swallow singing. "Listen," said he, "that small bird preaches the essential doctrine and proclaims the eternal truth." Then he went back to his room, giving no sermon.[135]

The letters of the alphabet, a, b, c, etc., have no meaning whatever. They are but artificial signs, but when spelt they can express any great idea that great thinkers may form. Trees, grass, mountains, rivers, stars, moons, suns. These are the alphabets with which the Zen Scripture is written. Even a, b, c, etc., when spelt, can express any great idea. Why not, then, these trees, grass, etc., the alphabets of Nature when they compose the Volume of the Universe? Even the meanest clod of earth proclaims the sacred law.
Hwui Chung[136] (E-chu) is said first to have given an expression to the Sermon of the Inanimate. "Do the inanimate preach the Doctrine?" asked a monk of Hwui Chung on one occasion. "Yes, they preach eloquently and incessantly. There is no pause in their orations," was the reply. "Why, then, do I not hear them?" asked the other again. "Even if you do not, there are many others who can hear them." "Who can hear them?" "All the sages hear and understand them," said Hwui Chung. Thus the Sermon of the Inanimate had been a favourite topic of discussion 900 years before

---

[135] Den-to-roku and E-gen.

[136] A direct disciple of the Sixth Patriarch.

Shakespeare who expressed the similar idea, saying:
"And this our life, exempt from public haunt,
Finds tongues in trees, books in the running brooks,
Sermons in stones, and good in everything."

"How wonderful is the Sermon of the Inanimate," says Tung Shan (To-zan). "You cannot hear it through your ears, but you can hear it through your eyes." You should hear it through your mind's eyes, through your heart's eyes, through your inmost soul's eyes, not through your intellect, not through your perception, not through your knowledge, not through your logic, not through your metaphysics. To understand it you have to divine, not to define; you have to observe, not to calculate; you have to sympathize, not to analyze; you have to see through, not to criticize; you have not to explain, but to feel; you have not to abstract, but to grasp; you have to see all in each, but not to know all in all; you have to get directly at the soul of things, penetrating their hard crust of matter by your rays of the innermost consciousness. "The falling leaves as well as the blooming flowers reveal to us the holy law of Buddha," says a Japanese Zenist.

Ye who seek for purity and peace, go to Nature. She will give you more than ye ask. Ye who long for strength and perseverance, go to Nature. She will train and strengthen you. Ye who aspire after an ideal, go to Nature. She will help you in its realization. Ye who yearn after Enlightenment, go to Nature. She will never fail to grant your request.

CHAPTER IV

BUDDHA, THE UNIVERSAL SPIRIT

The Ancient Buddhist Pantheon

The ancient Buddhist pantheon was full of deities or Buddhas, 3,000[137] in number, or rather countless, and also of Bodhisattvas no less than Buddhas. Nowadays, however, in every church of Mahayanism one Buddha or another together with some Bodhisattvas reigns supreme as the sole object of worship, while other supernatural beings sink in oblivion. These Enlightened Beings, regardless of their positions in the pantheon, were generally regarded as persons who in their past lives cultivated virtues, underwent austerities, and various sorts of penance, and at length attained to a complete Enlightenment, by virtue of which they secured not only peace and eternal bliss, but acquired divers supernatural powers, such as clairvoyance, clairaudience, all-knowledge, and what not. Therefore, it is natural that some Mahayanists[138] came to believe that, if they should go through the same course of discipline and study, they could attain to the same Enlightenment and Bliss, or the same Buddhahood, while other Mahayanists[139] came to believe in the doctrine that the believer is saved and led up to the eternal state of bliss, without undergoing these hard disciplines, by the power of a Buddha known as having boundless mercy and fathomless wisdom whom he invokes.

Zen is Iconoclastic

---

[137] Trikalpa-trisahasra-buddhanrama-sutra gives the names of 3,000 Buddhas, and Buddhabhisita-buddhanama-sutra enumerates Buddhas and Bodhisattvas 11,093 in number. See Nanjo's Catalogue, Nos. 404, 405, 406, 407.

[138] Those who believe in the doctrine of Holy Path. See 'A History of the Twelve Japanese Buddhist Sects,' pp. 109-111.

[139] Those who believe in the doctrine of the Pure Land.

For the followers of Bodhidharma, however, this conception of Buddha seemed too crude to be accepted unhesitatingly and the doctrine too much irrelevant with and uncongenial to actual life. Since Zen denounced, as we have seen in the previous chapter, the scriptural authority, it is quite reasonable to have given up this view of Buddha inculcated in the Mahayana sutras, and to set at naught those statues and images of supernatural beings kept in veneration by the orthodox Buddhists. Tan Hia (Tan-ka), a noted Chinese Zen master, was found warming himself on a cold morning by the fire made of a wooden statue of Buddha. On another occasion he was found mounting astride the statue of a saint. Chao Chen (Jo-shu) one day happened to find Wang Yuen (Bun-yen) worshipping the Buddha in the temple, and forthwith struck him with his staff. "Is there not anything good in the worshipping of the Buddha?" protested Wang Yuen. Then the master said: "Nothing is better than anything good."[140] These examples fully illustrate Zen's attitude towards the objects of Buddhist worship. Zen is not, nevertheless, iconoclastic in the commonly accepted sense of the term, nor is it idolatrous, as Christian missionaries are apt to suppose.

Zen is more iconoclastic than any of the Christian or the Mohammedan denominations in the sense that it opposes the acceptance of the petrified idea of Deity, so conventional and formal that it carries no inner conviction of the believers. Faith dies out whenever one comes to stick to one's fixed and immutable idea of Deity, and to deceive oneself, taking bigotry for genuine faith. Faith must be living and growing, and the living and growing faith should assume no fixed form. It might seem for a superficial observer to take a fixed form, as a running river appears constant, though it goes through ceaseless changes. The dead faith, immutable and conventional, makes its embracer appear religious and respectable, while it arrests his spiritual growth. It might give its owner comfort and pride, yet it at bottom proves to be fetters to his moral uplifting. It is on this account that Zen declares: "Buddha is nothing but spiritual chain or moral fetters," and, "If you remember even a name of Buddha, it would deprive you of purity of heart." The conventional or orthodox idea of Buddha or Deity might seem

---

[140] Zen-rin-rui-shu.

smooth and fair, like a gold chain, being polished and hammered through generations by religious goldsmiths; but it has too much fixity and frigidity to be worn by us.

"Strike off thy fetters, bonds that bind thee down
Of shining gold or darker, baser ore;
Know slave is slave caressed or whipped, not free;
For fetters tho' of gold, are not less strong to bind."

—The Song of the Sannyasin.

Buddha is Unnamable

Give a definite name to Deity, He would be no more than what the name implies. The Deity under the name of Brahman necessarily differs from the Being under the appellation of Jehovah, just as the Hindu differs from the Jew. In like manner the Being designated by God necessarily differs from One named Amitabha or from Him entitled Allah. To give a name to the Deity is to give Him tradition, nationality, limitation, and fixity, and it never brings us nearer to Him. Zen's object of worship cannot be named and determined as God, or Brahman, or Amitabha, or Creator, or Nature, or Reality, or Substance, or the like. Neither Chinese nor Japanese masters of Zen tried to give a definite name to their object of adoration. They now called Him That One, now This One, now Mind, now Buddha, now Tathagata, now Certain Thing, now the True, now Dharma-nature, now Buddha-nature, and so forth. Tung Shan[141] (To-zan) on a certain occasion declared it to be "A Certain Thing that pillars heaven above and supports the earth below; dark as lacquer and undefinable; manifesting itself through its activities, yet not wholly comprisable within them." So-kei[142] expressed it in the same wise: "There exists a Certain Thing, bright as a mirror, spiritual as a mind, not subjected to growth nor to decay." Huen Sha (Gen-sha) comparing it with a gem says: "There exists a bright gem illuminating

[141] Tung Shan Luh (To-zan-roku, 'Sayings and Doings of Ta-zan') is one of the best Zen books.

[142] So-kei, a Korean Zenist, whose work entitled Zen-ke-ki-kwan is worthy of our note as a representation of Korean Zen.

through the worlds in ten directions by its light."[143]

This certain thing or being is too sublime to be named after a traditional or a national deity, too spiritual to be symbolized by human art, too full of life to be formulated in terms of mechanical science, too free to be rationalized by intellectual philosophy, too universal to be perceived by bodily senses; but everybody can feel its irresistible power, see its invisible presence, and touch its heart and soul within himself. "This mysterious Mind," says Kwei Fung (Kei-ho), "is higher than the highest, deeper than the deepest, limitless in all directions. There is no centre in it. No distinction of east and west, and above and below. Is it empty? Yes, but not empty like space. Has it a form? Yes, but has no form dependent on another for its existence. Is it intelligent? Yes, but not intelligent like your mind. Is it non-intelligent? Yes, but not non-intelligent like trees and stone. Is it conscious? Yes, but not conscious like you when waking. Is it bright? Yes, but not bright like the sun or the moon." To the question, "What and who is Buddha?" Yuen Wu (En-go) replied: "Hold your tongue: the mouth is the gate of evils!" while Pao Fuh (Ho-fuku) answered to the same question: "No skill of art can picture Him." Thus Buddha is unnamable, indescribable, and indefinable, but we provisionally call Him Buddha.

Buddha, the Universal Life

Zen conceives Buddha as a Being, who moves, stirs, inspires, enlivens, and vitalizes everything. Accordingly, we may call Him the Universal Life in the sense that He is the source of all lives in the universe. This Universal Life, according to Zen, pillars the heaven, supports the earth, glorifies the sun and moon, gives voice to thunder, tinges clouds, adorns the pasture with flowers, enriches the field with harvest, gives animals beauty and strength. Therefore, Zen declares even a dead clod of earth to be imbued with the divine life, just as Lowell expresses a similar idea when he says:

"Every clod feels a stir of might,
An instinct within it that reaches and towers,

[143] Sho-bo-gen-zo.

And groping blindly above it for light,
Climbs to a soul in grass and flowers."

One of our contemporary Zenists wittily observed that 'vegetables are the children of earth, that animals which feed on vegetables are the grand-children of earth, and that men who subsist on animals are the great-grand-children of earth.' If there be no life in earth, how could life come out of it? If there be no life, the same as the animal's life in the vegetables, how could animals sustain their lives feeding on vegetables? If there be no life similar to ours in animals, how could we sustain our life by subsisting on them? The poet must be in the right, not only in his esthetic, but in his scientific point of view, in saying:

"I must
Confess that I am only dust.
But once a rose within me grew;
Its rootlets shot, its flowerets flew;
And all rose's sweetness rolled
Throughout the texture of my mould;
And so it is that I impart
Perfume to them, whoever thou art."

As we men live and act, so do our arteries; so does blood; so do corpuscles. As cells and protoplasm live and act, so do elements, molecules, and atoms. As elements and atoms live and act, so do clouds; so does the earth; so does the ocean, the Milky Way, and the Solar System. What is this life which pervades the grandest as well as the minutest works of Nature, and which may fitly be said 'greater than the greatest and smaller than the smallest?' It cannot be defined. It cannot be subjected to exact analysis. But it is directly experienced and recognized within us, just as the beauty of the rose is to be perceived and enjoyed, but not reduced to exact analysis. At any rate, it is something stirring, moving, acting and reacting continually. This something which can be experienced and felt and enjoyed directly by every one of us.

This life of living principle in the microcosmos is identical with that of the macrocosmos, and the Universal Life of the macrocosmos is the common source of all lives. Therefore, the Mahaparinirvana-sutra says:

"Tathagata (another name for Buddha) gives life to all beings, just as the lake Anavatapta gives rise to the four great rivers." "Tathagata," says the same sutra, "divides his own body into innumerable bodies, and also restores an infinite number of bodies to one body. Now be becomes cities, villages, houses, mountains, rivers, and trees; now he has a large body; now he has a small body; now he becomes men, women, boys, and girls."

Life and Change

A peculiar phase of life is change which appears in the form of growth and decay. Nobody can deny the transitoriness of life. One of our friends humorously observed: "Everything in the world may be doubtful to you, but it can never be doubted that you will die." Life is like a burning lamp. Every minute its flame dies out and is renewed. Life is like a running stream. Every moment it pushes onward. If there be anything constant in this world of change, it should be change itself. Is it not just one step from rosy childhood to snowy age? Is it not just one moment from the nuptial song to the funeral-dirge? Who can live the same moment twice? In comparison with an organism, inorganic matter appears to be constant and changeless; but, in fact, it is equally subjected to ceaseless alteration. Every morning, looking into the mirror, you will find your visage reflected in it just as it was on the preceding day; so also every morning, looking at the sun and the earth, you will find them reflected in your retina just as they were on the previous morning; but the sun and the earth are no less changeless than you. Why do the sun and the earth seem changeless and constant to you? Only because you yourself undergo change more quickly than they. When you look at the clouds sweeping across the face of the moon, they seem to be at rest, and the moon in rapid motion; but, in fact, the clouds, as well as the moon, incessantly move on.

Science might maintain the quantitative constancy of matter, but the so-called matter is mere abstraction. To say matter is changeless is as much as to say 2 is always 2, changeless and constant, because the arithmetical number is not more abstract than the physiological matter. The moon appears standing still when you look at her only a few moments. In like manner she seems to be free from change when you look at her in your short span of life. Astronomers, nevertheless, can tell you how she saw her better days, and is now in her wrinkles and white hair.

Pessimistic View of the Ancient Hindus

In addition to this, the new theory of matter has entirely over thrown the old conception of the unchanging atoms, and they are now regarded to be composed of magnetic forces, ions, and corpuscles in incessant motion. Therefore we have no inert matter in the concrete, no unchanging thing in the sphere of experience, no constant organism in the transient universe. These considerations often led many thinkers, ancient and modern, to the pessimistic view of life. What is the use of your exertion, they would say, in accumulating wealth, which is doomed to melt away in the twinkling of an eye? What is the use of your striving after power, which is more short-lived than a bubble? What is the use of your endeavour in the reformation of society, which does not endure any longer than the castle in the air? How do kings differ from beggars in the eye of Transience? How do the rich differ from the poor, how the beautiful from the ugly, bow the young from the old, how the good from the evil, how the lucky from the unlucky, how the wise from the unwise, in the court of Death? Vain is ambition. Vain is fame. Vain is pleasure. Vain are struggles and efforts. All is in vain. An ancient Hindu thinker[144] says:

"O saint, what is the use of the enjoyment of pleasures in this offensive, pithless body—a mere mass of bones, skins, sinews, marrow, and flesh? What is the use of the enjoyment of pleasures in this body, which is assailed by lust, hatred, greed, delusion, fear, anguish, jealousy, separation from what is loved, union with what is not loved, hunger, old age, death, illness, grief, and other evils? In such a world as this, what is the use of the enjoyment of pleasures, if he who has fed on them is to return to this world again and again? In this world I am like a frog in a dry well."

It is this consideration on the transitoriness of life that led some

144 Maitrayana Upanisad.

Taoist in China to prefer death to life, as expressed in Chwang Tsz (Su-shi):[145]

"When Kwang-zze went to Khu, he saw an empty skull, bleached indeed, but still retaining its shape. Tapping it with his horse-switch, he asked it saying: 'Did you, sir, in your greed of life, fail in the lessons of reason and come to this? Or did you do so, in the service of a perishing state, by the punishment of an axe? Or was it through your evil conduct, reflecting disgrace on your parents and on your wife and children? Or was it through your hard endurances of cold and hunger? Or was it that you had completed your term of life?'

"Having given expression to these questions, he took up the skull and made a pillow of it, and went to sleep. At midnight the skull appeared to him in a dream, and said: 'What you said to me was after the fashion of an orator. All your words were about the entanglements of men in their lifetime. There are none of those things after death. Would you like to hear me, sir, tell you about death?' 'I should,' said Kwang-zze, and the skull resumed: 'In death there are not (the distinctions of) ruler above minister below. There are none of the phenomena of the four seasons. Tranquil and at ease, our years are those of heaven and earth. No king in his court has greater enjoyment than we have.' Kwang-zze did not believe it, and said: 'If I could get the Ruler of our Destiny to restore your body to life with its bones and flesh and skin, and to give you back your father and mother, your wife and children, and all your village acquaintances, would you wish me to do so?' The skull stared fixedly at him, and knitted its brows and said: 'How should I cast away the enjoyment of my royal court, and undertake again the toils of life among mankind?'"

Hinayanism and its Doctrine

The doctrine of Transience was the first entrance gate of Hinayanism. Transience never fails to deprive us of what is dear and near to us. It disappoints us in our expectation and hope. It brings out grief, fear, anguish, and lamentation. It spreads terror and destruction among families,

---

[145] 'Chwang Tsz,' vol. vi., p. 23.

communities, nations, mankind. It threatens with perdition the whole earth, the whole universe. Therefore it follows that life is full of disappointment, sufferings, and miseries, and that man is like 'a frog in a dry well.' This is the doctrine called by the Hinayanists the Holy Truth of Suffering.

Again, when Transcience once gets hold of our imagination, we can easily foresee ruins and disasters in the very midst of prosperity and happiness, and also old age and ugliness in the prime and youth of beauty. It gives rise quite naturally to the thought that body is a bag full of pus and blood, a mere heap of rotten flesh and broken pieces of bone, a decaying corpse inhabited by innumerable maggots. This is the doctrine called by the Hinayanists the Holy Truth of Impurity.[146]

And, again, Transience holds its tyrannical sway not only over the material but over the spiritual world. At its touch Atman, or soul, is brought to nothing. By its call Devas, or celestial beings, are made to succumb to death. It follows, therefore, that to believe in Atman, eternal and unchanging, would be a whim of the ignorant. This is the doctrine called by the Hinayanists the Holy Truth of No-atman.

If, as said, there could be nothing free from Transience, Constancy should be a gross mistake of the ignorant; if even gods have to die, Eternity should be no more than a stupid dream of the vulgar; if all phenomena be flowing and changing, there could be no constant noumena underlying them. It therefore follows that all things in the universe are empty and unreal. This is the doctrine called by the Hinayanists the Holy Truth of Unreality. Thus Hinayana Buddhism, starting from the doctrine of Transience, arrived at the pessimistic view of life in its extreme form.

Change as seen by Zen

[146] Mahasaptipatthana Suttanta, 7, runs as follows: "And, moreover, bhikkhu, a brother, just as if he had been a body abandoned in the charnel-field, dead for one, two, or three days, swollen, turning black and blue, and decomposed, apply that perception to this very body (of his own), reflecting: 'This body, too, is even so constituted, is of such a nature, has not got beyond that (fate).'"

Zen, like Hinayanism, does not deny the doctrine of Transience, but it has come to a view diametrically opposite to that of the Hindus. Transience for Zen simply means change. It is a form in which life manifests itself. Where there is life there is change or Transience. Where there is more change there is more vital activity. Suppose an absolutely changeless body: it must be absolutely lifeless. An eternally changeless life is equivalent to an eternally changeless death. Why do we value the morning glory, which fades in a few hours, more than an artificial glass flower, which endures hundreds of years? Why do we prefer an animal life, which passes away in a few scores of years, to a vegetable life, which can exist thousands of years? Why do we prize changing organism more than inorganic matter, unchanging and constant? If there be no change in the bright hues of a flower, it is as worthless as a stone. If there be no change in the song of a bird, it is as valueless as a whistling wind. If there be no change in trees and grass, they are utterly unsuitable to be planted in a garden. Now, then, what is the use of our life, if it stand still? As the water of a running stream is always fresh and wholesome because it does not stop for a moment, so life is ever fresh and new because it does not stand still, but rapidly moves on from parents to children, from children to grandchildren, from grandchildren to great-grandchildren, and flows on through generation after generation, renewing itself ceaselessly.

We can never deny the existence of old age and death—nay, death is of capital importance for a continuation of life, because death carries away all the decaying organism in the way of life. But for it life would be choked up with organic rubbish. The only way of life's pushing itself onward or its renewing itself is its producing of the young and getting rid of the old. If there be no old age nor death, life is not life, but death.

Life and Change

Transformation and change are the essential features of life; life is not transformation nor change itself, as Bergson seems to assume. It is something which comes under our observation through transformation and change. There are, among Buddhists as well as Christians, not a few who covet constancy and fixity of life, being allured by such smooth names as eternal life, everlasting joy, permanent peace, and what not. They have forgotten that their souls can never rest content with things monotonous. If there be everlasting joy for their souls, it must be presented to them through incessant change. So also if there be eternal life granted for their souls, it must be given through ceaseless alteration. What is the difference between eternal life, fixed and constant, and eternal death? What is the difference between everlasting bliss, changeless and monotonous, and everlasting suffering? If constancy, instead of change, govern life, then hope or pleasure is absolutely impossible. Fortunately, however, life is not constant. It changes and becomes. Pleasure arises through change itself. Mere change of food or clothes is often pleasing to us, while the appearance of the same thing twice or thrice, however pleasing it may be, causes us little pleasure. It will become disgusting and tire us down, if it be presented repeatedly from time to time.

An important element in the pleasure we derive from social meetings, from travels, from sight-seeings, etc., is nothing but change. Even intellectual pleasure consists mainly of change. A dead, unchanging abstract truth, 2 and 2 make 4, excites no interest; while a changeable, concrete truth, such as the Darwinian theory of evolution, excites a keen interest.

Life, Change, and Hope

The doctrine of Transcience never drives us to the pessimistic view of life. On the contrary, it gives us an inexhaustible source of pleasure and hope. Let us ask you: Are you satisfied with the present state of things? Do you not sympathize with poverty-stricken millions living side by side with millionaires saturated with wealth? Do you not shed tears over those hunger-bitten children who cower in the dark lanes of a great city? Do you not wish to put down the stupendous oppressor—Might-is-right? Do you not want to do away with the so-called armoured peace among nations? Do you not need to mitigate the struggle for existence more sanguine than the war of weapons?

Life changes and is changeable; consequently, has its future. Hope is therefore possible. Individual development, social betterment, international peace, reformation of mankind in general, can be hoped. Our ideal, however unpractical it may seem at the first sight, can be realized. Moreover, the world itself, too, is changing and changeable. It reveals new phases from time to time, and can be moulded to subserve our purpose. We must not take life or the world as completed and doomed as it is now. No fact verifies the belief that the world was ever created by some other power and predestined to be as it is now. It lives, acts, and changes. It is transforming itself continually, just as we are changing and becoming. Thus the doctrine of Transience supplies us with an inexhaustible source of hope and comfort, leads us into the living universe, and introduces us to the presence of Universal Life or Buddha.

The reader may easily understand how Zen conceives Buddha as the living principle from the following dialogues: "Is it true, sir," asked a monk of Teu tsz (To-shi), "that all the voices of Nature are those of Buddha?" "Yes, certainly," replied Teu tsz. "What is, reverend sir," asked a man of Chao Cheu (Jo-shu), "the holy temple (of Buddha)?" "An innocent girl," replied the teacher. "Who is the master of the temple?" asked the other again. "A baby in her womb," was the answer. "What is, sir," asked a monk to Yen Kwan (Yen-kan), "the original body of Buddha Vairocana?"[147] "Fetch me a pitcher with water," said the teacher. The monk did as he was ordered. "Put it back in its place," said Yen Kwan again.[148]

Everything is Living according to Zen

Everything alive has a strong innate tendency to preserve itself, to assert itself, to push itself forward, and to act on its environment, consciously or unconsciously. The innate, strong tendency of the living is an undeveloped, but fundamental, nature of Spirit or Mind. It shows itself first in inert matter as impenetrability, or affinity, or mechanical force. Rock has a powerful tendency to preserve itself. And it is hard to crush it. Diamond has a robust tendency to assert itself. And it permits nothing to destroy it. Salt has the same strong tendency, for its particles act and react by

---

[147] Literally, All Illuminating Buddha, the highest of the Trikayas. See Eitel, p. 192.

[148] Zen-rin-rui-shu.

themselves, and never cease till its crystals are formed. Steam, too, should have the same, because it pushes aside everything in its way and goes where it will.

In the eye of simple folks of old, mountains, rivers, trees, serpents, oxen, and eagles were equally full of life; hence the deification of them. No doubt it is irrational to believe in nymphs, fairies, elves, and the like, yet still we may say that mountains stand of their own accord, rivers run as they will, just as we say that trees and grass turn their leaves towards the sun of their own accord. Neither is it a mere figure of speech to say that thunder speaks and hills respond, nor to describe birds as singing and flowers as smiling, nor to narrate winds as moaning and rain as weeping, nor to state lovers as looking at the moon, the moon as looking at them, when we observe spiritual element in activities of all this. Haeckel says, not without reason: "I cannot imagine the simple chemical and physical forces without attributing the movement of material particles to conscious sensation." The same author says again: "We may ascribe the feeling of pleasure and pain to all atoms, and so explain the electric affinity in chemistry."

The Creative Force of Nature and Humanity

The innate tendency of self-preservation, which manifests itself as mechanical force or chemical affinity in the inorganic nature, unfolds itself as the desire of the preservation of species in the vegetables and animals. See how vegetables fertilize themselves in a complicated way, and how they spread their seeds far and wide in a most mysterious manner. A far more developed form of the same desire is seen in the sexual attachment and parental love of animals. Who does not know that even the smallest birds defend their young against every enemy with self -sacrificing courage, and that they bring food whilst they themselves often starve and grow lean? In human beings we can observe the various transformations of the self-same desire. For instance, sorrow or despair is experienced when it is impossible; anger, when it is hindered by others; joy, when it is fulfilled; fear, when it is threatened; pleasure, when it is facilitated. Although it manifests itself as the sexual attachment and parental love in lower animals, yet its developed forms, such as sympathy, loyalty, benevolence, mercy, humanity, are observed in human beings. Again, the creative force in inorganic nature, in order to assert itself and act more effectively, creates the germ of organic nature, and gradually ascending the scale of evolution, develops the sense organs and the nervous system; hence intellectual powers, such as sensation, perception, imagination, memory, unfold themselves. Thus the creative force, exerting itself gradually, widens its sphere of action, and necessitates the union of individuals into families, clans, tribes, communities, and nations. For the sake of this union and co-operation they established customs, enacted laws, and instituted political and educational systems. Furthermore, to reinforce itself, it gave birth to languages and sciences; and to enrich itself, morality and religion.

Universal Life is Universal Spirit

These considerations naturally lead us to see that Universal Life is not a blind vital force, but Creative Spirit, or Mind, or Consciousness, which unfolds itself in myriads of ways. Everything in the universe, according to Zen, lives and acts, and at the same time discloses its spirit. To be alive is identically the same as to be spiritual. As the poet has his song, so does the nightingale, so does the cricket, so does the rivulet. As we are pleased or offended, so are horses, so are dogs, so are sparrows, ants, earthworms, and mushrooms. Simpler the body, simpler its spirit; more complicated the body, more complicated its spirit. 'Mind slumbers in the pebble, dreams in the plant, gathers energy in the animal, and awakens to self-conscious discovery in the soul of man.'

It is this Creative, Universal Spirit that sends forth Aurora to illuminate the sky, that makes Diana shed her benign rays and Æolus play on his harp, wreathes spring with flowers, that clothes autumn with gold, that induces plants to put forth blossoms, that incites animals to be energetic, and that awakens consciousness in man. The author of Mahavaipulya-purnabuddha-sutra expressly states our idea when he says: "Mountains, rivers, skies, the earth: all these are embraced in the True Spirit, enlightened and mysterious." Rin-zai also says: "Spirit is formless, but it penetrates through the world in the ten directions."[149] The Sixth Patriarch expresses the same idea more explicitly: "What creates the phenomena is Mind; what transcends all the phenomena is Buddha."[150]

Poetical Intuition and Zen

Since Universal Life or Spirit permeates the universe, the poetical intuition of man never fails to find it, and to delight in everything typical of that Spirit. "The leaves of the plantain," says a Zen poet, "unfold themselves, hearing the voice of thunder. The flowers of the hollyhock turn towards the sun, looking at it all day long." Jesus could see in the lily the Unseen Being who clothed it so lovely. Wordsworth found the most profound thing in all the world to be the universal spiritual life, which manifests itself most directly in nature, clothed in its own proper dignity and peace. "Through every star," says Carlyle, "through every grass blade, most through every soul, the glory of present God still beams."

It is not only grandeur and sublimity that indicate Universal Life, but smallness and commonplace do the same. A sage of old awakened to the faith[151] when he heard a bell ring; another, when he looked at the peach blossom; another, when he heard the frogs croaking; and another, when he saw his own form reflected in a river. The minutest particles of dust form a world. The meanest grain of sand under our foot proclaims a divine law. Therefore Teu Tsz Jo-shi), pointing to a stone in front of his temple, said: "All the Buddhas of the past, the present, and the future are living therein."[152]

---

[149] Rin-zai-roku.

[150] Roku-so-dan-kyo.

[151] Both the Chinese and the Japanese history of Zen are full of such incidents.

[152] Zen-rin-rui-shu and To-shi-go-roku.

Enlightened Consciousness

In addition to these considerations, which mainly depend on indirect experience, we can have direct experience of life within us. In the first place, we experience that our life is not a bare mechanical motion or change, but is a spiritual, purposive, and self-directing force. In the second place, we directly experience that it knows, feels, and wills. In the third place, we experience that there exists some power unifying the intellectual, emotional, and volitional activities so as to make life uniform and rational. Lastly, we experience that there lies deeply rooted within us Enlightened Consciousness, which neither psychologists treat of nor philosophers believe in, but which Zen teachers expound with strong conviction. Enlightened Consciousness is, according to Zen, the centre of spiritual life. It is the mind of minds, and the consciousness of consciousness. It is the Universal Spirit awakened in the human mind. It is not the mind that feels joy or sorrow; nor is it the mind that reasons and infers; nor is it the mind that fancies and dreams; nor is it the mind that hopes and fears; nor is it the mind that distinguishes good from evil. It is Enlightened Consciousness that holds communion with Universal Spirit or Buddha, and realizes that individual lives are inseparably united, and of one and the same nature with Universal Life. It is always bright as a burnished mirror, and cannot be dimmed by doubt and ignorance. It is ever pure as a lotus flower, and cannot be polluted by the mud of evil and folly. Although all sentient beings are endowed with this Enlightened Consciousness, they are not aware of its existence, excepting men who can discover it by the practice of Meditation. Enlightened consciousness is often called Buddha-nature, as it is the real nature of Universal Spirit. Zen teachers compare it with a precious stone ever fresh and pure, even if it be buried in the heaps of dust. Its divine light can never be extinguished by doubt or fear, just as the sunlight cannot be destroyed by mist and cloud. Let us quote a Chinese Zen poet to see how Zen treats of it:[153]

"I have an image of Buddha,
The worldly people know it not.
It is not made of clay or cloth,

---

[153] See Zen-gaku-ho-ten.

Nor is it carved out of wood,
Nor is it moulded of earth nor of ashes.
No artist can paint it;
No robber can steal it.
There it exists from dawn of time.
It's clean, although not swept and wiped.
Although it is but one,
Divides itself to a hundred thousand million forms."

Buddha Dwelling in the Individual Mind

Enlightened Consciousness in the individual mind acquires for its possessor, not a relative knowledge of things as his intellect does, but the profoundest insight in reference to universal brotherhood of all beings, and enables him to understand the absolute holiness of their nature, and the highest goal for which all of them are making. Enlightened Consciousness once awakened within us serves as a guiding principle, and leads us to hope, bliss, and life; consequently, it is called the Master[154] of both mind and body. Sometimes it is called the Original[155] Mind, as it is the mind of minds. It is Buddha dwelling in individuals. You might call it God in man, if you like. The following dialogues all point to this single idea:
On one occasion a butcher, who was used to kill one thousand sheep a day, came to Gotama, and, throwing down his butcher-knife, said "I am one of the thousand Buddhas." "Yes, really," replied Gotama. A monk, Hwui Chao (E-cha) by name, asked Pao Yen (Ho-gen): "What is Buddha?" "You are Hwui Chao," replied the master. The same question was put to Sheu Shan (Shu-zan), Chi Man (Chi-mon), and Teu Tsz (To-shi), the first of whom answered: "A bride mounts on a donkey and her mother-in-law drives it;" and the second: "He goes barefooted, his sandals being worn out;" while the third rose from his chair and stood still without saying a word. Chwen Hih (Fu-kiu) explains this point in unequivocal terms: "Night after night I sleep with Buddha, and every morning I get up with Him. He accompanies

---

[154] It is often called the Lord or Master of mind.

[155] Another name for Buddha is the Original Mind" (Kechi-myaku-ron).

me wherever I go. When I stand or sit, when I speak or be mute, when I am out or in, He never leaves me, even as a shadow accompanies body. Would you know where He is? Listen to that voice and word."[156]

Enlightened Consciousness is not an Intellectual Insight

Enlightened Consciousness is not a bare intellectual insight, for it is full of beautiful emotions. It loves, caresses, embraces, and at the same time esteems all beings, being ever merciful to them. It has no enemies to conquer, no evil to fight with, but constantly finds friends to help, good to promote. Its warm heart beats in harmony with those of all fellow beings. The author of Brahmajala-sutra fully expresses this idea as he says: "All women are our mothers; all men our fathers; all earth and water our bodies in the past existences; all fire and air our essence."

Thus relying on our inner experience, which is the only direct way of knowing Buddha, we conceive Him as a Being with profound wisdom and boundless mercy, who loves all beings as His children, whom He is fostering, bringing up, guiding, and teaching. "These three worlds are His, and all beings living in them are His children."[157] "The Blessed One is the mother of all sentient beings, and gives them all the milk of mercy."[158] Some people named Him Absolute, as He is all light, all hope, all mercy, and all wisdom; some, Heaven, as He is high and enlightened; some, God, as He is sacred and mysterious; some, Truth, as He is true to Himself; some, Buddha, as He is free from illusion; some, Creator, as He is the creative force immanent in the universe; some, Path, as He is the Way we must follow; some, Unknowable, as He is beyond relative knowledge; some, Self, as He is the Self of individual selves. All these names are applied to one Being, whom we designate by the name of Universal Life or Spirit.

---

[156] For such dialogues, see Sho-yo-roku, Mu-mon-kan,
Heki-gan-shu. Fu-kiu's words are repeatedly quoted by Zen masters.

[157] Saddharma-pundarika-sutra.

[158] Mahaparinirvana-sutra.

Our Conception of Buddha is not Final

Has, then, the divine nature of Universal Spirit been completely and exhaustively revealed in our Enlightened Consciousness? To this question we should answer negatively, for, so far as our limited experience is concerned, Universal Spirit reveals itself as a Being with profound wisdom and boundless mercy; this, nevertheless, does not imply that the conception is the only possible and complete one. We should always bear in mind that the world is alive, and changing, and moving. It goes on to disclose a new phase, or to add a new truth. The subtlest logic of old is a mere quibble of nowadays. The miracles of yesterday are the commonplaces of to-day. Now theories are formed, new discoveries are made, only to give their places to newer theories are discoveries. New ideals realized or new desires satisfied are sure to awaken newer and stronger desires. Not an instant life remains immutable, but it rushes on, amplifying and enriching itself from the dawn of time to the end of eternity.

Therefore Universal Life may in the future possibly unfold its new spiritual content, yet unknown to us because it has refined, lifted up, and developed living beings from the amœba to man, increasing the intelligence and range of individuals, until highly civilized man emerge into the plane of consciousness-consciousness of divine light in him. Thus to believe in Buddha is to be content and thankful for the grace of His, and to hope for the infinite unfoldment of His glories in man.

How to Worship Buddha

The author of Vimalakirtti-nirdeca-sutra well explains our attitude towards Buddha when he says: "We ask Buddha for nothing. We ask Dharma for nothing. We ask Samgha for nothing." Nothing we ask of Buddha. No worldly success, no rewards in the future life, no special blessing. Hwang Pah (O-baku) said: "I simply worship Buddha. I ask Buddha for nothing. I ask Dharma for nothing. I ask Samgha for nothing." Then a prince[159]

[159] Afterwards the Emperor Suen Tsung (Sen-so), of the Tang dynasty.

questioned him: "You ask Buddha for nothing. You ask Dharma for nothing. You ask Samgha for nothing. What, then, is the use of your worship?" The Prince earned a slap as an answer to his utilitarian question.[160] This incident well illustrates that worship, as understood by Zen masters, is a pure act of thanksgiving, or the opening of the grateful heart; in other words, the disclosing of Enlightened Consciousness. We are living the very life of Buddha, enjoying His blessing, and holding communion with Him through speech, thought, and action. The earth is not 'the vale of tears,' but the glorious creation of Universal Spirit; nor man 'the poor miserable sinner' but the living altar of Buddha Himself. Whatever we do, we do with grateful heart and pure joy sanctioned by Enlightened Consciousness; eating, drinking, talking, walking, and every other work of our daily life are the worship and devotion. We agree with Margaret Fuller when she says: "Reverence the highest; have patience with the lowest; let this day's performance of the meanest duty be thy religion. Are the stars too distant? Pick up the pebble that lies at thy feet, and from it learn all."

---

160 For the details, see Heki-gan-shu.

CHAPTER V

THE NATURE OF MAN

Man is Good-natured according to Mencius[161]

Oriental scholars, especially the Chinese men of letters, seem to have taken so keen an interest in the study of human nature that they proposed all the possible opinions respecting the subject in question-namely, (1) man is good-natured; (2) man is bad-natured; (3) man is good-natured and bad-natured as well; (4) man is neither good-natured nor bad-natured. The first of these opinions was proposed by a most reputed Confucianist scholar, Mencius, and his followers, and is still adhered to by the majority of the Japanese and the Chinese Confucianists. Mencius thought it as natural for man to do good as it is for the grass to be green. 'Suppose a person has happened,' he would say, 'to find a child on the point of tumbling down into a deep well. He would rescue it even at the risk of his life, no matter how morally degenerated he might be. He would have no time to consider that his act might bring him some reward from its parents, or a good reputation among his friends and fellow-citizens. He would do it barely out of his inborn good-nature.' After enumerating some instances similar to this one, Mencius concludes that goodness is the fundamental nature of man, even if he is often carried away by his brutal disposition.

[161] Mencius (372-282 B.C.) is regarded as the best expounder of the doctrine of Confucius. There exists a well-known work of his, entitled after his own name. See 'A History of Chinese Philosophy,' by R. Endo, and also 'A History of Chinese Philosophy' (pp. 38-50), by G. Nakauchi.

Man is Bad-natured according to Siun Tsz[162] (Jun-shi).

The weaknesses of Mencius's theory are fully exposed by another diametrically opposed theory propounded by Siun Tsz (Jun-shi) and his followers. 'Man is bad-natured,' says Siun Tsz, 'since he has inborn lust, appetite, and desire for wealth. As he has inborn lust and appetite, he is naturally given to intemperance and wantonness. As he has inborn desire for wealth, he is naturally inclined to quarrel and fight with others for the sake of gain.' Leave him without discipline or culture, he would not be a whit better than the beast. His virtuous acts, such as charity, honesty, propriety, chastity, truthfulness, are conduct forced by the teachings of ancient sages against his natural inclination. Therefore vices are congenial and true to his nature, while virtues alien and untrue to his fundamental nature.

These two theories are not only far from throwing light on the moral state of man, but wrap it in deeper gloom. Let us raise a few questions by way of refutation. If man's fundamental nature be good, as Mencius maintains, why is it easy for him to be vicious without instruction, while he finds it hard to be virtuous even with instruction. If you contend that good is man's primary nature and evil the secondary one, why is be so often overpowered by the secondary nature? If you answer saying that man is good-natured originally, but he acquires the secondary nature through the struggle for existence, and it gradually gains power over the primary nature by means of the same cause, then the primitive tribes should be more virtuous than the highly civilized nations, and children than grownup people. Is this not contrary to fact?

If, again, man's nature is essentially bad, as Siun Tsz holds, how can he cultivate virtue? If you contend that ancient sages invented so-called cardinal virtues and inculcated them against his natural inclination, why does he not give them up? If vices be congenial and true to man's nature, but virtues be alien and untrue to him, why are virtues honoured by him? If

---

162 Siun Tsz's date is later by some fifty years than Mencius. Siun Tsz gives the reason why man seeks after morality, saying that man seeks what he has not, and that he seeks after morality simply because he has not morality, just as the poor seek riches. See 'A History of Chinese Philosophy' (pp. 51-60), by G. Nakauchi, and 'A History of Development of Chinese Thought,' by R. Endo.

vices be genuine and virtue a deception, as you think, why do you call the inventors of that deceiving art sages? How was it possible for man to do good before these sages' appearance on earth?

Man is both Good-natured and Bad-natured according to Yan Hiung[163] (Yo-yu)

According to Yang Hiung and his followers, good is no less real than evil, and evil is no more unreal than good. Therefore man must be double-natured-that is, partly good and partly bad. This is the reason why the history of man is full of fiendish crimes, and, at the same time, it abounds with godly deeds. This is the reason why mankind comprises, on the one hand, a Socrates, a Confucius, a Jesus, and, on the other, a Nero and a Kieh. This is the reason why we find to-day a honest fellow in him whom we find a betrayer to-morrow.

This view of man's nature might explain our present moral state, yet it calls forth many questions bard to answer. If this assertion be true, is it not a useless task to educate man with the purpose of making him better and nobler? How could one extirpate man's bad nature implanted within him at his origin? If man be double-natured, how did he come to set good over evil? How did he come to consider that he ought to be good and ought not to be bad? How could you establish the authority of morality?

Man is neither Good-natured nor Bad-natured according to Su Shih (So-shoku)[164]

The difficulty may be avoided by a theory given by Su Shih and other scholars influenced by Buddhism, which maintains that man is neither good-natured nor bad-natured. According to this opinion man is not moral

---

[163] Yan Hiung (died A.D. 18) is the reputed author of Tai Huen (Tai-gen) and Fah Yen (Ho-gen). His opinion in reference to human nature is found in Fah Yen.

[164] Su Shih (1042-1101), a great man of letters, practiser of Zen, noted for his poetical works.

nor immoral by nature, but unmoral. He is morally a blank. He is at a crossroad, so to speak, of morality when he is first born. As he is blank, he can be dyed black or red. As he is at the cross-road, he can turn to the right or to the left. He is like fresh water, which has no flavour, and can be made sweet or bitter by circumstances. If we are not mistaken, this theory, too, has to encounter insurmountable difficulties. How could it be possible to make the unmoral being moral or immoral? We might as well try to get honey out of sand as to get good or evil out of the blank nature. There can be no fruit of good or evil where there is no seed of good or bad nature. Thus we find no satisfactory solution of the problem at issue in these four theories proposed by the Chinese scholars—the first theory being incompetent to explain the problem of human depravity; the second breaking down at the origin of morality; the third failing to explain the possibility of moral culture; the fourth being logically self-contradictory.

There is no Mortal who is Purely Moral

By nature man should be either good or bad; or he should be good as well as bad; or he should be neither good nor bad. There can be no alternative possible besides these four propositions, none of which can be accepted as true. Then there must be some misconception in the terms of which they consist. It would seem to some that the error can be avoided by limiting the sense of the term 'man,' saying some persons are good-natured, some persons are bad-natured, some persons are good-natured and bad-natured as well, and some persons are neither good-natured nor bad-natured. There is no contradiction in these modified propositions, but still they fail to explain the ethical state of man. Supposing them all to be true, let us assume that there are the four classes of people: (1) Those who are purely moral and have no immoral disposition; (2) those who are half moral and half immoral; (3) those who are neither moral nor immoral; (4) those who are purely immoral and have no moral disposition. Orthodox Christians, believing in the sinlessness of Jesus, would say he belongs to the first class, while Mohammedans and Buddhists, who deify the founder of their respective faith, would in such case regard their founder as the purely moral personage. But are your beliefs, we should ask, based on historical fact? Can you say that such traditional and self-contradictory records as the four gospels are history in the strict sense of the term? Can you assert that those traditions which deify Mohammed and Shakya are the statements of bare facts? Is not Jesus an abstraction and an ideal, entirely different from a concrete carpenter's son, who fed on the same kind of food, sheltered himself in the same kind of building, suffered from the same kind of pain, was fired by the same kind of anger, stung by the same kind of lust as our own? Can you say the person who fought many a sanguinary battle, who got through many cunning negotiations with enemies and friends, who personally experienced the troubles of polygamy, was a person sinless and divine? We might allow that these ancient sages are superhuman and divine, then our classification has no business with them, because they do not properly belong to mankind. Now, then, who can point out any sinless person in the present world? Is it not a fact that the more virtuous one grows the more sinful he feels himself? If there be any mortal, in the past, the present, and the future, who declares himself to be pure and sinless, his very declaration proves that he is not highly moral. Therefore the existence of the first class of people is open to question.

There is no Mortal who is Non-Moral or Purely Immoral

The same is the case with the third and the fourth class of people who are assumed as non-moral or purely immoral. There is no person, however morally degraded he may be, but reveals some good nature in his whole course of life. It is our daily experience that we find a faithful friend in the person even of a pickpocket, a loving father even in a burglar, and a kind neighbour even in a murderer. Faith, sympathy, friendship, love, loyalty, and generosity dwell not merely in palaces and churches, but also in brothels and gaols. On the other hand, abhorrent vices and bloody crimes often find shelter under the silk hat, or the robe, or the coronet, or the crown. Life may fitly be compared with a rope made of white and black straw, and to separate one from the other is to destroy the rope itself; so also life entirely independent of the duality of good and bad is no actual life. We must acknowledge, therefore, that the third and the fourth propositions are inconsistent with our daily experience of life, and that only the second proposition remains, which, as seen above, breaks down at the origin of morality.

Where, then, does the Error Lie?

Where, then, does the error lie in the four possible propositions respecting man's nature? It lies not in their subject, but in the predicate-that is to say, in the use of the terms 'good' and 'bad.' Now let us examine how does good differ from bad. A good action ever promotes interests in a sphere far wider than a bad action. Both are the same in their conducing to human interests, but differ in the extent in which they achieve their end. In other words, both good and bad actions are performed for one end and the same purpose of promoting human interests, but they differ from each other as to the extent of interests. For instance, burglary is evidently bad action, and is condemned everywhere; but the capturing of an enemy's property for the sake of one's own tribe or clan or nation is praised as a meritorious conduct. Both acts are exactly the same in their promoting interests; but the former relates to the interests of a single individual or of a single family, while the latter to those of a tribe or a nation. If the former be bad on account of its ignoring others' interests, the latter must be also bad on account of its ignoring the enemy's interests. Murder is considered bad everywhere; but the killing of thousands of men in a battle-field is praised and honoured, because the former is perpetrated to promote the private interests, while the latter those of the public. If the former be bad, because of its cruelty, the latter must also be bad, because of its inhumanity.

The idea of good and bad, generally accepted by common sense, may be stated as follows: 'An action is good when it promotes the interests of an individual or a family; better when it promotes those of a district or a country; best when it promotes those of the whole world. An action is bad when it inflicts injury on another individual or another family; worse when it is prejudicial to a district or a country; worst when it brings harm on the whole world. Strictly speaking, an action is good when it promotes interests, material or spiritual, as intended by the actor in his motive; and it is bad when it injures interests, material or spiritual, as intended by the actor in his motive.'

According to this idea, generally accepted by common sense, human actions may be classified under four different heads: (1) Purely good actions; (2) partly good and partly bad actions; (3) neither good nor bad actions; (4) purely bad actions. First, purely good actions are those actions which subserve and never hinder human interests either material or spiritual, such as humanity and love of all beings. Secondly, partly good and partly bad actions are those actions which are both for and against human interests, such as narrow patriotism and prejudiced love. Thirdly, neither good nor bad actions are such actions as are neither for nor against human interests —for example, an unconscious act of a dreamer. Lastly, purely bad actions, which are absolutely against human interests, cannot be possible for man except suicide, because every action promotes more or less the interests, material or spiritual, of the individual agent or of someone else. Even such horrible crimes as homicide and parricide are intended to promote some interests, and carry out in some measure their aim when performed. It follows that man cannot be said to be good or bad in the strict sense of the terms as above defined, for there is no human being who does the first class of actions and nothing else, nor is there any mortal who does the fourth class of actions and nothing else. Man may be called good and bad, and at the same time be neither good nor bad, in that he always performs the second and the third class of actions. All this, nevertheless, is a more play of words. Thus we are driven to conclude that the common-sense view of human nature fails to grasp the real state of actual life.

Man is not Good-natured nor Bad-natured, but Buddha-natured

We have had already occasion to observe that Zen teaches Buddha-nature, which all sentient beings are endowed with. The term 'Buddha-nature,'[165] as accepted generally by Buddhists, means a latent and undeveloped nature, which enables its owner to become Enlightened when it is developed and brought to actuality.[166] Therefore man, according to Zen, is not good-natured nor bad-natured in the relative sense, as accepted generally by common sense, of these terms, but Buddha-natured in the sense of non-duality. A good person (of common sense) differs from a bad person (of common sense), not in his inborn Buddha-nature, but in the extent of his expressing it in deeds. Even if men are equally endowed with that nature,

---

[165] For a detailed explanation of Buddha-nature, see the chapter entitled Buddha-nature in Sho-bo-gen-zo.

[166] Mahaparinirvana-sutra may be said to have been written for the purpose of stating this idea.

yet their different states of development do not allow them to express it to an equal extent in conduct. Buddha-nature may be compared with the sun, and individual mind with the sky. Then an Enlightened mind is like the sky in fair weather, when nothing prevents the beams of the sun; while an ignorant mind is like the sky in cloudy weather, when the sun sheds faint light; and an evil mind is like the sky in stormy weather, when the sun seems to be out of existence. It comes under our daily observation that even a robber or a murderer may prove to be a good father and a loving husband to his wife and children. He is an honest fellow when he remains at home. The sun of Buddha-nature gives light within the wall of his house, but without the house the darkness of foul crimes shrouds him.

The Parable of the Robber Kih[167]

Chwang Tsz (So-shi) remarks in a humorous way to the following effect: "The followers of the great robber and murderer Kih asked him saying: 'Has the robber also any moral principles in his proceedings?' He replied: 'What profession is there which has not its principles? That the robber comes to the conclusion without mistake that there are valuable deposits in an apartment shows his wisdom; that he is the first to enter it shows his bravery; that he makes an equal division of the plunder shows his justice; that he never betrays the fellow-robbers shows his faithfulness; and that he is generous to the followers shows his benevolence. Without all these five qualities no one in the world has ever attained to become a great robber.'" The parable clearly shows us Buddha-nature of the robber and murderer expresses itself as wisdom, bravery, justice, faithfulness, and benevolence in his society, and that if he did the same outside it, he would not be a great robber but a great sage.

---

[167] The parable is told for the purpose of undervaluing Confucian doctrine, but the author thereby accidentally touches human nature. We do not quote it here with the same purpose as the author's.

Wang Yang Ming (O-yo-mei) and a Thief

One evening when Wang was giving a lecture to a number of students on his famous doctrine that all human beings are endowed with Conscience,[168] a thief broke into the house and hid himself in the darkest corner. Then Wang declared aloud that every human being is born with Conscience, and that even the thief who had got into the house had Conscience just as the sages of old. The burglar, overhearing these remarks, came out to ask the forgiveness of the master; since there was no way of escape for him, and he was half-naked, he crouched behind the students. Wang's willing forgiveness and cordial treatment encouraged the man to ask the question how the teacher could know such a poor wretch as he was endowed with Conscience as the sages of old. Wang replied: "It is your Conscience that makes you ashamed of your nakedness. You yourself are a sage, if you abstain from everything that will put shame on you." We firmly believe that Wang is perfectly right in telling the thief that he was not different in nature from the sages of old. It is no exaggeration. It is a saving truth. It is also a most effective way of saving men out of darkness of sin. Any thief ceases to be a thief the moment he believes in his own Conscience, or Buddha-nature. You can never correct criminals by your severe reproach or punishment. You can save them only through your sympathy and love, by which you call forth their inborn Buddha-nature. Nothing can produce more pernicious effects on criminals than to treat them as if they were a different sort of people and confirm them in their conviction that they are bad-natured. We greatly regret that even in a civilized society authorities neglecting this saving truth are driving to perdition those criminals under their care, whom it is their duty to save.

---

[168] It is not conscience in the ordinary sense of the term. It is 'moral' principle, according to Wang, pervading through the Universe. 'It expresses itself as Providence in Heaven, as moral nature in man, and as mechanical laws in things.' The reader will notice that Wang's Conscience is the nearest approach to Buddha-nature.

The Bad are the Good in the Egg

This is not only the case with a robber or a murderer, but also with ordinary people. There are many who are honest and good in their homesteads, but turn out to be base and dishonest folk outside them. Similarly, there are those who, having an enthusiastic love of their local district, act unlawfully against the interests of other districts. They are upright and honourable gentlemen within the boundary of their own district, but a gang of rascals without it. So also there are many who are Washingtons and William Tells in their own, but at the same time pirates and cannibals in the other countries. Again, there are not a few persons who, having racial prejudices, would not allow the rays of their Buddha-nature to pass through a coloured skin. There are civilized persons who are humane enough to love and esteem any human being as their brother, but so unfeeling that they think lower creatures as their proper food. The highly enlightened person, however, cannot but sympathize with human beings and lower creatures as well, as Shakya Muni felt all sentient beings to be his children.

These people are exactly the same in their Buddha-nature, but a wide difference obtains among them in the extent of their expressing that nature in deeds. If thieves and murderers be called bad-natured, reformers and revolutionists should be called so. If, on the other hand, patriotism and loyalty be said to be good, treason and insurrection should likewise be so. Therefore it is evident that a so-called good person is none but one who acts to promote wider interests of life, and a so-called bad person is none but one who acts to advance narrower ones. In other words, the bad are the good in the egg, so to speak, and the good are the bad on the wing. As the bird in the egg is one and the same as the bird on the wing, so the good in the egg is entirely of the same nature as the bad on the wing. To show that human nature transcends the duality of good and evil, the author of Avatamsaka-sutra declares that 'all beings are endowed with the wisdom and virtue of Tathagata.' Kwei Fung (Kei-ho) also says: "All sentient beings have the Real Spirit of Original Enlightenment (within themselves). It is unchanging and pure. It is eternally bright and clear, and conscious. It is also named Buddha-nature, or Tathagata-garbha."

The Great Person and Small Person

For these reasons Zen proposes to call man Buddha-natured or Good-natured in a sense transcendental to the duality of good and bad. It conveys no sense to call some individuals good in case there is no bad individual. For the sake of convenience, however, Zen calls man good, as is exemplified by Shakya Muni, who was wont to address his hearers as 'good men and women,' and by the Sixth Patriarch in China, who called everybody 'a good and wise one.' This does not imply in the least that all human beings are virtuous, sinless, and saintly-nay, the world is full of vices and crimes. It is an undeniable fact that life is the warfare of good against evil, and many a valiant hero has fallen in the foremost ranks. It is curious, however, to notice that the champions on the both sides are fighting for the same cause. There can be no single individual in the world who is fighting against his own cause or interest, and the only possible difference between one party and the other consists in the extent of interests which they fight for. So-called bad persons, who are properly designated as 'small persons' by Chinese and Japanese scholars, express their Buddha-nature to a small extent mostly within their own doors, while so-called good persons, or 'great persons' as the Oriental scholars call them, actualize their Buddha-nature to a large extent in the whole sphere of a country, or of the whole earth.

Enlightened Consciousness, or Buddha-nature, as we have seen in the previous chapter, is the mind of mind and the consciousness of consciousness, Universal Spirit awakened in individual minds, which realizes the universal brotherhood of all beings and the unity of individual lives. It is the real self, the guiding principle, the Original Physiognomy[169] (nature), as it is called by Zen, of man. This real self lies dormant under the threshold of consciousness in the minds of the confused; consequently, each of them is inclined to regard petty individual as his self, and to exert himself to further the interests of the individual self even at the cost of those of the others. He is 'the smallest person' in the world, for his self is reduced to the smallest extent possible. Some of the less confused identify their selves with their families, and feel happy or unhappy in proportion as

[169] The expression first occurs in Ho-bo-dan-kyo of the Sixth Patriarch, and is frequently used by later Zenists.

their families are happy or unhappy, for the sake of which they sacrifice the interests of other families. On the other hand, some of the more enlightened unite their selves through love and compassion with their whole tribe or countrymen, and consider the rise or fall of the tribe or of the country as their own, and willingly sacrifice their own lives, if need be, for the cause of the tribe or the country. When they are fully enlightened, they can realize the unity of all sentient lives, and be ever merciful and helpful towards all creatures. They are 'the greatest persons' on earth, because their selves are enlarged to the greatest extent possible.

The Theory of Buddha-Nature adequately explains the Ethical States of Man

This theory of Buddha-nature enables us to get an insight into the origin of morality. The first awakening of Buddha-nature within man is the very beginning of morality, and man's ethical progress is the gradually widening expression of that nature in conduct. But for it morality is impossible for man. But for it not only moral culture or discipline, but education and social improvement must be futile. Again, the theory adequately explains the ethical facts that the standard of morality undergoes change in different times and places, that good and bad are so inseparably knit together, and that the bad at times become good all on a sudden, and the good grow bad quite unexpectedly. First, it goes without saying that the standard of morality is raised just in proportion as Buddha-nature or real self extends and amplifies itself in different times and places. Secondly, since good is Buddha-nature actualized to a large extent, and bad is also Buddha-nature actualized to a small extent, the existence of the former presupposes that of the latter, and the mess of duality can never be got rid of. Thirdly, the fact that the bad become good under certain circumstances, and the good also become bad often unexpectedly, can hardly be explained by the dualistic theory, because if good nature be so arbitrarily turned into bad and bad nature into good, the distinction of good and bad nature has no meaning whatever. According to the theory of Buddha-nature, the fact that the good become bad or the bad become good, does not imply in the least a change of nature, but the widening or the narrowing of its actualization. So that no matter how morally degenerated one may be, he can uplift himself to a high ethical plane by the widening of his self, and at the same time no matter how morally exalted one may be, he can descend to the level of the brute by the narrowing of his self. To be an angel or to be a devil rests with one's degrees of enlightenment and free choice. This is why such infinite varieties exist both among the good and the bad. This is why the higher the peak of enlightenment the people climb, the more widely the vista of moral possibilities open before them.

Buddha-Nature is the Common Source of Morals

Furthermore, Buddha-nature or real self, being the seat of love and the nucleus of sincerity, forms the warp and woof of all moral actions. He is an obedient son who serves his parents with sincerity and love. He is a loyal subject who serves his master with sincerity and love. A virtuous wife is she who loves her husband with her sincere heart. A trustworthy friend is he who keeps company with others with sincerity and love. A man of righteousness is he who leads a life of sincerity and love. Generous and humane is he who sympathizes with his fellow-men with his sincere heart. Veracity, chastity, filial piety, loyalty, righteousness, generosity, humanity, and what not-all-this is no other than Buddha-nature applied to various relationships of human brotherhood. This is the common source, ever fresh and inexhaustible, of morality that fosters and furthers the interests of all. To-ju[170] expresses the similar idea as follows:

"There exists the Inexhaustible Source (of morality) within me.
It is an invaluable treasure.
It is called Bright Nature of man.
It is peerless and surpasses all jewels.
The aim of learning is to bring out this Bright Nature.
This is the best thing in the world.
Real happiness can only be secured by it."

Thus, in the first place, moral conduct, which is nothing but the expression of Buddha-nature in action, implies the assertion of self and the

---

[170] To-ju Naka-e (died A.D. 1649), the founder of the Japanese Wang School of Confucianism, known as the Sage of Omi.

furtherance of one's interests. On this point is based the half-truth of the Egoistic theory. Secondly, it is invariably accompanied by a feeling of pleasure or satisfaction when it fulfils its end. This accidental concomitance is mistaken for its essence by superficial observers who adhere to the Hedonistic theory. Thirdly, it conduces to the furtherance of the material and spiritual interests of man, and it led the Utilitarians to the confusion of the result with the cause of morality. Fourthly, it involves the control or sacrifice of the lower and ignoble self of an individual in order to realize his higher and nobler self. This gave rise to the half-truth of the Ascetic theory of morality.

The Parable of a Drunkard

Now the question arises, If all human beings are endowed with Buddha-nature, why have they not come naturally to be Enlightened? To answer this question, the Indian Mahayanists[171] told the parable of a drunkard who forgets the precious gems put in his own pocket by one of his friends. The man is drunk with the poisonous liquor of selfishness, led astray by the alluring sight of the sensual objects, and goes mad with anger, lust, and folly. Thus he is in a state of moral poverty, entirely forgetting the precious gem of Buddha-nature within him. To be in an honourable position in society as the owner of that valuable property, he must first get rid himself of the influence of the liquor of self, and detach himself from sensual objects, gain control over his passion, restore peace and sincerity to his mind, and illumine his whole existence by his inborn divine light. Otherwise he has to remain in the same plight to all eternity.

Lot us avail ourselves of another figure to explain more clearly the point at issue. Universal Spirit may fitly be likened to the universal water, or water circulating through the whole earth. This universal water exists everywhere. It exists in the tree. It exists in the grass. It exists in the mountain. It exists in the river. It exists in the sea. It exists in the air. It exists in the cloud. Thus man is not only surrounded by water on all sides, but it penetrates his very body. But be can never appease his thirst without drinking water. In

---

[171] Mahaparinirvana-sutra.

like manner Universal Spirit exists everywhere. It exists in the tree. It exists in the grass. It exists in the ground. It exists in the mountain. It exists in the river. It exists in the sea. It exists in the bird. It exists in the beast. Thus man is not merely surrounded by Spirit on all sides, but it permeates through his whole existence. But he can never be Enlightened unless he awakens it within him by means of Meditation. To drink water is to drink the universal water; to awaken Buddha-nature is to be conscious of Universal Spirit.

Therefore, to get Enlightened we have to believe that all beings are Buddha-natured—that is, absolutely good-natured in the sense that transcends the duality of good and bad. "One day," to cite an example, "Pan Shan (Ban-zan) happened to pass by a meat-shop. He heard a customer saying: 'Give me a pound of fresh meat.' To which the shopkeeper, putting down his knife, replied: Certainly, sir. Could there be any meat that is not fresh in my shop?' Pan Shan, hearing these remarks, was Enlightened at once."

Shakya Muni and the Prodigal Son

A great trouble with us is that we do not believe in half the good that we are born with. We are just like the only son of a well-to-do, as the author of Saddharma-pundarika-sutra[172] tells us, who, being forgetful of his rich inheritance, leaves his home and leads a life of hand-to-mouth as a coolie. How miserable it is to see one, having no faith in his noble endowment, burying the precious gem of Buddha-nature into the foul rubbish of vices and crimes, wasting his excellent genius in the exertion that is sure to disgrace his name, falling a prey to bitter remorse and doubt, and casting himself away into the jaw of perdition. Shakya Muni, full of fatherly love towards all beings, looked with compassion on us, his prodigal son, and used every means to restore the half-starved man to his home. It was for this that he left the palace and the beloved wife and son, practised his self-mortification and prolonged Meditation, attained to Enlightenment, and preached Dharma for forty-nine years; in other words, all his strength and effort were focussed on that single aim, which was to bring the prodigal son to his rich mansion of Buddha-nature. He taught not only by words, but by his own actual example, that man has Buddha-nature, by the unfoldment of

---

[172] See 'Sacred Books of the East,' vol. xxi., chap. iv., pp. 98-118.

which he can save himself from the miseries of life and death, and bring himself to a higher realm than gods. When we are Enlightened, or when Universal Spirit awakens within us, we open the inexhaustible store of virtues and excellencies, and can freely make use of them at our will.

The Parable of the Monk and the Stupid Woman

The confused or unenlightened may be compared with a monk and a stupid woman in a Japanese parable which runs as follows: "One evening a monk (who was used to have his head shaved clean), getting drunk against the moral precepts, visited a woman, known as a blockhead, at her house. No sooner had he got into her room than the female fell asleep so soundly that the monk could not wake her nap. Thereupon he made up his mind to use every possible means to arouse her, and searched and searched all over the room for some instrument that would help him in his task of arousing her from death-like slumber. Fortunately, he found a razor in one of the drawers of her mirror stand. With it he gave a stroke to her hair, but she did not stir a whit. Then came another stroke, and she snored like thunder. The third and fourth strokes came, but with no better result. And at last her head was shaven clean, yet still she slept on. The next morning when she awoke, she could not find her visitor, the monk, as he had left the house in the previous night. 'Where is my visitor, where my dear monk?' she called aloud, and waking in a state of somnambulation looked for him in vain, repeating the outcry. When at length her hand accidentally touched her shaven head, she mistook it for that of her visitor, and exclaimed: 'Here you are, my dear, where am I myself gone then?" A great trouble with the confused is their forgetting of real self or Buddha-nature, and not knowing 'where it is gone.' Duke Ngai, of the State of Lu, once said to Confucius: "One of my subjects, Sir, is so much forgetful that he forgot to take his wife when be changed his residence." "That is not much, my lord," said the sage, "the Emperors Kieh[173] and Cheu[174] forgot their own selves."[175]

---

[173] The last Emperor of the Ha dynasty, notorious for his vices. His reign was 1818-1767 B.C.

[174] The last Emperor of the Yin dynasty, one of the worst despots. His reign was 1154-1122 B.C.

[175] Ko-shi-ke-go.

'Each Smile a Hymn, each Kindly Word a Prayer.'

The glorious sun of Buddha-nature shines in the zenith of Enlightened Consciousness, but men still dream a dream of illusion. Bells and clocks of the Universal Church proclaim the dawn of Bodhi, yet men, drunk with the liquors of the Three Poisons[176] Still slumber in the darkness of sin. Let us pray to Buddha, in whose bosom we live, for the sake of our own salvation. Let us invoke Buddha, whose boundless mercy ever besets us, for the Sake of joy and peace of all our fellow-beings. Let us adore Him through our sympathy towards the poor, through our kindness shown to the suffering, through our thought of the sublime and the good.

"O brother man, fold to thy heart thy brother;
Where pity dwells, the peace of God is there;
To worship rightly is to love each other,
Each smile a hymn, each kindly word a prayer."

—Whittier.

Let, then, your heart be so pure that you may not be unworthy of the sunshine beaming upon you the light of Universal Spirit. Let your thought be so noble that you may deserve fair flowers blooming before you, reminding you of merciful Buddha. Let your life be so good that you may not be ashamed of yourself in the presence of the Blessed One. This is the piety of Mahayanists, especially of Zenists.

The World is in the Making

Our assertion is far from assuming that life is now complete, and is in its best state. On the contrary, it is full of defects and shortcomings. We must not be puffed up with modern civilization, however great victory it has scored for its side. Beyond all doubt man is still in his cradle. He often stretches forth his hands to get at his higher ideal, yet is still satisfied with

[176] Lust, anger, and folly.

worthless playthings. It is too glaring a fact to be overlooked by us that faith in religion is dying out in the educated circles of society, that insincerity, cowardice, and double-tongue are found holding high positions in almost ever community, that Lucrese and Ezzeling are looking down upon the starving multitude from their luxurious palace, that Mammon and Bacchus are sometimes preying on their living victims, that even religion often sides with Contention and piety takes part in Cruelty, that Anarchy is ever ready to spring on the crowned beings, that philosophy is disposed to turn the deaf ear to the petition of peace, while science provides fuel for the fire of strife.

Was the golden age of man, then, over in the remote past? Is the doomsday coming instead? Do you bear the trumpet call? Do you feel the earth tremble? No, absolutely no, the golden age is not passed. It is yet to come. There are not a few who think that the world is in completion, and the Creator has finished His work. We witness, however, that He is still working and working, for actually we hear His hammer-strokes resounding through heaven above and earth beneath. Does He not show us new materials for His building? Does He not give new forms to His design? Does He not surprise us with novelties, extraordinaries, and mysteries? In a word, the world is in progress, not in retrogression.

A stream does not run in a straight line. It now turns to the right, now to the left, now leaps down a precipice, now waters rich fields, now runs back towards its source; but it is destined to find its outlet in the ocean. So it is with the stream of life. It now leaps down the precipice of revolution. Now it enriches the fertile field of civilization. Now it expands itself into a glassy lake of peace. Now it forms the dangerous whirlpool of strife. But its course is always toward the ocean of Enlightenment, in which the gems of equality and freedom, jewels of truth and beauty, and treasures of wisdom and bliss can be had.

The Progress and Hope of Life

How many myriads of years have passed since the germs of life first made appearance on earth none can tell; how many thousands of summers and winters it has taken to develop itself into higher animals, no scientist can calculate exactly. Slowly but steadily it has taken its swerving course, and ascending stop by step the series of evolution, has reached at length the plane of the rational animal. We cannot tell how many billions of years it takes to develop ourselves and become beings higher than man himself, yet we firmly believe that it is possible for us to take the same unerring course as the organic germs took in the past. Existing humanity is not the same as primitive one. It is quite another race. Our desires and hopes are entirely different from those of primitive man. What was gold for them is now iron for us. Our thoughts and beliefs are what they never dreamed of. Of our knowledge they had almost none. That which they kept in veneration we trample under our feet. Things they worshipped as deities now serve us as our slaves. Things that troubled and tortured them we now turn into utilities. To say nothing of the customs and manners and mode of living which underwent extraordinary change, we are of a race in body and mind other than the primitive forefathers of good old days. In addition to this we have every reason to believe in the betterment of life. Let us cast a glance to the existing state of the world. While the Turco-Italian war was raising its ferocious outcry, the Chinese revolution lifted its head before the trembling throne. Who can tell whether another sanguinary affair will not break out before the Bulgarian bloodshed comes to an end? Still we believe that, as fire drives out fire, to borrow Shakespeare's phrase, so war is driving out war. As an ocean, which separated two nations in the past, serves to unite them now, so a war, which separated two people in the past, brings them to unity now. It goes without saying, that every nation groans under the burden of cannons and warships, and heartily desires peace. No nation can willingly wage war against any other nation. It is against the national conscience. It is no exaggeration to say the world is wholly the ear to hear the news from the goddess of peace. A time will surely come, if our purpose be steady and our resolution firm, when universal peace will be restored, and Shakya Muni's precept, 'not to kill,' will be realized by all mankind.

The Betterment of Life

Again, people nowadays seem to feel keenly the wound of the economical results of war, but they are unfeeling to its moral injuries. As elements have their affinities, as bodies have their attractions, as creatures have their instinct to live together, so men have their inborn mutual love. 'God divided man into men that they might help each other.' Their strength lies in their mutual help, their pleasure is in their mutual love, and their perfection is in their giving and receiving of alternate good. Therefore Shakya Muni says: "Be merciful to all living beings." To take up arms against any other person is unlawful for any individual. It is the violation of the universal law of life. We do not deny that there are not a few who are so wretched that they rejoice in their crimes, nor that there is any person but has more or less stain on his character, nor that the means of committing crimes are multiplied in proportion as modern civilization advances; yet still we believe that our social life is ever breaking down our wolfish disposition that we inherited from our brute ancestors, and education is ever wearing out our cannibalistic nature which we have in common with wild animals. On the one hand, the signs of social morals are manifest in every direction, such as asylums for orphans, poorhouses, houses of correction, lodgings for the penniless, asylums for the poor, free hospitals, hospitals for domestic animals, societies for the prevention of cruelty to animals, schools for the blind and the dumb, asylums for the insane, and so forth; on the other hand, various discoveries and inventions have been made that may contribute to the social improvement, such as the discovery of the X rays and of radium, the invention of the wireless telegraph and that of the aeroplane and what not. Furthermore, spiritual wonders such as clairvoyance, clairaudience, telepathy, etc., remind us of the possibilities of further spiritual unfoldment in man which he never dreamed of. Thus life is growing richer and nobler step by step, and becoming more and more hopeful as we advance in the Way of Buddha.

The Buddha of Mercy

Milton says:
"Virtue may be assailed, but never hurt;
Surprised by unjust force, but not enthralled.
But evil on itself shall back recoil,
And mix no more with goodness. If this fail,
The pillared firmament is rottenness,
And earth's base built on stubble."

The world is built on the foundation of morality, which is another name for Universal Spirit, and moral order sustains it. We human beings, consciously or unconsciously, were, are, and will be at work to bring the world into perfection. This idea is allegorically expressed in the Buddhist sutra,[177] which details the advent of a merciful Buddha named Maitreya in the remote future. At that time, it says, there will be no steep hills, no filthy places, no epidemic, no famine, no earthquake, no storm, no war, no revolution, no bloodshed, no cruelty, and no suffering; the roads will be paved smoothly, grass and trees always blooming, birds ever singing, men contented and happy; all sentient beings will worship the Buddha of Mercy, accept His doctrine, and attain to Enlightenment. This prophecy will be fulfilled, according to the sutra, 5,670,000,000 years after the death of Shakya Muni. This evidently shows us that the Mahayanist's aim of life is to bring out man's inborn light of Buddha-nature to illumine the world, to realize the universal brotherhood of all sentient beings, to attain to Enlightenment, and to enjoy peace and joy to which Universal Spirit leads us.

---

[177] See Nanjo's Catalogue, Nos. 204-209.

CHAPTER VI

ENLIGHTENMENT

Enlightenment is beyond Description and Analysis

In the foregoing chapters we have had several occasions to refer to the central problem of Zen or Enlightenment, whose content it is futile to attempt to explain or analyze. We must not explain or analyze it, because by doing so we cannot but mislead the reader. We can as well represent Enlightenment by means of explanation or analysis as we do personality by snapshots or by anatomical operations. As our inner life, directly experienced within us, is anything but the shape of the head, or the features of the face, or the posture of the body, so Enlightenment experienced by Zenists at the moment of their highest Samadhi[178] is anything but the psychological analysis of mental process, or the epistemological explanation of cognition, or the philosophical generalization of concepts. Enlightenment can be realized only by the Enlightened, and baffles every attempt to describe it, even by the Enlightened themselves. The effort of the confused to guess at Enlightenment is often likened by the Zenists to the effort of the blind who feel an elephant to know what it looks like. Some of them who happen to feel the trunk would declare it is like a rope, but those who happen to feel the belly would declare it is like a huge drum; while those who happen to feel the feet would declare it is like the trunk of a tree. But none of these conjectures can approach the living elephant.

---

[178] Abstract Contemplation, which the Zenists distinguish from Samadhi, practised by the Brahmins. The author of 'An Outline of Buddhist Sects' points out the distinction, saying: "Contemplation of outside religionists is practised with the heterodox view that the lower worlds (the worlds for men, beasts, etc.) are disgusting, but the upper worlds (the worlds for Devas) are desirable; Contemplation of common people (ordinary lay believers of Buddhism) is practised with the belief in the law of Karma, and also with disgust (for the lower worlds) and desire (for the upper worlds); Contemplation of Hinayana is practised with an insight into the truth of Anatman (non-soul); Contemplation of Mahayana is practised with an insight of Unreality of Atman (soul) as well as of Dharma (thing); Contemplation of the highest perfection is practised with the view that Mind is pure in its nature, it is endowed with unpolluted wisdom, free from passion, and it is no other than Buddha himself."

Enlightenment implies an Insight into the Nature of Self

We cannot pass over, however, this weighty problem without saying a word. We shall try in this chapter to present Enlightenment before the reader in a roundabout way, just as the painter gives the fragmentary sketches of a beautiful city, being unable to give even a bird's-eye view of it. Enlightenment, first of all, implies an insight into the nature of Self. It is an emancipation of mind from illusion concerning Self. All kinds of sin take root deep in the misconception of Self, and putting forth the branches of lust, anger, and folly, throw dark shadows on life. To extirpate this misconception Buddhism[179] strongly denies the existence of the individual soul as conceived by common sense-that is, that unchanging spiritual entity provided with sight, hearing, touch, smell, feeling, thought, imagination, aspiration, etc., which survives the body. It teaches us that there is no such thing as soul, and that the notion of soul is a gross illusion. It treats of body as a temporal material form of life doomed to be destroyed by death and reduced to its elements again. It maintains that mind is also a temporal spiritual form of life, behind which there is no immutable soul.

An illusory mind tends either to regard body as Self and to yearn after its material interests, or to believe mind dependent on soul as Ego. Those who are given to sensual pleasures, consciously or unconsciously, bold body to be the Self, and remain the life-long slave to the objects of sense. Those who regard mind as dependent on soul as the Self, on the other hand, undervalue body as a mere tool with which the soul works, and are inclined to denounce life as if unworthy of living. We must not undervalue body, nor must we overestimate mind. There is no mind isolated from body, nor is there any body separated from mind. Every activity of mind produces chemical and physiological changes in the nerve-centres, in the organs, and eventually in the whole body; while every activity of body is sure to bring

---

[179] Both Mahayana and Hinayana Buddhism teach the doctrine of Anatman, or Non-self. It is the denial of soul as conceived by common sense, and of Atman as conceived by Indian heterodox thinkers. Some Mahayanists believe in the existence of real Self instead of individual self, as we see in Mahaparinirvana-sutra, whose author says: "There is real self in non-self." It is worthy of note that the Hinayanists set forth Purity, Pleasure, Atman, and Eternity, as the four great misconceptions about life, while the same author regards them as the four great attributes of Nirvana itself.

out the corresponding change in the mental function, and eventually in the whole personality. We have the inward experience of sorrow when we have simultaneously the outward appearance of tears and of pallor; when we have the outward appearance of the fiery eyes and short breath, we have simultaneously the inward feeling of anger. Thus body is mind observed outwardly in its relation to the senses; mind is body inwardly experienced in its relation to introspection. Who can draw a strict line of demarcation between mind and body? We should admit, so far as our present knowledge is concerned, that mind, the intangible, has been formed to don a garment of matter in order to become an intelligible existence at all; matter, the solid, has faded under examination into formlessness, as that of mind. Zen believes in the identification of mind and body, as Do-gen[180] says: "Body is identical with mind; appearance and reality are one and the same thing." Bergson denies the identification of mind and body, saying:[181]

"It (experience) shows us the interdependence of the mental and the physical, the necessity of a certain cerebral substratum for the psychical state-nothing more. From the fact that two things are mutually dependent, it does not follow that they are equivalent. Because a certain screw is necessary for a certain machine, because the machine works when the screw is there and stops when the screw is taken away, we do not say that the screw is equivalent of the machine." Bergson's simile of a screw and a machine is quite inadequate to show the interdependence of mind and body, because the screw does cause the machine to work, but the machine does not cause the screw to work; so that their relation is not interdependence. On the contrary, body causes mind to work, and at the same time mind causes body to work; so that their relation is perfectly interdependent, and the relation is not that of an addition of mind to body, or of body to mind, as the screw is added to the machine. Bergson must have compared the working of the machine with mind, and the machine itself with body, if be wanted to show the real fact. Moreover, he is not right in asserting that "from the fact that two things are mutually dependent, it does not follow that they are equivalent," because there are

180 The master strongly condemns the immortality of the soul as the heterodox doctrine in his Sho-bo-gen-zo. The same argument is found in Mu-chu-mon-do, by Mu-so Koku-shi.

181 'Creative Evolution,' pp. 354, 355.

several kinds of interdependence, in some of which two things can be equivalent. For instance, bricks, mutually dependent in their forming an arch, cannot be equivalent one with another; but water and waves, being mutually dependent, can be identified. In like manner fire and heat, air and wind, a machine and its working, mind and body.[182]

The Irrationality of the Belief of Immortality

Occidental minds believe in a mysterious entity under the name of soul, just as Indian thinkers believe in the so-called subtle body entirely distinct from the gross body of flesh and blood. Soul, according to this belief, is an active principle that unites body and mind so as to form an harmonious whole of mental as well as bodily activities. And it acts through the instrumentality of the mind and body in the present life, and enjoys an eternal life beyond the grave. It is on this soul that individual immortality is based. It is immortal Self. Now, to say nothing of the origin of soul, this long-entertained belief is hardly good for anything. In the first place, it throws no light upon the relation of mind and body, because soul is an empty name for the unity of mind and body, and serves to explain nothing. On the contrary, it adds another mystery to the already mysterious relationships between matter and spirit. Secondly, soul should be conceived as a psychical individual, subject to spacial determinations—but since it has to be deprived by death of its body which individualizes it, it will cease to be individuality after death, to the disappointment of the believer. How could you think anything purely spiritual and formless existing without blending together with other things? Thirdly, it fails to gratify the desire, cherished by the believer, of enjoying eternal life, because soul has to lose its body, the sole important medium

---

182 Bergson, arguing against the dependence of the mind on brain, says: "That there is a close connection between a state of consciousness and the brain we do not dispute. But there is also a close connection between a coat and the nail on which it hangs, for if the nail is pulled out, the coat will fall to the ground. Shall we say, then, that the shape of the nail gave the shape of the coat, or in any way corresponds to it? No more are we entitled to conclude, because the psychical fact is hung on to a cerebral state, that there is any parallelism between the two series, psychical and physiological." We have to ask, in what respects does the interrelation between mind and body resemble the relation between a coat and a nail?

through which it may enjoy life. Fourthly, soul is taken as a subject matter to receive in the future life the reward or the punishment from God for our actions in this life; but the very idea of eternal punishment is inconsistent with the boundless love of God. Fifthly, it is beyond all doubt that soul is conceived as an entity, which unifies various mental faculties and exists as the foundation of individual personality. But the existence of such soul is quite incompatible with the well-known pathological fact that it is possible for the individual to have double or treble or multiple personalities. Thus the belief in the existence of soul conceived by the common sense turns out not only to be irrational, but a useless encumbrance on the religious mind. Therefore Zen declares that there is no such thing as soul, and that mind and body are one. Hwui Chung (Ye-chu), a famous disciple of the Sixth Patriarch in China, to quote an example, one day asked a monk: "Where did you come from?" "I came, sir, from the South," replied the man. "What doctrine do the masters of the South teach?" asked Hwui Chung again. "They teach, sir, that body is mortal, but mind is immortal," was the answer. "That," said the master, "is the heterodox doctrine of the Atman!" "How do you, sir," questioned the monk, "teach about that?" "I teach that the body and mind are one," was the reply.[183]

Fiske,[184] in his argument against materialism, blames the denial of immortality, saying: "The materialistic assumption that there is no such state of things, and that the life of the soul ends accordingly with the life of the body, is perhaps the most colossal instance of baseless assumption that is known to the history of philosophy." But we can say with equal force that the common-sense assumption that the life of soul continues beyond the grave is, perhaps, the most colossal instance of baseless assumption that is known to the history of thought, because, there being no scientific evidences that give countenance to the assumption, even the spiritualists themselves hesitate to assert the existence of a ghost or soul. Again he[185] says: "With this illegitimate hypothesis of annihilation the materialist transgresses the bounds of experience quite as widely as the poet who sings

---

[183] For further explanation, see Sho-bo-gen-zo and Mu-chu-mon-do.

[184] 'The Destiny of Man,' p. 110.

[185] 'The Destiny of Man,' pp. 110, 111.

of the New Jerusalem with its river of life and its street of gold. Scientifically speaking, there is not a particle of evidence for either view." This is as much as to say there is not a particle of evidence, scientifically speaking, for the common-sense view of soul, because the poet's description of the New Jerusalem is nothing but the result of the common-sense belief of immortality.

The Examination of the Notion of Self

The belief in immortality is based on the strong instinct of self-preservation that calls forth an insatiable longing for longevity. It is another form of egoism, one of the relics of our brute forefathers. We must bear in mind that this illusion of the individual Self is the foundation on which every form of immorality has its being. I challenge my readers to find in the whole history of mankind any crime not based on egoism. Evil-doers have been as a rule pleasure-hunters, money-seekers, seekers after self-interests, characterized by lust, folly, and cruelty. Has there been anyone who committed theft that he might further the interests of his villagers? Has there been any paramour who disgraced himself that lie might help his neighbours? Has there been any traitor who performed the ignoble conduct to promote the welfare of his own country or society at large?

To get Enlightened, therefore, we have to correct, first of all, our notions concerning Self. Individual body and mind are not the only important constituents of Self. There are many other indispensable elements in the notion of Self. For instance, I have come into existence as another form of my parents. I am theirs, and may justly be called the reincarnation of them. And again, my father is another form of his parents; my mother of hers; his and her parents of theirs; and ad infinitum. In brief, all my forefathers live and have their being in me. I cannot help, therefore, thinking that my physical state is the result of the sum total of my good and bad actions in the past lives I led in the persons of my forefathers, and of the influence I received therein;[186] and that my psychical state is the result of that which I received, felt, imagined, conceived, experienced, and thought in my past

[186] This is the law of Karma.

existences in the persons of my ancestors.

Besides this, my brothers, my sisters, my neighbours—nay, all my follow-men and fellow-women are no other than the reincarnation of their parents and forefathers, who are also mine. The same blood invigorated the king as well as the beggar; the same nerve energized the white as well as the black men; the same consciousness vitalized the wise as well as the unwise. Impossible it is to conceive myself independent of my fellow-men and fellow-women, for they are mine and I am theirs—that is, I live and move in them, and they live and move in me.

It is bare nonsense to say that I go to school, not to be educated as a member of society, but simply to gratify my individual desire for knowledge; or that I make a fortune, not to lead the life of a well-to-do in society, but to satisfy my individual money-loving instinct; or that I seek after truth, neither to do good to my contemporaries nor to the future generations, but only for my individual curiosity or that I live neither to live with my family nor with my friends nor with anyone else, but to live my individual life. It is as gross absurdity to say that I am an individual absolutely independent of society as to say I am a husband with no wife, or I am a son to no parents. Whatever I do directly or indirectly I contribute to the common fortune of man; whatever anyone else does directly or indirectly determines my fate. Therefore we must realize that our Selves necessarily include other members of the community, while other members' Selves necessarily comprehend us.

Nature is the Mother of All Things

Furthermore, man has come into existence out of Nature. He is her child. She provided him food, raiment, and shelter. She nourishes him, strengthens him, and vitalizes him. At the same time she disciplines, punishes, and instructs him. His body is of her own formation, his knowledge is of her own laws, and his activities are the responses to her own addresses to him. Modern civilization is said by some to be the conquest of man over Nature; but, in fact, it is his faithful obedience to her. "Bacon truly said," says Eucken,[187] "that to rule nature man must first serve

[187] Eucken's 'Philosophy of Life,' by W. R. Royce Gibbon, p. 51.

her. He forgot to add that, as her ruler, he is still destined to go on serving her." She can never be attacked by any being unless he acts in strict conformity to her laws. To accomplish anything against her law is as impossible as to catch fishes in a forest, or to make bread of rock. How many species of animals have perished owing to their inability to follow her steps! How immense fortunes have been lost in vain from man's ignorance of her order! How many human beings disappeared on earth from their disobedience to her unbending will! She is, nevertheless, true to those who obey her rules. Has not science proved that she is truthful? Has not art found that she is beautiful?

Has not philosophy announced that she is spiritual? Has not religion proclaimed that she is good? At all events, she is the mother of all beings. She lives in all things and they live in her. All that she possesses is theirs, and all that they want she supplies. Her life is the same vitality that stirs all sentient beings. Chwang Tsz[188] (So-shi) is right when he says: "Heaven, Earth, and I were produced together, and all things and I are one." And again: "If all things be regarded with love, Heaven and Earth are one with me." Sang Chao (So-jo) also says: "Heaven and Earth are of the same root as we. All things in the world are of one substance with Me."[189]

Real Self

If there be no individual soul either in mind or body, where does personality lie? What is Real Self? How does it differ from soul? Self is living entity, not immutable like soul, but mutable and ever-changing life, which is body when observed by senses, and which is mind when experienced by introspection. It is not an entity lying behind mind and body, but life existent as the union of body and mind. It existed in our forefathers in the past, is existing in the present, and will exist in the future generations. It also discloses itself to some measure in vegetables and animals, and shadows itself forth in inorganic nature. It is Cosmic life and Cosmic spirit, and at the same time individual life and individual spirit. It is

---

188 Chwang Tsz, vol. i., p. 20.

189 This is a favourite subject of discussion by Zenists.

one and the same life which embraces men and nature. It is the self-existent, creative, universal principle that moves on from eternity to eternity. As such it is called Mind or Self by Zenists. Pan Shan (Ban-zan) says: "The moon of mind comprehends all the universe in its light." A man asked Chang Sha (Cho-sha): "How can you turn the phenomenal universe into Self ?" "How can you turn Self into the phenomenal universe?" returned the master.

When we get the insight into this Self, we are able to have the open sesame to the mysteries of the universe, because to know the nature of a drop of water is to know the nature of the river, the lake, and the ocean—nay, even of vapour, mist, and cloud; in other words, to get an insight into individual life is the key to the secret of Universal Life. We must not confine Self within the poor little person called body. That is the root of the poorest and most miserable egoism. We should expand that egoism into family-egoism, then into nation-egoism, then into race-egoism, then into human-egoism, then into living-being-egoism, and lastly into universe-egoism, which is not egoism at all. Thus we deny the immortality of soul as conceived by common sense, but assume immortality of the Great Soul, which animates, vitalizes, and spiritualizes all sentient beings. It is Hinayana Buddhism that first denied the existence of atman or Self so emphatically inculcated in the Upanisads, and paved the way for the general conception of Universal Self, with the eulogies of which almost every page of Mahayana books is filled.

The Awakening of the Innermost Wisdom

Having set ourselves free from the misconception of Self, next we must awaken our innermost wisdom, pure and divine, called the Mind of Buddha,[190] or Bodhi,[191] or Prajnya[192] by Zen masters. It is the divine light, the inner heaven, the key to all moral treasures, the centre of thought and consciousness, the source of all influence and power, the seat of kindness,

190 Zen is often called the Sect of Buddha-mind, as it lays stress on the awakening of the Mind of Buddha. The words 'the Mind of Buddha' were taken from a passage in Lankavatara-sutra.

191 That knowledge by which one becomes enlightened.

192 Supreme wisdom.

justice, sympathy, impartial love, humanity, and mercy, the measure of all things. When this innermost wisdom is fully awakened, we are able to realize that each and everyone of us is identical in spirit, in essence, in nature with the universal life or Buddha, that each ever lives face to face with Buddha, that each is beset by the abundant grace of the Blessed One, that He arouses his moral nature, that He opens his spiritual eyes, that He unfolds his new capacity, that He appoints his mission, and that life is not an ocean of birth, disease, old age, and death, nor the vale of tears, but the holy temple of Buddha, the Pure Land,[193] where be can enjoy the bliss of Nirvana.

Then our minds go through an entire revolution. We are no more troubled by anger and hatred, no more bitten by envy and ambition, no more stung by sorrow and chagrin, no more overwhelmed by melancholy and despair. Not that we become passionless or simply intellectual, but that we have purified passions, which, instead of troubling us, inspire us with noble aspirations, such as anger and hatred against injustice, cruelty, and dishonesty, sorrow and lamentation for human frailty, mirth and joy for the welfare of follow-beings, pity and sympathy for suffering creatures. The same change purifies our intellect. Scepticism and sophistry give way to firm conviction; criticism and hypothesis to right judgment; and inference and argument to realization.

What we merely observed before we now touch with heart as well. What we knew in relation of difference before we now understand in relation of unity as well. How things happen was our chief concern before, but now we consider as well bow much value they have. What was outside us before now comes within us. What was dead and indifferent before grows now alive and lovable to us. What was insignificant and empty before becomes now important, and has profound meaning. Wherever we go we find beauty; whomever we meet we find good; whatever we get we receive with gratitude. This is the reason why the Zenists not only regarded all their fellow-beings as their benefactors, but felt gratitude even towards fuel and water. The present writer knows a contemporary Zenist who would not drink even a cup of water without first making a salutation to it. Such an attitude of Zen toward things may well be illustrated by the following

[193] Sukhavati, or the land of bliss.

example: Sueh Fung (Sep-po) and Kin Shan (Kin-zan), once travelling through a mountainous district, saw a leaf of the rape floating down the stream. Thereon Kin Shan said: "Let us go up, dear brother, along the stream that we may find a sage living up on the mountain. I hope we shall find a good teacher in him." "No," replied Sueh Fung, "for he cannot be a sage who wastes even a leaf of the rape. He will be no good teacher for us."

Zen is not Nihilistic

Zen judged from ancient Zen masters' aphorisms may seem, at the first sight, to be idealistic in an extreme form, as they say: "Mind is Buddha" or, "Buddha is Mind," or, "There is nothing outside mind," or, "Three worlds are of but one mind." And it may also appear to be nihilistic, as they say: "There has been nothing since all eternity," "By illusion you see the castle of the Three Worlds"; "by Enlightenment you see but emptiness in ten directions."[194] In reality, however, Zen[195] is neither idealistic nor nihilistic. Zen makes use of the nihilistic idea of Hinayana Buddhism, and calls its students' attention to the change and evanescence of life and of the world, first to destroy the error of immutation, next to dispel the attachment to the sensual objects.

It is a misleading tendency of our intellect to conceive things as if they were immutable and constant. It often leaves changing and concrete individual objects out of consideration, and lays stress on the general, abstract, unchanging aspect of things. It is inclined to be given to generalization and abstraction. It often looks not at this thing or at that thing, but at things in general. It loves to think not of a good thing nor of a bad thing, but of bad and good in the abstract. This intellectual tendency hardens and petrifies the living and growing world, and leads us to take the

---

194 These words were repeatedly uttered by Chinese and Japanese Zenists of all ages. Chwen Hih (Fu-dai-shi) expressed this very idea in his Sin Wang Ming (Shin-o-mei) at the time of Bodhidharma.

195 The Rin-zai teachers mostly make use of the doctrine of unreality of all things, as taught in Prajnya-paramita-sutras. We have to note that there are some differences between the Mahayana doctrine of unreality and the Hinayana doctrine of unreality.

universe as a thing dead, inert, and standing still. This error of immutation can be corrected by the doctrine of Transcience taught by Hinayana Buddhism. But as medicine taken in an undue quantity turns into poison, so the doctrine of Transcience drove the Hinayanists to the suicidal conclusion of nihilism. A well-known scholar and believer of Zen, Kwei Fung (Kei-ha) says in his refutation of nihilism:[196]

"If mind as well as external objects be unreal, who is it that knows they are so? Again, if there be nothing real in the universe, what is it that causes unreal objects to appear? We stand witness to the fact that there is no one of the unreal things on earth that is not made to appear by something real. If there be no water of unchanging fluidity, how can there be the unreal and temporary forms of waves? If there be no unchanging mirror, bright and clean, bow can there be the various images, unreal and temporary, reflected in it? If mind as well as external objects be nothing at all, no one can tell what it is that causes these unreal appearances. Therefore this doctrine (of the unreality of all things) can never clearly disclose spiritual Reality. So that Mahabheri-harakaparivarta-sutra says: " All the sutras that teach the unreality of things belong to the imperfect doctrine " (of the Shakya Muni). Mahaprajnya-paramita-sutra says The doctrine of unreality is the entrance-gate of Mahayana."

Zen and Idealism

Next Zen makes use of Idealism as explained by the Dharmalaksana School of Mahayana Buddhism.[197] For instance, the Fourth Patriarch says: "Hundreds and thousands of laws originate with mind. Innumerable mysterious virtues proceed from the mental source." Niu Teu (Go-zu) also says: "When mind arises, various things arise; when mind ceases to exist, various things cease to exist." Tsao Shan (So-zan) carried the point so far that he cried out, on hearing the bell: "It hurts, it pains." Then an attendant of his asked "What is the matter?" "It is my mind," said he, that is

[196] See the appendix, chap. ii., 'The Mahayana Doctrine of Nihilism.'

[197] Appendix, chap. ii., 'The Mahayana Doctrine of Dharmalaksana.'

struck."[198]

We acknowledge the truth of the following considerations: There exists no colour, nor sound, nor odour in the objective world, but there are the vibrations of ether, or the undulations of the air, or the stimuli of the sensory nerves of smell. Colour is nothing but the translation of the stimuli into sensation by the optical nerves, so also sounds by the auditory, and odours by the smelling. Therefore nothing exists objectively exactly as it is perceived by the senses, but all are subjective. Take electricity, for example, it appears as light when perceived through the eye; it appears as sound when perceived through the ear; it appears as taste when perceived through the tongue; but electricity in reality is not light, nor sound, nor taste. Similarly, the mountain is not high nor low; the river is not deep nor shallow; the house is not large nor small; the day is not long nor short; but they seem so through comparison. It is not objective reality that displays the phenomenal universe before us, but it is our mind that plays an important part. Suppose that we have but one sense organ, the eye, then the whole universe should consist of colours and of colours only. If we suppose we were endowed with the sixth sense, which entirely contradicts our five senses, then the whole world would be otherwise. Besides, it is our reason that finds the law of cause and effect in the objective world, that discovered the law of uniformity in Nature, and that discloses scientific laws in the universe so as to form a cosmos. Some scholars maintain that we cannot think of non-existence of space, even if we can leave out all objects in it; nor can we doubt the existence of time, for the existence of mind itself presupposes time. Their very argument, however, proves the subjectivity of time and space, because, if they were objective, we should be able to think them non-existent, as we do with other external objects. Even space and time, therefore are no more than subjective.

Idealism is a Potent Medicine for Self-created Mental Disease

In so far as Buddhist idealism refers to the world of sense, in so far as it does not assume that to to be known is identical with to be, in so far as it does not assert that the phenomenal universe is a dream and a vision, we

[198] Zen-rin-rui-shu.

may admit it as true. On the one hand, it serves us as a purifier of our hearts polluted with materialistic desires, and uplifts us above the plain of sensualism; on the other hand, it destroys superstitions which as a rule arise from ignorance and want of the idealistic conception of things. It is a lamentable fact that every country is full of such superstitions people as described by one of the New Thought writers: 'Tens of thousands of women in this country believe that if two people look in a mirror at the same time, or if one thanks the other for a pin, or if one gives a knife or a sharp instrument to a friend, it will break up friendship. If a young lady is presented with a thimble, she will be an old maid. Some people think that after leaving a house it is unlucky to go back after any article which has been forgotten, and, if one is obliged to do so, one should sit down in a chair before going out again; that if a broom touches a person while someone is sweeping, bad luck will follow; and that it is unlucky to change one's place at a table. A man took an opal to a New York jeweller and asked him to buy it. He said that it had brought him nothing but bad luck, that since it had come into his possession he had failed in business, that there bad been much sickness in his family, and all sorts of misfortune had befallen him. He refused to keep the cursed thing any longer. The jeweller examined the stone, and found that it was not an opal after all, but an imitation.'

Idealism is a most potent medicine for these self-created mental diseases. It will successfully drive away devils and spirits that frequent ignorant minds, just as Jesus did in the old days. Zen makes use of moral idealism to extirpate, root and branch, all such idle dreams and phantasmagoria of illusion and opens the way to Enlightenment.

Idealistic Scepticism concerning Objective Reality

But extreme Idealism identifies 'to be' with 'to be known,' and assumes all phenomena to be ideas as illustrated in Mahayana-vidyamatra-siddhitridaca-castra[199] and Vidyamatra-vincati-castra,[200] by Vasubandhu. Then it necessarily parts company with Zen, which believes in Universal Life existing in everything instead of behind it. Idealism shows us its dark side in three sceptic views: (1) scepticism respecting objective reality; (2) scepticism respecting religion; (3) scepticism respecting morality.

First it assumes that things exist in so far as they are known by us. It is as a matter of course that if a tree exists at all, it is known as having a trunk long or short, branches large or small, leaves green or yellow, flowers yellow or purple, etc., all of which are ideas. But it does not imply in the least that 'to be known' is equivalent to 'to be existent.' Rather we should say that to be known presupposes to be existent, for we cannot know anything non-existent, even if we admit that the axioms of logic subsist. Again, a tree may stand as ideas to a knower, but it can stand at the same time as a shelter in relation to some birds, as food in relation to some insects, as a world in relation to some minute worms, as a kindred organism to other vegetables. How could you say that its relation to a knower is the only and fundamental relation for the existence of the tree? The disappearance of its knower no more affects the tree than of its feeder; nor the appearance of its knower affects the tree any more than that of kindred vegetables.

Extreme idealism erroneously concludes that what is really existent, or what is directly proved to be existent, is only our sensations, ideas, thoughts; that the external world is nothing but the images reflected on the mirror of the mind, and that therefore objective reality of things is doubtful-nay, more, they are unreal, illusory, and dreams. If so, we can no longer distinguish the real from the visionary; the waking from the dreaming; the sane from the insane; the true from the untrue. Whether life is real or an empty dream, we are at a loss to understand.

---

[199] A philosophical work on Buddhist idealism by Vasubandhu, translated into Chinese by Hiuen Tsang in A.D. 648. There exists a famous commentary on it, compiled by Dharmapala, translated into Chinese by Hiuen Tsang in A.D. 659. See Nanjo's Catalogue, Nos. 1197 and 1125.

[200] A simpler work on Idealism, translated into Chinese by Hiuen Tsang in A.D. 661. See Nanjo's Catalogue, Nos. 1238, 1239, and 1240.

Idealistic Scepticism concerning Religion and Morality

Similarly, it is the case with religion and morality. If we admit extreme idealism as true, there can be nothing objectively real. God is little more than a mental image. He must be a creature of mind instead of a Creator. He has no objective reality. He is when we think He is. He is not when we think He is not. He is at the mercy of our thought. How much more unreal the world must be, which is supposed to have been created by an unreal God! Providence, salvation, and divine grace—what are they? A bare dream dreamed in a dream!

What is morality, then? It is subjective. It has no objective validity. A moral conduct highly valued by our fathers is now held to be immoral by us. Immoral acts now strongly denounced by us may be regarded as moral by our posterity. Good deeds of the savage are not necessarily good in the eyes of the civilized, nor evil acts of the Orientals are necessarily evil before the face of the Occidentals. It follows, then, that there is no definite standard of morality in any place at any time.

If morality be merely subjective, and there be no objective standard, how can you distinguish evil from good? How can you single out angels from among devils? Was not Socrates a criminal? Was not Jesus also a criminal? How could you know Him to be a Divine man different from other criminals who were crucified with Him? What you honour may I not denounce as disgrace? What you hold as duty may I not condemn as sin? Every form of idealism is doomed, after all, to end in such confusion and scepticism. We cannot embrace radical idealism, which holds these threefold sceptical views in her womb.

An Illusion concerning Appearance and Reality

To get Enlightened we must next dispel an illusion respecting appearance and reality. According. to certain religionists, all the phenomena of the universe are to succumb to change. Worldly things one and all are evanescent. They are nought in the long run. Snowcapped mountains may sink into the bottom of the deep, while the sands in the fathomless ocean may soar into the azure sky at some time or other. Blooming flowers are destined to fade and to bloom again in the next year. So destined are growing trees, rising generations, prospering nations, glowing suns, moons, and stars. This, they would say, is only the case with phenomena or appearances, but not with reality. Growth and decay, birth and death, rise and fall, all these are the ebb and flow of appearances in the ocean of reality, which is always the same. Flowers may fade and be reduced to dust, yet out of that dust come flowers. Trees may die out, yet they are reproduced somewhere else. The time may come when the earth will become a dead sphere quite unsuitable for human habitation, and the whole of mankind will perish; yet who knows that whether another earth may not be produced as man's home? The sun might have its beginning and end, stars, moons, theirs as well; yet an infinite universe would have no beginning nor end.

Again, they say, mutation is of the world of sense or phenomenal appearances, but not of reality. The former are the phases of the latter shown to our senses. Accordingly they are always limited and modified by our senses, just as images are always limited and modified by the mirror in which they are reflected. On this account appearances are subject to limitations, while reality is limitless. And it follows that the former are imperfect, while the latter is perfect; that the former is transient, while the latter is eternal; that the former is relative, while the latter is absolute; that the former is worldly, while the latter is holy; that the former is knowable, while the latter is unknowable.

These considerations naturally lead us to an assertion that the world of appearances is valueless, as it is limited, short-lived, imperfect, painful, sinful, hopeless, and miserable; while the realm of reality is to be aspired for, as it is eternal, perfect, comfortable, full of hope, joy, and peace-hence the eternal divorce of appearance and reality. Such a view of life tends to make one minimize the value of man, to neglect the present existence, and to yearn after the future.

Some religionists tell us that we men are helpless, sinful, hopeless, and miserable creatures. Worldly riches, temporal honours, and social positions-nay, even sublimities and beauties of the present existence, are to be ignored and despised. We have no need of caring for those things that pass away in a twinkling moment. We must prepare for the future life which is eternal. We must accumulate wealth for that existence. We must endeavour to hold rank in it. We must aspire for the sublimity and beauty and glory of that realm.

Where does the Root of the Illusion Lie?

Now let us examine where illusion lies hidden from the view of these religionists. It lies deeply rooted in the misconstruction of reality, grows up into the illusive ideas of appearances, and throws its dark shadow on life. The most fundamental error lies in their construing reality as something unknowable existing behind appearances.

According to their opinion, all that we know, or perceive, or feel, or imagine about the world, is appearances or phenomena, but not reality itself. Appearances are 'things known as,' but not 'things as they are.' Thing-in-itself, or reality, lies behind appearances permanently beyond our ken. This is probably the most profound metaphysical pit into which philosophical minds have ever fallen in their way of speculation. Things appear, they would say, as we see them through our limited senses; but they must present entirely different aspects to those that differ from ours, just as the vibration of ether appears to us as colours, yet it presents quite different aspects to the colour-blind or to the purblind. The phenomenal universe is what appears to the human mind, and in case our mental constitution undergoes change, it would be completely otherwise.

This argument, however, is far from proving that the reality is unknowable, or that it lies hidden behind appearances or presentations. Take, for instance, a reality which appears as a ray of the sun. When it goes through a pane of glass it appears to be colourless, but it exhibits a beautiful spectrum when it passes through a prism. Therefore you assume that a reality appearing as the rays of the sun is neither colourless nor coloured in itself, since these appearances are wholly due to the difference that obtains between the pane of glass and the prism.

We contend, however, that the fact does not prove the existence of the reality named the sun's ray beyond or behind the white light, nor its existence beyond or behind the spectrum. It is evident that the reality exists in white light, and that it is known as the white light when it goes through a pane of glass; and that the same reality exists in the spectrum, and is known as the spectrum when it goes through the prism. The reality is known as the white light on the one hand, and as the spectrum on the other. It is not unknowable, but knowable.

Suppose that one and the same reality exhibits one aspect when it stands in relation to another object; two aspects when it stands in relation in two different objects; three aspects when it stands in relation to three different objects. The reality of one aspect never proves the unreality of another aspect, for all these three aspects can be equally real. A tree appears to us as a vegetable; it appears to some birds as a shelter; and it appears to some worms as a food. The reality of its aspect as a vegetable never proves the unreality of its aspect as food, nor the reality of its aspect as food disproves the reality of its aspect as shelter. The real tree does not exist beyond or behind the vegetable. We can rely upon its reality, and make use of it to a fruitful result. At the same time, the birds can rely on its reality as a shelter, and build their nests in it; the worms, too, can rely on its reality as food, and eat it-to their satisfaction. A reality which appears to me as my wife must appear to my son as his mother, and never as his wife. But the same real woman is in the wife and in the mother; neither is unreal.

Thing-in-Itself means Thing-Knowerless

How, then, did philosophers come to consider reality to be unknowable and hidden behind or beyond appearances? They investigated all the possible presentations in different relationships, and put them all aside as appearances, and brooded on the thing-in-itself, shut out from all possible relationship, and declared it unknowable. Thing-in-itself means thing cut off from all possible relationships. To, put it in another way: thing-in-itself means thing deprived of its relation to its knower—that is to say, thing-knower-less. So that to declare thing-in-itself unknowable is as much as to declare thing-unknowable unknowable; there is no doubt about it, but what does it prove?

Deprive yourself of all the possible relationships, and see what you are. Suppose you are not a son to your parents, nor the husband to your wife, nor the father to your children, nor a relative to your kindred, nor a friend to your acquaintances, nor a teacher to your students, nor a citizen to your country, nor an individual member to your society, nor a creature to your God, then you get you-in-yourself. Now ask yourself what is you-in-yourself? You can never answer the question. It is unknowable, just because it is cut off from all knowable relations. Can you thus prove that you-in-yourself exist beyond or behind you?

In like manner our universe appears to us human beings as the phenomenal world or presentation. It might appear to other creatures of a different mental constitution as something else. We cannot ascertain how it might seem to Devas, to Asuras, to angels, and to the Almighty, if there be such beings. However different it might seem to these beings, it does not imply that the phenomenal world is unreal, nor that the realm of reality is unknowable.

'Water,' the Indian tradition has it, 'seems to man as a drink, as emerald to Devas, as bloody pus to Pretas, as houses to fishes.' Water is not a whit less real because of its seeming as houses to fishes, and fishes' houses are not less real because of its seeming as emerald to Devas. There is nothing that proves the unreality of it. It is a gross illusion to conceive reality as transcendental to appearances. Reality exists as appearances, and appearances are reality known to human beings. You cannot separate appearances from reality, and hold out the latter as the object of aspiration at the cost of the former. You must acknowledge that the so-called realm of reality which you aspire after, and which you seek for outside or behind the phenomenal universe, exists here on earth. Let Zen teachers tell you that "the world of birth and death is the realm of Nirvana"; "the earth is the pure land of Buddha."

The Four Alternatives and the Five Categories

There are, according to Zen, the four classes of religious and philosophical views, technically called the Four Alternatives,[201] of life and of the world. The first is 'the deprivation of subject and the non-deprivation of object' that is to say, the denial of subject, or mind, or Atman, or soul, and the non-denial of object, or matter, or things—a view which denies the reality of mind and asserts the existence of things. Such a view was held by a certain school of Hinayanism, called Sarvastivada, and still is held by some philosophers called materialists or naturalists. The second is the 'deprivation of object and the non-deprivation of subject'—that is to say, the denial of object, or matter, or things, and the non-denial of subject, or mind, or spirit-a view which denies the reality of material object, and asserts the existence of spirit or ideas. Such a view was held by the Dharmalaksana

[201] Shi-rya-ken in Japanese, the classification mostly made use of by masters of the Rin Zai School of Zen. For the details, see Ki-gai-kwan, by K. Watanabe.

School of Mahayanism, and is still held by some philosophers called idealists. The third is 'the deprivation of both subject and object'—that is to say, the denial of both subject or spirit, and of object or matter-a view which denies the reality of both physical and mental phenomena, and asserts the existence of reality that transcends the phenomenal universe. Such a view was held by the Madhyamika School of Mahayanism, and is still held by some religionists and philosophers of the present day. The fourth is 'the non-deprivation of both subject and object'—that is to say, the non-denial of subject and object—a view which holds mind and body as one and the same reality. Mind, according to this view, is reality experienced inwardly by introspection, and body is the selfsame reality observed outwardly by senses. They are one reality and one life. There also exist other persons and other beings belonging to the same life and reality; consequently all things share in one reality, and life in common with each other. This reality or life is not transcendental to mind and body, or to spirit and matter, but is the unity of them. In other words, this phenomenal world of ours is the realm of reality. This view was held by the Avatamsaka School of Mahayanism, and is still held by Zenists. Thus Zen is not materialistic, nor idealistic, nor nihilistic, but realistic and monistic in its view of the world.

There are some scholars that erroneously maintain that Zen is based on the doctrine of unreality of all things expounded by Kumarajiva and his followers. Ko-ben,[202] known as Myo-ye Sho-nin, said 600 years ago: "Yang Shan (Kyo-zan) asked Wei Shan (I-san): 'What shall we do when hundreds, thousands, and millions of things beset us all at once?' 'The blue are not the yellow,' replied Wei Shan, 'the long are not the short. Everything is in its own place. It has no business with you.' Wei Shan was a great Zen master. He did not teach the unreality of all things. Who can say that Zen is nihilistic?"

Besides the Four Alternatives, Zen uses the Five Categories[203] in order to explain the relation between reality and phenomena. The first is 'Relativity

---

202 A well-known scholar (1173-1232) of the Anatamsaka School of Mahayanism.

203 Go-i in Japanese, mostly used by the So-To School of Zen.
The detailed explanation is given in Go-i-ken-ketsu.

in Absolute,' which means that the universe appears to be consisting in relativities, owing to our relative knowledge; but these relativities are based on absolute reality. The second is 'Absolute in Relativity,' which means Absolute Reality does not remain inactive, but manifests itself as relative phenomena. The third is 'Relativity out of Absolute,' which means Absolute Reality is all in all, and relative phenomena come out of it as its secondary and subordinate forms. The fourth is 'Absolute up to Relativity,' which means relative phenomena always play an important part on the stage of the world; it is through these phenomena that Absolute Reality comes to be understood. The fifth is the 'Union of both Absolute and Relativity,' which means Absolute Reality is not fundamental or essential to relative phenomena, nor relative phenomena subordinate or secondary to Absolute Reality—that is to say, they are one and the same cosmic life, Absolute Reality being that life experienced inwardly by intuition, while relative phenomena are the same life outwardly observed by senses. The first four Categories are taught to prepare the student's mind for the acceptance of the last one, which reveals the most profound truth.

Personalism of B. P. Bowne

B. P. Bowne[204] says: They (phenomena) are not phantoms or illusions, nor are they masks of a back-lying reality which is trying to peer through them." "The antithesis," he continues,[205] "of phenomena and noumena rests on the fancy that there is something that rests behind phenomena which we ought to perceive but cannot, because the masking phenomena thrusts itself between the reality and us." Just so far we agree with Bowne, but we think he is mistaken in sharply distinguishing between body and self, saying:[206] "We ourselves are invisible. The physical organism is only an instrument for expressing and manifesting the inner life, but the living self is never seen." "Human form," he argues,[207] "as an object in space apart from our

204 'Personalism,' p. 94.

205 Ibid., p. 95.

206 Ibid., p. 268.

207 Ibid., p. 271.

experience of it as the instrument and expression of personal life, would have little beauty or attraction; and when it is described in anatomical terms, there is nothing in it that we should desire it. The secret of its beauty and its value lies in the invisible realm." "The same is true," he says again, "of literature. It does not exist in space, or in time, or in books, or in libraries . . . all that could be found there would be black marks on a white paper, and collections of these bound together in various forms, which would be all the eyes could see. But this would not be literature, for literature has its existence only in mind and for mind as an expression of mind, and it is simply impossible and meaningless in abstraction from mind." "Our human history"—he gives another illustration[208]—"never existed in space, and never could so exist. If some visitor from Mars should come to the earth and look at all that goes on in space in connection with human beings, he would never get any hint of its real significance. He would be confined to integrations and dissipations of matter and motion. He could describe the masses and grouping of material things, but in all this be would get no suggestion of the inner life which gives significance to it all. As conceivably a bird might sit on a telegraph instrument and become fully aware of the clicks of the machine without any suspicion of the existence or meaning of the message, or a dog could see all that eye can see in a book yet without any hint of its meaning, or a savage could gaze at the printed score of an opera without ever suspecting its musical import, so this supposed visitor would be absolutely cut off by an impassable gulf from the real seat and significance of human history. The great drama of life, with its likes and dislikes, its loves and hates, its ambitions and strivings, and manifold ideas, inspirations, aspirations, is absolutely foreign to space, and could never in any way be discovered in space. So human history has its seat in the invisible."

In the first place, Bowne's conception of the physical organism as but an instrument for the expression of the inner, personal life, just as the telegraphic apparatus is the instrument for the expression of messages, is erroneous, because body is not a mere instrument of inner personal life, but an essential constituent of it. Who can deny that one's physical

[208] 'Personalism,' pp. 272, 273.

conditions determine one's character or personality? Who can overlook the fact that one's bodily conditions positively act upon one's personal life? There is no physical organism which remains as a mere passive mechanical instrument of inner life within the world of experience. Moreover, individuality, or personality, or self, or inner life, whatever you may call it, conceived as absolutely independent of physical condition, is sheer abstraction. There is no such concrete personality or individuality within our experience.

In the second place, he conceives the physical organism simply as a mark or symbol, and inner personal life as the thing marked or symbolized; so he compares physical forms with paper, types, books, and libraries, and inner life, with literature. In so doing he overlooks the essential and inseparable connection between the physical organism and inner life, because there is no essential inseparable connection between a mark or symbol and the thing marked or symbolized. The thing may adopt any other mark or symbol. The black marks on the white paper, to use his figure, are not essential to literature. Literature may be expressed by singing, or by speech, or by a series of pictures. But is there inner life expressed, or possible to be expressed, in any other form save physical organism? We must therefore acknowledge that inner life is identical with physical organism, and that reality is one and the same as appearance.

All the Worlds in Ten Directions are Buddha's Holy Land

We are to resume this problem in the following chapter. Suffice it to say for the present it is the law of Universal Life that manifoldness is in unity, and unity is in manifoldness; difference is in agreement, and agreement in difference; confliction is in harmony, and harmony in confliction; parts are in the whole, and the whole is in parts; constancy is in change, and change in constancy; good is in bad, and bad in good; integration is in disintegration, and disintegration is in integration; peace is in disturbance, and disturbance in peace. We can find something celestial among the earthly. We can notice something glorious in the midst of the base and degenerated.

'There are nettles everywhere, but are not smooth, green grasses more common still?' Can you recognize something awe-inspiring in the rise and fall of nations? Can you not recognize something undisturbed and peaceful among disturbance and trouble? Has not even grass some meaning? Does not even a stone tell the mystery of Life? Does not the immutable law of good sway over human affairs after all, as Tennyson says-

"I can but trust that good shall fall
At last-far off-at last, to all."

Has not each of us a light within him, whatever degrees of lustre there may be? Was Washington in the wrong when he said: "Labour to keep alive in your heart that little spark of celestial fire called conscience."
We are sure that we can realize the celestial bliss in this very world, if we keep alive the Enlightened Consciousness, of which Bodhidharma and his followers showed the example. 'All the worlds in ten directions are Buddha's Holy Lands!' That Land of Bliss and Glory exists above us, under us, around us, within us, without us, if we open our eyes to see. 'Nirvana is in life itself,' if we enjoy it with admiration and love. "Life and death are the life of Buddha," says Do-gen. Everywhere the Elysian gates stand open, if we do not shut them up by ourselves. Shall we starve ourselves refusing to accept the rich bounty which the Blessed Life offers to us? Shall we perish in the darkness of scepticism, shutting our eyes to the light of Tathagata? Shall we suffer from innumerable pains in the self-created hell where remorse, jealousy, and hatred feed the fire of anger? Let us pray to Buddha, not in word only, but in the deed of generosity and tolerance, in the character noble and loving, and in the personality sublime and good. Let us pray to Buddha to save us from the hell of greed and folly, to deliver us from the thraldom of temptation. Let us 'enter the Holy of Holies in admiration and wonder.'

CHAPTER VII

LIFE

Epicureanism and Life

There are a good many people always buoyant in spirit and mirthful in appearance as if born optimists. There are also no fewer persons constantly crestfallen and gloomy as if born pessimists. The former, however, may lose their buoyancy and sink deep in despair if they are in adverse circumstances. The latter, too, may regain their brightness and grow exultant if they are under prosperous conditions. As there is no evil however small but may cause him to groan under it, who has his heart undisciplined, so there is no calamity however great but may cause him to despair, who has his feelings in control. A laughing child would cry, a crying child would laugh, without a sufficient cause. 'It can be teased or tickled into anything.' A grown-up child is he who cannot hold sway over his passions.

He should die a slave to his heart, which is wayward and blind, if he be indulgent to it. It is of capital importance for us to discipline the heart,[209] otherwise it will discipline us. Passions are like legs. They should be guided by the eye of reason. No wise serpent is led by its tail, so no wise man is led by his passion. Passions that come first are often treacherous and lead us astray. We must guard ourselves against them. In order to gratify them there arise mean desires-the desires to please sight, hearing, smell, taste, and touch. These five desires are ever pursuing or, rather, driving us. We must not spend our whole lives in pursuit of those mirage-like objects which gratify our sensual desires. When we gratify one desire, we are silly enough to fancy that we have realized true happiness. But one desire gratified begets another stronger and more insatiable. Thirst allayed with salt water becomes more intense than ever.

Shakya Muni compared an Epicurean with a dog chewing a dry bone,

[209] Compare Gaku-do-yo-jin-shu, chap. i., and Zen-kwan-saku shin.

mistaking the blood out of a wound in his mouth for that of the bone. The author of Mahaparinirvana-sutra[210] has a parable to the following effect: 'Once upon a time a hunter skilled in catching monkeys alive went into the wood. He put something very sticky on the ground, and hid himself among the bushes. By-and-by a monkey came out to see what it was, and supposing it to be something eatable, tried to feed on it. It stuck to the poor creature's snout so firmly that he could not shake it off. Then he attempted to tear it off with both his paws, which also stuck to it. Thereupon he strove to kick it off with both his hind-legs, which were caught too. Then the hunter came out, and thrusting his stick through between the paws and hind-legs of the victim, and thus carrying it on his shoulder, went home.' In like manner an Epicurean (the monkey), allured by the objects of sense (something sticky), sticks to the five desires (the snout and the four limbs), and being caught by Temptation (the hunter), loses his life of Wisdom.

We are no more than a species of monkeys, as evolutionists hold. Not a few testify to this truth by their being caught by means of 'something eatable.' We abolished slavery and call ourselves civilized nations. Have we not, nevertheless, hundreds of life-long slaves to cigars among us? Have we not thousands of life-long slaves to spirits among us? Have we not hundreds of thousands of life-long slaves to gold among us? Have we not myriads of lifelong slaves to vanity among us? These slaves are incredibly loyal to, and incessantly work for, their masters, who in turn bestow on them incurable diseases, poverty, chagrin, and disappointment.

A poor puppy with an empty can tied to his tail, Thomas Carlyle wittily observes, ran and ran on, frightened by the noise of the can. The more rapidly he ran, the more loudly it rang, and at last he fell exhausted of running. Was it not typical of a so-called great man of the world? Vanity tied an empty can of fame to his tail, the hollow noise of which drives him through life until he falls to rise no more. Miserable!

Neither these men of the world nor Buddhist ascetics can be optimists. The latter rigorously deny themselves sensual gratifications, and keep themselves aloof from all objects of pleasure. For them to be pleased is equivalent to sin, and to laugh, to be cursed. They would rather touch an adder's head

---

[210] The sutra translated by Hwui Yen and Hwui Kwan, A.D. 424-453.

than a piece of money.[211] They would rather throw themselves into a fiery furnace than to come in contact with the other sex. Body for them is a bag full of blood and pus;[212] life, an idle, or rather evil, dream. Vegetarianism and celibacy are their holy privileges. Life is unworthy of having; to put an end to it is their deliverance.[213]Such a view of life is hardly worth our refutation.

The Errors of Philosophical Pessimists and Religious Optimists

Philosophical pessimists[214] maintain that there are on earth many more causes of pain than of pleasure; and that pain exists positively, but pleasure is a mere absence of pain because we are conscious of sickness but not of health; of loss, but not of possession. On the contrary, religious optimists insist that there must not be any evil in God's universe, that evil has no independent nature, but simply denotes a privation of good—that is, evil is null, is nought, is silence implying sound.'

No matter what these one-sided observers' opinion may be, we are certain that we experience good as well as evil, and feel pain and pleasure as well. Neither can we alleviate the real sufferings of the sick by telling them that sickness is no other than the absence of health, nor can we make the poor a whit richer by telling them that poverty is a mere absence of riches. How could we save the dying by persuading them that death is a bare privation of life? Is it possible to dispirit the happy by telling them that happiness is unreal, or make the fortunate miserable by telling them that fortune has no objective reality, or to make one welcome evil by telling one that it is only the absence of good?

You must admit there are no definite external causes of pain nor those of pleasure, for one and the same thing causes pain at one time and pleasure at

---

211 Such is the precept taught in the Vinaya of Hinayanists.

212 See Mahasatiptthana Suttanta, 2-13.

213 This is the logical conclusion of Hinayanism.

214

another. A cause of delight to one person turns out to be that of aversion to another. A dying miser might revive at the sight of gold, yet a Diogenes would pass without noticing it. Cigars and wine are blessed gifts of heaven to the intemperate,[215] but accursed poison to the temperate. Some might enjoy a long life, but others would heartily desire to curtail it. Some might groan under a slight indisposition, while others would whistle away a life of serious disease. An Epicure might be taken prisoner by poverty, yet an Epictetus would fearlessly face and vanquish him. How, then, do you distinguish the real cause of pain from that of pleasure? How do you know the causes of one are more numerous than the causes of the other?

Expose thermometers of several kinds to one and the same temperature. One will indicate, say, 60°, another as high as 100°, another as low as 15°. Expose the thermometers of human sensibilities, which are of myriads of different kinds, to one and the same temperature of environment. None of them will indicate the same degrees. In one and the same climate, which we think moderate, the Eskimo would be washed with perspiration, while the Hindu would shudder with cold. Similarly, under one and the same circumstance some might be extremely miserable and think it unbearable, yet others would be contented and happy. Therefore we may safely conclude that there are no definite external causes of pain and pleasure, and that there must be internal causes which modify the external.

The Law of Balance

Nature governs the world with her law of balance. She puts things ever in pairs,[216] and leaves nothing in isolation. Positives stand in opposition to negatives, actives to passives, males to females, and so on. Thus we get the ebb in opposition to the flood tide; the centrifugal force to the centripetal; attraction to repulsion; growth to decay; toxin to antitoxin; light to shade; action to reaction; unity to variety; day to night; the animate to the inanimate. Look at our own bodies: the right eye is placed side by side with the left; the left shoulder with the right; the right lung with the left; the left

---

215

216 Zenists call them 'pairs of opposites.'

hemisphere of the brain with that of the right; and so forth.
It holds good also in human affairs: advantage is always accompanied by disadvantage; loss by gain; convenience by inconvenience; good by evil; rise by fall; prosperity by adversity; virtue by vice; beauty by deformity; pain by pleasure; youth by old age; life by death. 'A handsome young lady of quality,' a parable in Mahaparinirvana-sutra tells us, 'who carries with her an immense treasure is ever accompanied by her sister, an ugly woman in rags, who destroys everything within her reach. If we win the former, we must also get the latter.' As pessimists show intense dislike towards the latter and forget the former, so optimists admire the former so much that they are indifferent to the latter.

Life Consists in Conflict

Life consists in conflict. So long as man remains a social animal he cannot live in isolation. All individual hopes and aspirations depend on society. Society is reflected in the individual, and the individual in society. In spite of this, his inborn free will and love of liberty seek to break away from social ties. He is also a moral animal, and endowed with love and sympathy. He loves his fellow-beings, and would fain promote their welfare; but he must be engaged in constant struggle against them for existence. He sympathizes even with animals inferior to him, and heartily wishes to protect them; yet he is doomed to destroy their lives day and night. He has many a noble aspiration, and often soars aloft by the wings of imagination into the realm of the ideal; still his material desires drag him down to the earth. He lives on day by day to continue his life, but he is unfailingly approaching death at every moment.

The more he secures new pleasure, spiritual or material, the more he incurs pain not yet experienced. One evil removed only gives place to another; one advantage gained soon proves itself a disadvantage. His very reason is the cause of his doubt and suspicion; his intellect, with which he wants to know everything, declares itself to be incapable of knowing anything in its real state; his finer sensibility, which is the sole source of finer pleasure, has to experience finer suffering. The more he asserts himself, the more he has to sacrifice himself. These conflictions probably led Kant to call life "a trial time, wherein most succumb, and in which even the best does not rejoice in his life." "Men betake themselves," says Fichte, "to the chase after felicity. . . . But as soon as they withdraw into themselves and ask themselves, 'Am I now happy?' the reply comes distinctly from the depth of their soul, 'Oh no; thou art still just as empty and destitute as before!' . . . They will in the future life just as vainly seek blessedness as they have sought it in the present life."

It is not without reason that the pessimistic minds came to conclude that 'the unrest of unceasing willing and desiring by which every creature is goaded is in itself unblessedness,' and that 'each creature is in constant danger, constant agitation, and the whole, with its restless, meaningless motion, is a tragedy of the most piteous kind.' 'A creature like the carnivorous animal, who cannot exist at all without continually destroying and tearing others, may not feel its brutality, but man, who has to prey on other sentient beings like the carnivorous, is intelligent enough, as hard fate would have it, to know and feel his own brutal living.' He must be the most miserable of all creatures, for he is most conscious of his own misery. Furthermore, 'he experiences not only the misfortunes which actually befall him, but in imagination he goes through every possibility of evil.' Therefore none, from great kings and emperors down to nameless beggars, can be free from cares and anxieties, which 'ever flit around them like ghosts.'

The Mystery of Life

Thus far we have pointed out the inevitable conflictions in life in order to prepare ourselves for an insight into the depth of life. We are far from being pessimistic, for we believe that life consists in confliction, but that confliction does not end in confliction, but in a new form of harmony. Hope comes to conflict with fear, and is often threatened with losing its hold on mind; then it renews its life and takes root still deeper than before. Peace is often disturbed with wars, but then it gains a still firmer ground than ever. Happiness is driven out of mind by melancholy, then it is re-enforced by favourable conditions and returns with double strength. Spirit is dragged down by matter from its ideal heaven, then, incited by shame, it tries a higher flight. Good is opposed by evil, then it gathers more strength and vanquishes its foe. Truth is clouded by falsehood, then it issues forth with its greater light. Liberty is endangered by tyranny, then it overthrows it with a splendid success.

Manifoldness stands out boldly against unity; difference against agreement; particularity against generality; individuality against society. Manifoldness, nevertheless, instead of annihilating, enriches unity; difference, instead of destroying agreement, gives it variety; particularities, instead of putting an end to generality, increase its content; individuals, instead of breaking the harmony of society, strengthen the power of it.

Thus 'Universal Life does not swallow up manifoldness nor extinguish differences, but it is the only means of bringing to its full development the detailed content of reality; in particular, it does not abolish the great oppositions of life and world, but takes them up into itself and brings them into fruitful relations with each other.' Therefore 'our life is a mysterious blending of freedom and necessity, power and limitation, caprice and law; yet these opposites are constantly seeking and finding a mutual adjustment.'

6. Nature Favours Nothing in Particular.

There is another point of view of life, which gave the present writer no small contentment, and which he believes would cure one of pessimistic complaint. Buddha, or Universal Life conceived by Zen, is not like a capricious despot, who acts not seldom against his own laws. His manifestation as shown in the Enlightened Consciousness is lawful, impartial, and rational. Buddhists believe that even Shakya Muni himself was not free from the law of retribution, which includes, in our opinion, the law of balance and that of causation.

Now let us briefly examine how the law of balance holds its sway over life and the world. When the Cakravartin, according to an Indian legend, the universal monarch, would come to govern the earth, a wheel would also appear as one of his treasures, and go on rolling all over the world, making everything level and smooth. Buddha is the spiritual Cakravartin, whose wheel is the wheel of the law of balance, with which he governs all things equally and impartially. First let us observe the simplest cases where the law of balance holds good. Four men can finish in three days the same amount of work as is done by three men in four days. The increase in the number of men causes the decrease in that of days, the decrease in the number of men causes the increase in that of days, the result being always the same. Similarly the increase in the sharpness of a knife is always accompanied by a decrease in its durability, and the increase of durability by a decrease of sharpness. The more beautiful flowers grow, the uglier their fruits become; the prettier the fruits grow, the simpler become their flowers. 'A strong soldier is ready to die; a strong tree is easy to be broken; hard leather is easy to be torn. But the soft tongue survives the hard teeth.' Horned creatures are destitute of tusks, the sharp-tusked creatures lack horns. Winged animals are not endowed with paws, and handed animals are provided with no wings. Birds of beautiful plumage have no sweet voice, and sweet-voiced songsters no feathers of bright colours. The finer in quality, the smaller in quantity, and bulkier in size, the coarser in nature.

Nature favours nothing in particular. So everything has its advantage and disadvantage as well. What one gains on the one hand one loses on the other. The ox is competent in drawing a heavy cart, but he is absolutely incompetent in catching mice. A shovel is fit for digging, but not for ear-picking. Aeroplanes are good for aviation, but not for navigation. Silkworms feed on mulberry leaves and make silk from it, but they can do nothing with other leaves. Thus everything has its own use or a mission appointed by Nature; and if we take advantage of it, nothing is useless, but if not, all are useless. 'The neck of the crane may seem too long to some idle on-lookers, but there is no surplus in it. The limbs of the tortoise may appear too short, but there is no shortcoming in them.' The centipede, having a hundred limbs, can find no useless feet; the serpent, having no foot, feels no want.

The Law of Balance in Life

It is also the case with human affairs. Social positions high or low, occupations spiritual or temporal, work rough or gentle, education perfect or imperfect, circumstances needy or opulent, each has its own advantage as well as disadvantage. The higher the position the graver the responsibilities, the lower the rank the lighter the obligation. The director of a large bank can never be so careless as his errand-boy who may stop on the street to throw a stone at a sparrow; nor can the manager of a large plantation have as good a time on a rainy day as his day-labourers who spend it in gambling. The accumulation of wealth is always accompanied by its evils; no Rothschild nor Rockefeller can be happier than a poor pedlar.

A mother of many children may be troubled by her noisy little ones and envy her sterile friend, who in turn may complain of her loneliness; but if they balance what they gain with what they lose, they will find the both sides are equal. The law of balance strictly forbids one's monopoly of happiness. It applies its scorpion whip to anyone who is given to pleasures. Joy in extremity lives next door to exceeding sorrow. "Where there is much light," says Goethe, "shadow is deep." Age, withered and disconsolate, lurks under the skirts of blooming youth. The celebration of birthday is followed by the commemoration of death. Marriage might be supposed to be the luckiest event in one's life, but the widow's tears and the orphan's sufferings also might be its outcome. But for the former the latter can never be. The death of parents is indeed the unluckiest event in the son's life, but it may result in the latter's inheritance of an estate, which is by no means unlucky. The disease of a child may cause its parents grief, but it is a matter of course that it lessens the burden of their livelihood. Life has its pleasures, but also its pains. Death has no pleasure of life, but also none of its pain. So that if we balance their smiles and tears, life and death are equal. It is not wise for us, therefore, to commit suicide while the terms of our life still remain, nor to fear death when there is no way of avoiding it.

Again, the law of balance does not allow anyone to take the lion's share of nature's gifts. Beauty in face is accompanied by deformity in character. Intelligence is often uncombined with virtue. "Fair girls are destined to be unfortunate," says a Japanese proverb, "and men of ability to be sickly." "He makes no friend who never makes a foe." "Honesty is next to idiocy." "Men of genius," says Longfellow, "are often dull and inert in society; as the blazing meteor when it descends to earth is only a stone." Honour and shame go hand in hand. Knowledge and virtue live in poverty, while ill health and disease are inmates of luxury.

Every misfortune begets some sort of fortune, while every good luck gives birth to some sort of bad luck. Every prosperity never fails to sow seeds of adversity, while every fall never fails to bring about some kind of rise. We must not, then, despair in days of frost and snow, reminding ourselves of sunshine and flowers that follow them; nor must we be thoughtless in days of youth and health, keeping in mind old age and ill health that are in the rear of them. In brief, all, from crowns and coronets down to rags and begging bowls, have their own happiness and share heavenly grace alike.

The Application of the Law of Causation to Morals

Although it may be needless to state here the law of causation at any length, yet it is not equally needless to say a few words about its application to morals as the law of retribution, which is a matter of dispute even among Buddhist scholars. The kernel of the idea is very simple-like seed, like fruit; like cause, like effect; like action, like influence—nothing more. As fresh air strengthens and impure air chokes us, so good conduct brings about good consequence, and bad conduct does otherwise.[217]

Over against these generalizations we raise no objection, but there are many cases, in practical life, of doubtful nature. An act of charity, for example, might do others some sort of damage, as is often the case with the giving of alms to the poor, which may produce the undesirable consequence of encouraging beggary. An act of love might produce an injurious effect, as the mother's love often spoils her children. Some[218] may think these are cases of good cause and bad effect. We have, however, to analyze these causes and effects in order to find in what relation they stand. In the first case the good action of almsgiving produces the good effect of lessening the sufferings of the poor, who should be thankful for their benefactor. The giver is rewarded in his turn by the peace and satisfaction of his conscience. The poor, however, when used to being given alms are inclined to grow lazy and live by means of begging. Therefore the real cause of the bad effect is the thoughtlessness of both the giver and the given, but not charity itself. In the second case the mother's love and kindness produce a good effect on her and her children, making them all happy, and enabling them to enjoy the pleasure of the sweet home; yet carelessness and folly on the part of the mother and ingratitude on the part of the children may bring about the bad effect.

History is full of numerous cases in which good persons were so unfortunate as to die a miserable death or to live in extreme poverty, side by side with those cases in which bad people lived in health and prosperity, enjoying a long life. Having these cases in view, some are of the opinion

---

217 Zen lays much stress on this law. See Shu-sho-gi and Ei-hei-ka-kun, by Do-gen.

218 Dr. H. Kato seems to have thought that good cause may bring out bad effect when he attacked Buddhism on this point.

that there is no law of retribution as believed by the Buddhists. And even among the Buddhist scholars themselves there are some who think of the law of retribution as an ideal, and not as a law governing life. This is probably due to their misunderstanding of the historical facts. There is no reason because he is good and honourable that he should be wealthy or healthy; nor is there any reason because he is bad that he should be poor or sickly. To be good is one thing, and to be healthy or rich is another. So also to be bad is one thing, And to be poor and sick is another. The good are not necessarily the rich or the healthy, nor are the bad necessarily the sick or the poor. Health must be secured by the strict observance of hygienic rules, and not by the keeping of ethical precepts; nor can wealth ever be accumulated by bare morality, but by economical and industrial activity. The moral conduct of a good person has no responsibility for his ill health or poverty; so also the immoral action of a bad person has no concern with his wealth or health. You should not confuse the moral with the physical law, since the former belongs only to human life, while the latter to the physical world.

The good are rewarded morally, not physically; their own virtues, honours, mental peace, and satisfaction are ample compensation for their goodness. Confucius, for example, was never rich nor high in rank; he was, nevertheless, morally rewarded with his virtues, honours, and the peace of mind. The following account of him,[219] though not strictly historical, well explains his state of mind in the days of misfortune:
"When Confucius was reduced to extreme distress between Khan and Zhai, for seven days he had no cooked meat to eat, but only some soup of coarse vegetables without any rice in it. His countenance wore the appearance of great exhaustion, and yet be kept playing on his lute and singing inside the house. Yen Hui (was outside) selecting the vegetables, while Zze Lu and Zze Kung were talking together, and said to him: 'The master has twice been driven from Lu; he had to flee from Wei; the tree beneath which he rested was cut down in Sung; he was reduced to extreme distress in Shang and Kau; he is held in a state of siege here between Khan and Zhai; anyone who kills him will be held guiltless; there is no prohibition against making him a prisoner. And yet he keeps playing and singing, thrumming his lute

[219] The account is given by Chwang Tsz in his book, vol. xviii., p. 17.

without ceasing. Can a superior man be without the feeling of shame to such an extent as this?' Yen Hui gave them no reply, but went in and told (their words) to Confucius, who pushed aside his lute and said: 'Yu and Zhze are small men. Call them here, and I will explain the thing to them.'

"When they came in, Zze Lu said: 'Your present condition may be called one of extreme distress!' Confucius replied: 'What words are these? When the superior man has free course with his principles, that is what we call his success; when such course is denied, that is what we call his failure. Now I hold in my embrace the principles of righteousness and benevolence, and with them meet the evils of a disordered age; where is the proof of my being in extreme distress? Therefore, looking inwards and examining myself, I have no difficulties about my principles; though I encounter such difficulties (as the present), I do not lose my virtue. It is when winter's cold is come, and the hoar-frost and snow are falling, that we know the vegetative power of the pine and cypress. This distress between Khan and Zhai is fortunate for me.' He then took back his lute so that it emitted a twanging sound, and began to play and sing. (At the same time) Zze Lu hurriedly seized a shield and began to dance, while Zze Kung said: 'I did not know (before) the height of heaven nor the depth of earth!'"

Thus the good are unfailingly rewarded with their own virtue, and the wholesome consequences of their actions on society at large. And the bad are inevitably recompensed with their own vices, and the injurious effects of their actions on their fellow-beings. This is the unshaken conviction of humanity, past, present, and future. It is the pith and marrow of our moral ideal. It is the crystallization of ethical truths, distilled through long experiences from time immemorial to this day. We can safely approve Edwin Arnold, as he says:

"Lo I as hid seed shoots after rainless years,
So good and evil, pains and pleasures, hates
And loves, and all dead deeds come forth again,
Bearing bright leaves, or dark, sweet fruit or sour."

Longfellow also says:
"No action, whether foul or fair,
Is ever done, but it leaves somewhere
A record-as a blessing or a curse."

Retribution[220] in the Past, the Present, and the Future Life

Then a question suggests itself: If there be no soul that survives body (as shown in the preceding chapter), who will receive the retributions of our actions in the present life? To answer this question, we have to restate our conviction that life is one and the same; in other words, the human beings form one life or one self—that is to say, our ancestors in the past formed man's past life. We ourselves now form man's present life, and our posterity will form the future life. Beyond all doubt, all actions of man in the past have brought their fruits on the present conditions of man, and all actions of the present man are sure to influence the conditions of the future man. To put it in another way, we now reap the fruits of what we sowed in our past life (or when we lived as our fathers), and again shall reap the fruits of what we now sow in our future life (or when we shall live as our posterity). There is no exception to this rigorous law of retribution, and we take it as the will of Buddha to leave no action without being retributed. Thus it is Buddha himself who kindles our inward fire to save ourselves from sin and crimes. We must purge out all the stains in our hearts, obeying Buddha's command audible in the innermost self of ours. It is the great mercy of His that, however sinful, superstitious, wayward, and thoughtless, we have still a light within us which is divine in its nature. When that light shines forth, all sorts of sin are destroyed at once. What is our sin, after all? It is nothing but illusion or error originating in ignorance and folly. How true it is, as an Indian Mahayanist declares, that 'all frost and the dewdrops of sin disappear in the sunshine of wisdom!'[221] Even if we might be imprisoned in the bottomless bell, yet let once the Light of Buddha shine upon us, it would be

---

220 The retribution cannot be explained by the doctrine of the transmigration of the soul, for it is incompatible with the fundamental doctrine of non-soul. See Abhidharmamahavibhasa-castra, vol. cxiv.

221 Samantabhadra-dhyana-sutra.

changed into heaven. Therefore the author of Mahakarunika-sutra[222] says: "When I climb the mountain planted with swords, they would break under my tread. When I sail on the sea of blood, it will be dried up. When I arrive at Hades, they will be ruined at once."

The Eternal Life as taught by Professor Munsterberg

Some philosophical pessimists undervalue life simply because it is subject to limitation. They ascribe all evils to that condition, forgetting that without limitation life is a mere blank. Suppose our sight could see all things at once, then sight has no value nor use for us, because it is life's purpose to choose to see one thing or another out of many; and if all things be present at once before us through sight, it is of no purpose. The same is true of intellect, bearing, smell, touch, feeling, and will. If they be limitless, they cease to be useful for us. Individuality necessarily implies limitation, hence if there be no limitation in the world, then there is no room for individuality. Life without death is no life at all.

Professor Hugo Munsterberg finds no value, so it seems to me, in 'such life as beginning with birth and ending with death.' He says:[223] "My life as a causal system of physical and psychological processes, which lies spread out in time between the dates of my birth and of my death, will come to an end with my last breath; to continue it, to make it go on till the earth falls into the sun, or a billion times longer, would be without any value, as that kind of life which is nothing but the mechanical occurrence of physiological and psychological phenomena had as such no ultimate value for me or for you, or for anyone, at any time. But my real life, as a system of interrelated-will-attitudes, has nothing before or after because it is beyond time. It is independent of birth and death because it cannot be related to biological events; it is not born, and will not die; it is immortal; all possible thinkable time is enclosed in it; it is eternal."

Professor Munsterberg tries to distinguish sharply life as the causal system of physiological and psychological processes, and life as a system of

---

[222] Nanjo's Catalogue, No. 117.

[223] 'The Eternal Life,' p. 26.

interrelated-will-attitudes, and denounces the former as fleeting and valueless, in order to prize the latter as eternal and of absolute value. How could he, however, succeed in his task unless he has two or three lives, as some animals are believed to have? Is it not one and the same life that is treated on the one hand by science as a system of physiological and psychological processes, and is conceived on the other by the Professor himself as a system of interrelated-will-attitudes? It is true that science treats of life as it is observed in time, space, and causality, and it estimates it of no value, since to estimate the value of things is no business of science. The same life observed as a system of interrelated-will-attitudes is independent of time, space, and causality as he affirms. One and the same life includes both phases, the difference being in the points of view of the observers.

Life as observed only from the scientific point of view is bare abstraction; it is not concrete life; nor is life as observed only in the interrelated-will-attitude point of view the whole of life. Both are abstractions. Concrete life includes both phases. Moreover, Professor Munsterberg sees life in the relationship entirely independent-of time, space, and causality, saying: "If you agree or disagree with the latest act of the Russian Czar, the only significant relation which exists between him and you has nothing to do with the naturalistic fact that geographically 'an ocean lies between you; and if you are really a student of Plato, your only important relation to the Greek philosopher has nothing to do with the other naturalistic fact that biologically two thousand years lie between you"; and declares life (seen from that point of view) to be immortal and eternal. This is as much as to say that life, when seen in the relationship independent of time and space, is independent of time and space-that is, immortal and eternal. Is it not mere tautology? He is in the right in insisting that life can be seen from the scientific point of view as a system of physiological and psychological processes, and at the same time as a system of interrelated-will-attitudes independent of time and space. But he cannot by that means prove the existence of concrete individual life which is eternal and immortal, because that which is independent of time and space is the relationship in which he observes life, but not life itself. Therefore we have to notice that life held by Professor Munsterberg to be eternal and immortal is quite a different thing from the eternal life or immortality of soul believed by common sense.

Life in the Concrete

Life in the concrete, which we are living, greatly differs from life in the abstract, which exists only in the class-room. It is not eternal; it is fleeting; it is full of anxieties, pains, struggles, brutalities, disappointments, and calamities. We love life, however, -not only for its smoothness, but for its roughness; not only for its pleasure, but for its pain; not only for its hope, but for its fear; not only for its flowers, but for its frost and snow. As Issai[224] (Sato) has aptly put it: "Prosperity is like spring, in which we have green leaves and flowers wherever we go; while adversity is like winter, in which we have snow and ice. Spring, of course, pleases us; winter, too, displeases us not." Adversity is salt to our lives, as it keeps them from corruption, no matter how bitter to taste it way be. It is the best stimulus to body and mind, since it brings forth latent energy that may remain dormant but for it. Most people hunt after pleasure, look for good luck, hunger after success, and complain of pain, ill-luck, and failure. It does not occur to them that 'they who make good luck a god are all unlucky men,' as George Eliot has wisely observed. Pleasure ceases to be pleasure when we attain to it; another sort of pleasure displays itself to tempt us. It is a mirage, it beckons to us to lead us astray. When an overwhelming misfortune looks us in the face, our latent power is sure to be aroused to grapple with it. Even delicate girls exert the power of giants at the time of emergency; even robbers or murderers are found to be kind and generous when we are thrown into a common disaster. Troubles and difficulties call forth our divine force, which lies deeper than the ordinary faculties, and which we never before dreamed we possessed.

Difficulties are no Match for the Optimist

How can we suppose that we, the children of Buddha, are put at the mercy of petty troubles, or intended to be crushed by obstacles? Are we not endowed with inner force to fight successfully against obstacles and difficulties, and to wrest trophies of glory from hardships? Are we to be slaves to the vicissitudes of fortune? Are we doomed to be victims for the

---

[224] A noted scholar (1772-1859) and author, who belonged to the Wang School of Confucianism. See Gen-shi-roku.

jaws of the environment? It is not external obstacles themselves, but our inner fear and doubt that prove to be the stumbling-blocks in the path to success; not material loss, but timidity and hesitation that ruin us for ever. Difficulties are no match for the optimist, who does not fly from them, but welcomes them. He has a mental prism which can separate the insipid white light of existence into bright hues. He has a mental alchemy by which he can produce golden instruction out of the dross of failure. He has a spiritual magic which makes the nectar of joy out of the tears of sorrow. He has a clairvoyant eye that can perceive the existence of hope through the iron walls of despair. Prosperity tends to make one forget the grace of Buddha, but adversity brings forth one's religious conviction. Christ on the cross was more Christ than Jesus at the table. Luther at war with the Pope was more Luther than he at peace. Nichi-ren[225] laid the foundation of his church when sword and sceptre threatened him with death. Shin-ran[226] and Hen-en[227] established their respective faiths when they were exiled. When they were exiled, they complained not, resented not, regretted not, repented not, lamented not, but contentedly and joyously they met with their inevitable calamity and conquered it. Ho-nen is said to have been still more joyous and contented when be bad suffered from a serious disease, because he had the conviction that his desired end was at hand.

A Chinese monk, E Kwai by name, one day seated himself in a quiet place among hills and practised Dhyana. None was there to disturb the calm enjoyment of his meditation. The genius of the hill was so much stung by his envy that he made up his mind to break by surprise the mental serenity of the monk. Having supposed nothing ordinary would be effective, he appeared all on a sudden before the man, assuming the frightful form of a headless monster. E Kwai being disturbed not a whit, calmly eyed the

---

[225] The founder (1222-1282) of the Nichi Ren Sect, who was exiled in 1271 to the Island of Sado. For the history and doctrine of the Sect, see I A Short History of the Twelve Japanese Buddhist Sects,' by B. Nanjo, pp. 132-147.

[226] The founder (1173-1262) of the Shin Sect, who was banished to the province of Eechigo in 1207. See Nanjo's 'History,' pp. 122-131.

[227] The founder (1131 1212) of the Jo Do Sect, who was exiled to the Island of Tosa in 1207. See Nanjo's 'History,' pp. 104-113.

monster, and observed with a smile: "Thou hast no head, monster! How happy thou shouldst be, for thou art in no danger of losing thy head, nor of suffering from headache!"

Were we born headless, should we not be happy, as we have to suffer from no headache? Were we born eyeless, should we not be happy, as we are in no danger of suffering from eye disease? Ho Ki Ichi,[228] a great blind scholar, was one evening giving a lecture, without knowing that the light had been put out by the wind. When his pupils requested him to stop for a moment, he remarked with a smile: "Why, how inconvenient are your eyes!" Where there is contentment, there is Paradise.

Do Thy Best and Leave the Rest to Providence

There is another point of view which enables us to enjoy life. It is simply this, that everything is placed in the condition best for itself, as it is the sum total of the consequences of its actions and reactions since the dawn of time. Take, for instance, the minutest grains of dirt that are regarded by us the worst, lifeless, valueless, mindless, inert matter. They are placed in their best condition, no matter how poor and worthless they may seem. They can never become a thing higher nor lower than they. To be the grains of dirt is best for them. But for these minute microcosms, which, flying in the air, reflect the sunbeams, we could have no azure sky. It is they that scatter the sun's rays in mid-air and send them into our rooms. It is also these grains of dirt that form the nuclei of raindrops and bring seasonable rain. Thus they are not things worthless and good for nothing, but have a hidden import and purpose in their existence. Had they mind to think, heart to feel, they should be contented and happy with their present condition.

Take, for another example, the flowers of the morning glory. They bloom and smile every morning, fade and die in a few hours. How fleeting and ephemeral their lives are! But it is that short life itself that makes them frail, delicate, and lovely. They come forth all at once as bright and beautiful as a rainbow or as the Northern light, and disappear like dreams. This is the best

---

[228] Hanawa (1746-1821), who published Gun-sho-rui-zu in 1782.

condition for them, because, if they last for days together, the morning glory shall no longer be the morning glory. It is so with the cherry-tree that puts forth the loveliest flowers and bears bitter fruits. It is so with the apple-tree, which bears the sweetest of fruits and has ugly blossoms. It is so with animals and men. Each of them is placed in the condition best for his appointed mission.

The newly-born baby sucks, sleeps, and cries. It can do no more nor less. Is it not best for it to do so? When it attained to its boyhood, he goes to school and is admitted to the first-year class. He cannot be put in a higher nor lower class. It is best for him to be the first-year class student. When his school education is over, he may get a position in society according to his abilities, or may lead a miserable life owing to his failure of some sort or other. In any case he is in a position best for his special mission ordained by Providence or the Hum-total of the fruits of his actions and reactions since all eternity. He should be contented and happy, and do what is right with might and main. Discontent and vexation only make him more worthy of his ruin Therefore our positions, no matter, how high or low, no matter how favourable or unfavourable our environment, we are to be cheerful. "Do thy best and leave the rest to Providence," says a Chinese adage. Longfellow also says:

"Do thy best; that is best.
Leave unto thy Lord the rest."

CHAPTER VIII

THE TRAINING OF THE MIND AND THE PRACTICE OF MEDITATION

The Method of Instruction Adopted by Zen Masters

Thus far we have described the doctrine of Zen inculcated by both Chinese and Japanese masters, and in this chapter we propose to sketch the practice of mental training and the method of practising Dhyana or Meditation. Zen teachers never instruct their pupils by means of explanation or argument, but urge them to solve by themselves through the practice of Meditation such problems as—'What is Buddha?' What is self?' 'What is the spirit of Bodhidharma?' 'What is life and death?' 'What is the real nature of mind?' and so on. Ten Shwai (To-sotsu), for instance, was wont to put three questions[229] to the following effect: (1) Your study and discipline aim at the understanding of the real nature of mind. Where does the real nature of mind exist? (2) When you understand the real nature of mind, you are free from birth and death. How can you be saved when you are at the verge of death? (3) When you are free from birth and death, you know where you go after death. Where do you go when your body is reduced to elements? The pupils are not requested to express their solution of these problems in the form of a theory or an argument, but to show how they have grasped the profound meaning implied in these problems, how they have established their conviction, and how they can carry out what they grasped in their daily life.

A Chinese Zen master[230] tells us that the method of instruction adopted by Zen may aptly be compared with that of an old burglar who taught his son the art of burglary. The burglar one evening said to his little son, whom he desired to instruct in the secret of his trade: "Would you not, my dear boy,

---

[229] The famous three difficult questions, known as the Three Gates of Teu Shwai (To Sotsu San Kwan), who died in 1091. See Mu Mon Kwan, xlvii.

[230] Wu Tsu (Go So), the teacher of Yuen Wu (En Go).

be a great burglar like myself?" "Yes, father," replied the promising young man." "Come with me, then. I will teach you the art." So saying, the man went out, followed by his son. Finding a rich mansion in a certain village, the veteran burglar made a hole in the wall that surrounded it. Through that hole they crept into the yard, and opening a window with complete ease broke into the house, where they found a huge box firmly locked up as if its contents were very valuable articles. The old man clapped his hands at the lock, which, strange to tell, unfastened itself. Then he removed the cover and told his son to get into it and pick up treasures as fast as he could. No sooner had the boy entered the box than the father replaced the cover and locked it up. He then exclaimed at the top of his voice: "Thief! thief! thief! thief!" Thus, having aroused the inmates, he went out without taking anything. All the house was in utter confusion for a while; but finding nothing stolen, they went to bed again. The boy sat holding his breath a short while; but making up his mind to get out of his narrow prison, began to scratch the bottom of the box with his finger-nails. The servant of the house, listening to the noise, supposed it to be a mouse gnawing at the inside of the box; so she came out, lamp in hand, and unlocked it. On removing the cover, she was greatly surprised to find the boy instead of a little mouse, and gave alarm. In the meantime the boy got out of the box and went down into the yard, hotly pursued by the people. He ran as fast as possible toward the well, picked up a large stone, threw it down into it, and hid himself among the bushes. The pursuers, thinking the thief fell into the well, assembled around it, and were looking into it, while the boy crept out unnoticed through the hole and went home in safety. Thus the burglar taught his son how to rid himself of overwhelming difficulties by his own efforts; so also Zen teachers teach their pupils how to overcome difficulties that beset them on all sides and work out salvation by themselves.

The First Step in the Mental Training

Some of the old Zen masters are said to have attained to supreme Enlightenment after the practice of Meditation for one week, some for one day, some for a score of years, and some for a few months. The practice of Meditation, however, is not simply a means for Enlightenment, as is usually supposed, but also it is the enjoyment of Nirvana, or the beatitude of Zen. It is a matter, of course, that we have fully to understand the doctrine of Zen, and that we have to go through the mental training peculiar to Zen in order to be Enlightened.

The first step in the mental training is to become the master of external things. He who is addicted to worldly pleasures, however learned or ignorant he may be, however high or low his social position may be, is a servant to mere things. He cannot adapt the external world to his own end, but he adapts himself to it. He is constantly employed, ordered, driven by sensual objects. Instead of taking possession of wealth, he is possessed by wealth. Instead of drinking liquors, he is swallowed up by his liquors. Balls and music bid him to run mad. Games and shows order him not to stay at home. Houses, furniture, pictures, watches, chains, hats, bonnets, rings, bracelets, shoes—in short, everything has a word to command him. How can such a person be the master of things? To Ju (Na-kae) says: "There is a great jail, not a jail for criminals, that contains the world in it. Fame, gain, pride, and bigotry form its four walls. Those who are confined in it fall a prey to sorrow and sigh for ever."

To be the ruler of things we have first to shut up all our senses, and turn the currents of thoughts inward, and see ourselves as the centre of the world, and meditate that we are the beings of highest intelligence; that Buddha never puts us at the mercy of natural forces; that the earth is in our possession; that everything on earth is to be made use of for our noble ends; that fire, water, air, grass, trees, rivers, hills, thunder, cloud, stars, the moon, the sun, are at our command; that we are the law-givers of the natural phenomena; that we are the makers of the phenomenal world; that it is we that appoint a mission through life, and determine the fate of man.

The Next Step in the Mental Training

In the next place we have to strive to be the master of our bodies. With most of the unenlightened, body holds absolute control over Self. Every order of the former has to be faithfully obeyed by the latter. Even if Self revolts against the tyranny of body, it is easily trampled down under the brutal hoofs of bodily passion. For example, Self wants to be temperate for the sake of health, and would fain pass by the resort for drinking, but body would force Self into it. Self at times lays down a strict dietetic rule for himself, but body would threaten Self to act against both the letter and spirit of the rule. Now Self aspires to get on a higher place among sages, but body pulls Self down to the pavement of masses. Now Self proposes to give some money to the poor, but body closes the purse tightly. Now Self admires divine beauty, but body compels him to prefer sensuality. Again, Self likes spiritual liberty, but body confines him in its dungeons.

Therefore, to get Enlightened, we must establish the authority of Self over the whole body. We must use our bodies as we use our clothes in order to accomplish our noble purposes. Let us command body not to shudder under a cold shower-bath in inclement weather, not to be nervous from sleepless nights, not to be sick with any sort of food, not to groan under a surgeon's knife, not to succumb even if we stand a whole day in the midsummer sun, not to break down under any form of disease, not to be excited in the thick of battlefield—in brief, we have to control our body as we will.

Sit in a quiet place and meditate in imagination that body is no more bondage to you, that it is your machine for your work of life, that you are not flesh, that you are the governor of it, that you can use it at pleasure, and that it always obeys your order faithfully. Imagine body as separated from you. When it cries out, stop it instantly, as a mother does her baby. When it disobeys you, correct it by discipline, as a master does his pupil. When it is wanton, tame it down, as a horse-breaker does his wild horse. When it is sick, prescribe to it, as a doctor does to his patient. Imagine that you are not a bit injured, even if it streams blood; that you are entirely safe, even if it is drowned in water or burned by fire.

E-Shun, a pupil and sister of Ryo-an,[231] a famous Japanese master, burned herself calmly sitting cross-legged on a pile of firewood which consumed her. She attained to the complete mastery of her body. Socrates' self was never poisoned, even if his person was destroyed by the venom he took. Abraham Lincoln himself stood unharmed, even if his body was laid low by the assassin. Masa-shige was quite safe, even if his body was hewed by the traitors' swords. Those martyrs that sang at the stake to the praise of

[231] Ryo an (E-myo, died 1411), the founder of the monastery of Sai-jo-ji, near the city of Odawara. See To-jo-ren-to-roku.

God could never be burned, even if their bodies were reduced to ashes, nor those seekers after truth who were killed by ignorance and superstition. Is it not a great pity to see a man endowed with divine spirit and power easily upset by a bit of headache, or crying as a child under a surgeon's knife, or apt to give up the ghost at the coming of little danger, or trembling through a little cold, or easily laid low by a bit of indisposition, or yielding to trivial temptation?

It is no easy matter to be the dictator of body. It is not a matter of theory, but of practice. You must train your body that you may enable it to bear any sort of suffering, and to stand unflinched in the face of hardship. It is for this that So-rai[232] (Ogiu) laid himself on a sheet of straw-mat spread on the ground in the coldest nights of winter, or was used to go up and down the roof of his house, having himself clad in heavy armour. It is for this that ancient Japanese soldiers led extremely simple lives, and that they often held the meeting-of-perseverance,[233] in which they exposed themselves to the coldest weather in winter or to the hottest weather in summer. It is for this that Katsu Awa practised fencing in the middle of night in a deep forest.[234]

Ki-saburo, although he was a mere outlaw, having his left arm half cut at the elbow in a quarrel, ordered his servant to cut it off with a saw, and during the operation he could calmly sit talking and laughing with his friends. Hiko-kuro (Takayama),[235] a Japanese loyalist of note, one evening happened to come to a bridge where two robbers were lying in wait for him. They lay fully stretching themselves, each with his head in the middle of the bridge, that he might not pass across it without touching them. Hiko-kuro was not excited nor disheartened, but calmly approached the vagabonds and passed the bridge, treading upon their heads, which act so frightened them that they took to their heels without doing any harm to

---

[232] One of the greatest scholars of the Tokugawa period, who died in 1728. See Etsu-wa-bun-ko.

[233] The soldiers of the Tokugawa period were used to hold such a meeting.

[234] Kai-shu-gen-ko-roku.

[235] A well-known loyalist in the Tokugawa period, who died in 1793.

him.[236]

The history of Zen is full of the anecdotes that show Zen priests were the lords of their bodies. Here we quote a single example by way of illustration: Ta Hwui (Dai-ye), once having had a boil on his hip, sent for a doctor, who told him that it was fatal, that he must not sit in Meditation as usual. Then Ta Hwui said to the physician: "I must sit in Meditation with all my might during my remaining days, for if your diagnosis be not mistaken, I shall die before long." He sat day and night in constant Meditation, quite forgetful of his boil, which was broken and gone by itself.[237]

The Third Step in the Mental Training

To be the lord of mind is more essential to Enlightenment, which, in a sense, is the clearing away of illusions, the putting out of mean desires and passions, and the awakening of the innermost wisdom. He alone can attain to real happiness who has perfect control over his passions tending to disturb the equilibrium of his mind. Such passions as anger, hatred, jealousy, sorrow, worry, grudge, and fear always untune one's mood and break the harmony of one's mind. They poison one's body, not in a figurative, but in a literal sense of the word. Obnoxious passions once aroused never fail to bring about the physiological change in the nerves, in the organs, and eventually in the whole constitution, and leave those injurious impressions that make one more liable to passions of similar nature.

We do not mean, however, that we ought to be cold and passionless, as the most ancient Hinayanists were used to be. Such an attitude has been blamed by Zen masters. "What is the best way of living for us monks?" asked a monk to Yun Ku (Un-go), who replied: "You had better live among mountains." Then the monk bowed politely to the teacher, who questioned: "How did you understand me?" "Monks, as I understood," answered the man, "ought to keep their hearts as immovable as mountains, not being

236 Etsu-wa-bun-ko.

237 Sho-bo-gen-zo-zui-mon-ki, by Do-gen.

moved either by good or by evil, either by birth or by death, either by prosperity or by adversity." Hereupon Yun Ku struck the monk with his stick and said: "You forsake the Way of the old sages, and will bring my followers to perdition!" Then, turning to another monk, inquired: "How did you understand me?" "Monks, as I understand," replied the man, "ought to shut their eyes to attractive sights and close their ears to musical notes." "You, too," exclaimed Yun Ka, "forsake the Way of the old sages, and will bring my followers to perdition!" An old woman, to quote another example repeatedly told by Zen masters, used to give food and clothing to a monk for a score of years. One day she instructed a young girl to embrace and ask him: "How do you feel now?" "A lifeless tree," replied the monk coolly, "stands on cold rock. There is no warmth, as if in the coldest season of the year." The matron, being told of this, observed: "Oh that I have made offerings to such a vulgar fellow for twenty years!" She forced the monk to leave the temple and reduced it to ashes.[238]

If you want to secure Dhyana, let go of your anxieties and failures in the past; let bygones be bygones; cast aside enmity, shame, and trouble, never admit them into your brain; let pass the imagination and anticipation of future hardships and sufferings; let go of all your annoyances, vexations, doubts, melancholies, that impede your speed in the race of the struggle for existence. As the miser sets his heart on worthless dross and accumulates it, so an unenlightened person clings to worthless mental dross and spiritual rubbish, and makes his mind a dust-heap. Some people constantly dwell on the minute details of their unfortunate circumstances, to make themselves more unfortunate than they really are; some go over and over again the symptoms of their disease to think themselves into serious illness; and some actually bring evils on them by having them constantly in view and waiting for them. A man asked Poh Chang (Hyaku-jo): "How shall I learn the Law?" "Eat when you are hungry," replied the teacher; " sleep when you are tired. People do not simply eat at table, but think of hundreds of things; they do not simply sleep in bed, but think of thousands of things."[239]
A ridiculous thing it is, in fact, that man or woman, endowed with the same nature as Buddha's, born the lord of all material objects, is ever upset by

---

[238] These instances are quoted from Zen-rin-rui-shu.

[239] E-gen and Den-to-roku.

petty cares, haunted by the fearful phantoms of his or her own creation, and burning up his or her energy in a fit of passion, wasting his or her vitality for the sake of foolish or insignificant things.

It is a man who can keep the balance of his mind under any circumstances, who can be calm and serene in the hottest strife of life, that is worthy of success, reward, respect, and reputation, for he is the master of men. It was at the age of forty-seven that Wang Yang Ming[240] (O-yo-mei) won a splendid victory over the rebel army which threatened the throne of the Ming dynasty. During that warfare Wang was giving a course of lectures to a number of students at the headquarters of the army, of which he was the Commander-in-chief. At the very outset of the battle a messenger brought him the news of defeat of the foremost ranks. All the students were terror-stricken and grew pale at the unfortunate tidings, but the teacher was not a whit disturbed by it. Some time after another messenger brought in the news of complete rout of the enemy. All the students, enraptured, stood up and cheered, but he was as cool as before, and did not break off lecturing. Thus the practiser of Zen has so perfect control over his heart that he can keep presence of mind under an impending danger, even in the presence of death itself.

It was at the age of twenty-three that Haku-in got on board a boat bound for the Eastern Provinces, which met with a tempest and was almost wrecked. All the passengers were laid low with fear and fatigue, but Haku-in enjoyed a quiet sleep during the storm, as if he were lying on a comfortable bed. It was in the fifth of Mei-ji era that Doku-on[241] lived for some time in the city of Tokyo, whom some Christian zealots attempted to murder. One day he met with a few young men equipped with swords at the gate of his temple. "We want to see Doku-on; go and tell him," said they to the priest. "I am Doku-on," replied he calmly, "whom you want to see, gentlemen. What can I do for you?" "We have come to ask you a favour; we are Christians; we want your hoary head." So saying they were ready to attack him, who, smiling, replied: "All right, gentlemen. Behead me forthwith, if

240 The founder of the Wang School of Confucianism, a practiser of Meditation, who was born in 1472, and died at the age of fifty-seven in 1529.

241 Doku On (Ogino), a distinguished Zen master, an abbot of So-koku-ji, who was born in 1818, and died in 1895.

you please." Surprised by this unexpected boldness on the part of the priest, they turned back without harming even a hair of the old Buddhist.[242]

These teachers could through long practice constantly keep their minds buoyant, casting aside useless encumbrances of idle thoughts; bright, driving off the dark cloud of melancholy; tranquil, putting down turbulent waves of passion; pure, cleaning away the dust and ashes of illusion; and serene, brushing off the cobwebs of doubt and fear. The only means of securing all this is to realize the conscious union with the Universal Life through the Enlightened Consciousness, which can be awakened by dint of Dhyana.

Zazen, or the Sitting in Meditation

Habit comes out of practice, and forms character by degrees, and eventually works out destiny. Therefore we must practically sow optimism, and habitually nourish it in order to reap the blissful fruit of Enlightenment. The sole means of securing mental calmness is the practice of Zazen, or the sitting in Meditation. This method was known in India as Yoga as early as the Upanisad period, and developed by the followers of the Yoga system.[243] But Buddhists sharply distinguished Zazen from Yoga, and have the method peculiar to themselves. Kei-zan[244] describes the method to the following effect: 'Secure a quiet room neither extremely light nor extremely dark, neither very warm nor very cold, a room, if you can, in the Buddhist temple located in a beautiful mountainous district. You should not practise Zazen in a place where a conflagration or a flood or robbers may be likely to disturb you, nor should you sit in a place close by the sea or drinking-shops or brothel-houses, or the houses of widows and of maidens or buildings for music, nor should you live in close proximity to the place

---

242 Kin-sei-zen-rin-gen-ko-roku, by D. Mori.

243 See Yoga Sutra with the Commentary of Bhoja Raja (translated by Rajendralala Mitra), pp. 102-104.

244 Kei-zan (Jo-kin), the founder of So-ji-ji, the head temple of the So To Sect of Zen, who died at the age of fifty-eight in 1325. He sets forth the doctrine of Zen and the method of practising Zazen in his famous work, entitled Za-zen-yo-jin-ki.

frequented by kings, ministers, powerful statesmen, ambitious or insincere persons. You must not sit in Meditation in a windy or very high place lest you should get ill. Be sure not to let the wind or smoke get into your room, not to expose it to rain and storm. Keep your room clean. Keep it not too light by day nor too dark by night. Keep it warm in winter and cool in summer. Do not sit leaning against a wall, or a chair, or a screen. You must not wear soiled clothes or beautiful clothes, for the former are the cause of illness, while the latter the cause of attachment. Avoid the Three Insufficiencies-that is to say, insufficient clothes, insufficient food, and insufficient sleep. Abstain from all sorts of uncooked or hard or spoiled or unclean food, and also from very delicious dishes, because the former cause troubles in your alimentary canal, while the latter cause you to covet after diet. Eat and drink just too appease your hunger and thirst, never mind whether the food be tasty or not. Take your meals regularly and punctually, and never sit in Meditation immediately after any meal. Do not practise Dhyana soon after you have taken a heavy dinner, lest you should get sick thereby. Sesame, barley, corn, potatoes, milk, and the like are the best material for your food. Frequently wash your eyes, face, hands, and feet, and keep them cool and clean.

'There are two postures in Zazen—that is to say, the crossed-leg sitting, and the half crossed-leg sitting. Seat yourself on a thick cushion, putting it right under your haunch. Keep your body so erect that the tip of the nose and the navel are in one perpendicular line, and both ears and shoulders are in the same plane. Then place the right foot upon the left thigh, the left foot on the right thigh, so as the legs come across each other. Next put your right hand with the palm upward on the left foot, and your left hand on the right palm with the tops of both the thumbs touching each other. This is the posture called the crossed-leg sitting. You may simply place the left foot upon the right thigh, the position of the hands being the same as in the cross-legged sitting. This posture is named the half crossed-leg sitting.'

'Do not shut your eyes, keep them always open during whole Meditation. Do not breathe through the mouth; press your tongue against the roof of the mouth, putting the upper lips and teeth together with the lower. Swell your abdomen so as to hold the breath in the belly; breathe rhythmically through the nose, keeping a measured time for inspiration and expiration. Count for some time either the inspiring or the expiring breaths from one to ten, then beginning with one again. Concentrate your attention on your breaths going in and out as if you are the sentinel standing at the gate of the nostrils. If you do some mistake in counting, or be forgetful of the breath, it is evident that your mind is distracted.'

Chwang Tsz seems to have noticed that the harmony of breathing is typical of the harmony of mind, since he says: "The true men of old did not dream when they slept. Their breathing came deep and silently. The breathing of true men comes (even) from his heels, while men generally breathe (only) from their throats."[245] At any rate, the counting of breaths is an expedient for calming down of mind, and elaborate rules are given in the Zen Sutra,[246] but Chinese and Japanese Zen masters do not lay so much stress on this point as Indian teachers.

The Breathing Exercise of the Yogi

Breathing exercise is one of the practices of Yoga, and somewhat similar in its method and end to those of Zen. We quote here[247] Yogi Ramacharaka to show how modern Yogis practise it: "(1) Stand or sit erect. Breathing through the nostrils, inhale steadily, first filling the lower part of the lungs, which is accomplished by bringing into play the diaphragm, which, descending, exerts a gentle pressure on the abdominal organs, pushing forward the front walls of the abdomen. Then fill the middle part of the lungs, pushing out the lower ribs, breastbone, and chest. Then fill the higher portion of the lungs, protruding the upper chest, thus lifting the chest, including the upper six or seven pairs of ribs. In the final movement the lower part of the abdomen will be slightly drawn in, which movement gives the lungs a support, and also helps to fill the highest part of the lungs. At the first reading it may appear that this breath consists of three distinct movements. This, however, is not the correct idea. The inhalation is continuous, the entire chest cavity from the lower diaphragm to the highest point of the chest in the region of the collar-bone being expanded with a uniform movement. Avoid a jerking series of inhalations, and strive to

245 Chwang Tsz, vol. iii., p. 2.

246 Dharmatara-dhyana-sutra.

247 Hatha Yoga, pp. 112, 113.

attain a steady, continuous action. Practice will soon overcome the tendency to divide the inhalation into three movements, and will result in a uniform continuous breath. You will be able to complete the inhalation in a couple of seconds after a little practice. (2) Retain the breath a few seconds. (3) Exhale quite slowly, holding the chest in a firm position, and drawing the abdomen in a little and lifting it upward slowly as the air leaves the lungs. When the air is entirely exhaled, relax the chest and abdomen. A little practice will render this part of exercise easy, and the movement once acquired will be afterwards performed almost automatically."

Calmness of Mind

The Yogi breathing above mentioned is fit rather for physical exercise than for mental balance, and it will be beneficial if you take that exercise before or after Meditation. Japanese masters mostly bold it very important to push forward. The lowest part of the abdomen during Zazen, and they are right so far as the present writer's personal experiences go.

'If you feel your mind distracted, look at the tip of the nose; never lose sight of it for some time, or look at your own palm, and let not your mind go out of it, or gaze at one spot before you.' This will greatly help you in restoring the equilibrium of your mind. Chwang Tsz[248] thought that calmness of mind is essential to sages, and said: "The stillness of the sages does not belong to them as a consequence of their skilful ability; all things are not able to disturb their minds; it is on this account that they are still. When water is still, its clearness shows the beard and eyebrows (of him who looks into it). It is a perfect level, and the greatest artificer takes his rule from it. Such is the clearness of still water, and how much greater is that of the human spirit? The still mind of the sage is the mirror of heaven and earth, the glass of all things."

Forget all worldly concerns, expel all cares and anxieties, let go of passions and desires, give up ideas and thoughts, set your mind at liberty absolutely, and make it as clear as a burnished mirror. Thus let flow your inexhaustible fountain of purity, let open your inestimable treasure of virtue, bring forth your inner hidden nature of goodness, disclose your innermost divine

---

[248] Chwang Tsz, vol. v., p. 5.

wisdom, and waken your Enlightened Consciousness to see Universal Life within you. "Zazen enables the practiser," says Kei-zan,[249] "to open up his mind, to see his own nature, to become conscious of mysteriously pure and bright spirit, or eternal light within him."

Once become conscious of Divine Life within you, yon can see it in your brethren, no matter how different they may be in circumstances, in abilities, in characters, in nationalities, in language, in religion, and in race. You can see it in animals, vegetables, and minerals, no matter how diverse they may be in form, no matter how wild and ferocious some may seem in nature, no matter how unfeeling in heart some may seem, no matter how devoid of intelligence some may appear, no matter how insignificant some may be, no matter how simple in construction some may be, no matter how lifeless some may seem. You can see that the whole universe is Enlightened and penetrated by Divine Life.

Zazen and the Forgetting of Self

Zazen is a most effectual means of destroying selfishness, the root of all Sin, folly, vice, and evil, since it enables us to see that every being is endowed with divine spirituality in common with men. It is selfishness that throws dark shadows on life, just as it is not the sun but the body that throws shadow before it. It is the self-same selfishness that gave rise to the belief in the immortality of soul, in spite of its irrationality, foolishness, and superstition. Individual self should be a poor miserable thing if it were not essentially connected with the Universal Life. We can always enjoy pure happiness when we are united with nature, quite forgetful of our poor self. When you look, for example, into the smiling face of a pretty baby, and smile with it, or listen to the sweet melody of a songster and sing with it, you completely forget your poor self at that enraptured moment. But your feelings of beauty and happiness are for ever gone when you resume your self, and begin to consider them after your own selfish ideas. To forget self and identify it with nature is to break down its limitation and to set it at liberty. To break down petty selfishness and extend it into Universal Self is

[249] Za-zen-yo-jin-ki.

to unfetter and deliver it from bondage. It therefore follows that salvation can be secured not by the continuation of individuality in another life, but by the realization of one's union with Universal Life, which is immortal, free, limitless, eternal, and bliss itself. This is easily effected by Zazen.

Zen and Supernatural Power

Yoga[250] claims that various supernatural powers can be acquired by Meditation, but Zen does not make any such absurd claims. It rather disdains those who are believed to have acquired supernatural powers by the practice of austerities. The following traditions clearly show this spirit: "When Fah Yung (Ho-yu) lived in Mount Niu Teu[251] (Go-zu-san) he used to receive every morning the offerings of flowers from hundreds of birds, and was believed to have supernatural powers. But after his Enlightenment by the instruction of the Fourth Patriarch, the birds ceased to make offering, because be became a being too divine to be seen by inferior animals." "Hwang Pah (O-baku), one day going up Mount Tien Tai (Ten-dai-san), which was believed to have been inhabited by Arhats with supernatural powers, met with a monk whose eyes emitted strange light. They went along the pass talking with each other for a short while until they came to a river roaring with torrent. There being no bridge, the master bad to stop at the shore; but his companion crossed the river walking on the water and beckoned to Hwang Pah to follow him. Thereupon Hwang Pah said: 'If I knew thou art an Arhat, I would have doubled you up before thou got over there!' The monk then understood the spiritual attainment of Hwang Pah, and praised him as a true Mahayanist." "On one occasion Yang Shan (Kyo-zan) saw a stranger monk flying through the air. When that monk came down and approached him with a respectful salutation, he asked: 'Where art thou from? 'Early this morning,' replied the other, 'I set out from India.' 'Why,' said the teacher, 'art thou so late?' 'I stopped,' responded the man, 'several times to look at beautiful sceneries.' Thou mayst have supernatural powers,' exclaimed Yang Shan, 'yet thou must give

250 'Yoga Aphorisms of Patanyjali,' chap. iii.

251 A prominent disciple of the Fourth Patriarch, the founder of the Niu Teu School (Go-zu-zen) of Zen, who died in A.D. 675.

back the Spirit of Buddha to me.' Then the monk praised Yang Shan saying: 'I have come over to China in order to worship Manyjucri,[252] and met unexpectedly with Minor Shakya,' and, after giving the master some palm leaves he brought from India, went back through the air.'"[253]

It is quite reasonable that Zenists distinguish supernatural powers from spiritual uplifting, the former an acquirement of Devas, or of Asuras, or of Arhats, or of even animals, and the latter as a nobler accomplishment attained only by the practisers of Mahayanism. Moreover, they use the term supernatural power in a meaning entirely different from the original one. Lin Tsi (Rin-zai) says, for instance: "There are six supernatural powers of Buddha: He is free from the temptation of form, living in the world of form; He is free from the temptation of sound, living in the world of sound; He is free from the temptation of smell, living in the world of smell; He is free from the temptation of taste, living in the world of taste; He is free from the temptation of Dharma,[[254] living in the world of Dharma. These are six supernatural powers."[255]

Sometimes Zenists use the term as if it meant what we call Zen Activity, or the free display of Zen in action, as you see in the following examples. Tung Shan (To-Zan) was on one occasion attending on his teacher Yun Yen (Un-gan), who asked: "What are your supernatural powers?" Tung Shan, saying nothing, clasped his hands on his breast, and stood up before Yun Yen. "How do you display your supernatural powers?" questioned the teacher again. Then Tung Shan said farewell and went out. Wei Shan (E-san) one day was taking a nap, and seeing his disciple Yang Shan (Kyo-zan) coming into the room, turned his face towards the wall. "You need not, Sir," said Yang Shan, "stand on ceremony, as I am your disciple." Wei Shan seemed to try to get up, so Yang Shan went out; but Wei Shan called him back and said: "I shall tell you of a dream I dreamed." The other inclined

---

[252] Manyjucri is a legendary Bodhisattva, who became an object of worship of some Mahayanists. He is treated as a personification of transcendental wisdom.

[253] Hwui Yuen (E-gen) and Sho-bo-gen-zo.

[254] The things or objects, not of sense, but of mind.

[255] Lin Tsi Luh (Rin-zai-roku).

his head as if to listen. "Now," said Wei Shan, "divine my fortune by the dream." Thereupon Yang Shan fetched a basin of water and a towel and gave them to the master, who washed his face thereby. By-and-by Hiang Yen (Kyo-gen) came in, to whom Wei Shan said: "We displayed supernatural powers a moment ago. It was not such supernatural powers as are shown by Hinayanists." "I know it, Sir," replied the other, "though I was down below." "Say, then, what it was," demanded the master. Then Hiang Yen made tea and gave a cup to Wei Shan, who praised the two disciples, saying: "You surpass Çariputra[256] and Maudgalyayana[257] in your wisdom and supernatural powers."[258]

Again, ancient Zenists did not claim that there was any mysterious element in their spiritual attainment, as Do-gen says[259] unequivocally respecting his Enlightenment: "I recognized only that my eyes are placed crosswise above the nose that stands lengthwise, and that I was not deceived by others. I came home from China with nothing in my hand. There is nothing mysterious in Buddhism. Time passes as it is natural, the sun rising in the east, and the moon setting into the west."

True Dhyana

To sit in Meditation is not the only method of practising Zazen. "We practise Dhyana in sitting, in standing, and in walking," says one of the Japanese Zenists. Lin Tsi (Rin-Zai) also says: "To concentrate one's mind, or to dislike noisy places, and seek only for stillness, is the characteristic of heterodox Dhyana." It is easy to keep self-possession in a place of tranquillity, yet it is by no means easy to keep mind undisturbed amid the bivouac of actual life. It is true Dhyana that makes our mind sunny while the storms of strife rage around us. It is true Dhyana that secures the harmony of heart, while the surges of struggle toss us violently. It is true

[256] One of the prominent disciples of Shakya Muni, who became famous for his wisdom.

[257] One of the eminent disciples of Shakya Muni, noted for his supernatural powers.

[258] Zen-rin-rui-sku.

[259] Ei-hei-ko-roku.

Dhyana that makes us bloom and smile, while the winter of life covets us with frost and snow.

"Idle thoughts come and go over unenlightened minds six hundred and fifty times in a snap of one's fingers," writes an Indian teacher,[260] "and thirteen hundred million times every twenty-four hours." This might be an exaggeration, yet we cannot but acknowledge that one idle thought after another ceaselessly bubbles up in the stream of consciousness. "Dhyana is the letting go," continues the writer—"that is to say, the letting go of the thirteen hundred million of idle thoughts." The very root of these thirteen hundred million idle thoughts is an illusion about one's self. He is indeed the poorest creature, even if he be in heaven, who thinks himself poor. On the contrary, he is an angel who thinks himself hopeful and happy, even though he be in hell. "Pray deliver me," said a sinner to Sang Tsung (So-san).[261] "Who ties you up?" was the reply. You tie yourself up day and night with the fine thread of idle thoughts, and build a cocoon of environment from which you have no way of escape. 'There is no rope, yet you imagine yourself bound.' Who could put fetters on your mind but your mind itself? Who could chain your will but your own will? Who could blind your spiritual eyes, unless you yourself shut them up? Who could prevent you from enjoying moral food, unless you yourself refuse to eat? "There are many," said Sueh Fung (Sep-po) on one occasion, "who starve in spite of their sitting in a large basket full of victuals. There are many who thirst in spite of seating themselves on the shore of a sea." "Yes, Sir," replied Huen Sha (Gen-sha), "there are many who starve in spite of putting their heads into the basket full of victuals. There are many who thirst in spite of putting their heads into the waters of the sea."[262] Who could cheer him up who abandons himself to self-created misery? Who could save him who denies his own salvation?

---

260 The introduction to Anapana-sutra by Khin San Hwui, who came to China A.D. 241.

261 The Third Patriarch.

262 Hwui Yuen (Œ-gen).

Let Go of your Idle Thoughts[263]

A Brahmin, having troubled himself a long while with reference to the problem of life and of the world, went out to call on Shakya Muni that he might be instructed by the Master. He got some beautiful flowers to offer them as a present to the Muni, and proceeded to the place where He was addressing his disciples and believers. No sooner had he come in sight of the Master than he read in his mien the struggles going on within him. "Let go of that," said the Muni to the Brahmin, who was going to offer the flowers in both his hands. He dropped on the ground the flowers in his right hand, but still holding those in his left. "Let go of that," demanded the Master, and the Brahmin dropped the flowers in his left hand rather reluctantly. "Let go of that, I say," the Muni commanded again; but the Brahmin, having nothing to let go of, asked: "What shall I let go of, Reverend Sir? I have nothing in my hands, you know." "Let go of that, you have neither in your right nor in your left band, but in the middle." Upon these words of the Muni a light came into the sufferer's mind, and he went home satisfied and in joy.[264] "Not to attach to all things is Dhyana," writes an ancient Zenist, "and if you understand this, going out, staying in, sitting, and lying are in Dhyana." Therefore allow not your mind to be a receptacle for the dust of society, or the ashes of life, or rags and waste paper of the world. You bear too much burden upon your shoulders with which you have nothing to do.

Learn the lesson of forgetfulness, and forget all that troubles you, deprives you of sound sleep, and writes wrinkles on your forehead. Wang Yang Ming, at the age of seventeen or so, is said to have forgotten the day 'on which he was to be married to a handsome young lady, daughter of a man of high position. It was the afternoon of the very day on which their nuptials had to be held that he went out to take a walk. Without any definite purpose he went into a temple in the neighbourhood, and there he found a recluse apparently very old with white hair, but young in countenance like a

---

263 A famous Zenist, Mu-go-koku-shi, is said to have replied to every questioner, saying: "Let go of your idle thoughts."

264 'Sutra on the Brahmacarin Black-family,' translated into Chinese by K' Khien, of the Wu dynasty (A.D. 222-280).

child. The man was sitting absorbed in Meditation. There was something extremely calm and serene in that old man's look and bearing that attracted the young scholar's attention. Questioning him as to his name, age, and birthplace, Wang found that the venerable man had enjoyed a life so extraordinarily long that he forgot his name and age, but that he had youthful energy so abundantly that be could talk with a voice sounding as a large bell. Being asked by Wang the secret of longevity, the man replied: "There is no secret in it; I merely kept my mind calm and peaceful." Further, he explained the method of Meditation according to Taoism and Buddhism. Thereupon Wang sat face to face with the old man and began to practise Meditation, utterly forgetful of his bride and nuptial ceremony. The sun began to cast his slanting rays on the wall of the temple, and they sat motionless; twilight came over them, and night wrapped them with her sable shroud, and they sat as still as two marble statues; midnight, dawn, at last the morning sun rose to find them still in their reverie. The father of the bride, who had started a search during the night, found to his surprise the bridegroom absorbed in Meditation on the following day.[265]

It was at the age of forty-seven that Wang gained a great victory over the rebel army, and wrote to a friend saying: "It is so easy to gain a victory over the rebels fortifying themselves among the mountains, yet it is not so with those rebels living in our mind."[266] Tsai Kiun Mu (Sai-kun-bo) is said to have had an exceedingly long and beautiful beard, and when asked by the Emperor, who received him in audience, whether he should sleep with his beard on the comforters or beneath them, be could not answer, since he had never known how he did. Being distracted by this question, he went home and tried to find out how he had been used to manage his beard in bed. First he put his beard on the comforters and vainly tried to sleep; then he put it beneath the comforters and thought it all right. Nevertheless, he was all the more disturbed by it. So then, putting on the comforters, now putting it beneath them, he tried to sleep all night long, but in vain. You must therefore forget your mental beard that annoys you all the time.

---

[265] O-yo-mei-shutsu-shin-sei-ran-roku.

[266] Ibid.

Men of longevity never carried troubles to their beds. It is a well-known fact that Zui-o (Shi-ga)[267] enjoyed robust health at the age of over one hundred years. One day, being asked whether there is any secret of longevity, he replied affirmatively, and said to the questioner: "Keep your mind and body pure for two weeks, abstaining from any sort of impurity, then I shall tell you of the secret." The man did as was prescribed, and came again to be instructed in the secret. Zui-o said: "Now I might tell you, but be cautious to keep yourself pure another week so as to qualify yourself to learn the secret." When that week was over the old man said: "Now I might tell you, but will you be so careful as to keep yourself pure three days more in order to qualify yourself to receive the secret?" The man did as he was ordered, and requested the instruction. Thereupon Zui-o took the man to his private room and softly whispered, with his mouth close to the ear of the man: "Keep the secret I tell you now, even at the cost of your life. It is this-don't be passionate. That is all."[268]

'The Five Ranks of Merit'

Thus far we have stated how to train our body and mind according to the general rules and customs established by Zenists. And here we shall describe the different stages of mental uplifting through which the student of Zen has to go. They are technically called 'The Five Ranks of Merit.'[269] The first stage is called the Rank of Turning,[270] in which the student 'turns' his mind from the external objects of sense towards the inner Enlightened Consciousness. He gives up all mean desires and aspires to spiritual elevation. He becomes aware that he is not doomed to be the slave of material things, and strives to conquer over them. Enlightened Consciousness is likened to the King, and it is called the Mind-King, while the student who now turns towards the King is likened to common people. Therefore in this first stage the student is in the rank of common people.

---

[267] This famous old man died in A.D. 1730.

[268] Se-ji-hyaku-dan.

[269] Ko-kun-go-i. For further details, see So-to-ni-shi-roku.

[270] Ko in Japanese.

The second stage is called the Rank of Service,[271] in which the student distinguishes himself by his loyalty to the Mind-King, and becomes a courtier to 'serve' him. He is in constant 'service' to the King, attending him with obedience and love, and always fearing to offend him. Thus the student in this stage is ever careful not to neglect rules and precepts laid down by the sages, and endeavours to uplift himself in spirituality by his fidelity. The third stage is called the Rank of Merit,[272] in which the student distinguishes himself by his 'meritorious' acts of conquering over the rebel army of passion which rises against the Mind-King. Now, his rank is not the rank of a courtier, but the rank of a general. In other words, his duty is not only to keep rules and instructions of the sages, but to subjugate his own passion and establish moral order in the mental kingdom.

The fourth stage is called the Rank of Co-operative Merit,[273] in which the student 'co-operates' with other persons in order to complete his merit. Now, he is not compared with a general who conquers his foe, but with the prime-minister who co-operates with other officials to the benefit of the people. Thus the student in this stage is not satisfied with his own conquest of passion, but seeks after spiritual uplifting by means of extending his kindness and sympathy to his fellow-men.

The fifth stage is called the Rank of Merit-over-Merit,[274] which means the rank of meritless-merit. This is the rank of the King himself. The King does nothing meritorious, because all the governmental works are done by his ministers and subjects. All that he has to do is to keep his inborn dignity and sit high on his throne. Therefore his conduct is meritless, but all the meritorious acts of his subjects are done through his authority. Doing nothing, he does everything. Without any merit, he gets all merits. Thus the student in this stage no more strives to keep precepts, but his doings are naturally in accord with them. No more he aspires for spiritual elevation, but his, heart is naturally pure from material desires. No more he makes an

---

[271] Bu in Japanese.

[272] Ko in Japanese.

[273] Gu-ko in Japanese.

[274] Ko-ko in Japanese.

effort to vanquish his passion, but no passion disturbs him. No more he feels it his duty to do good to others, but he is naturally good and merciful. No more he sits in Dhyana, but he naturally lives in Dhyana at all times. It is in this fifth stage that the student is enabled to identify his Self with the Mind-King or Enlightened Consciousness, and to abide in perfect bliss.

'The Ten Pictures of the Cowherd.'[275]

Besides these Five Ranks of Merit, Zenists make use of the Ten Pictures of the Cowherd, in order to show the different stages of mental training through which the student of Zen has to go. Some poems were written by Chinese and Japanese teachers on each of these pictures by way of explanation, but they are too ambiguous to be translated into English, and we rest content with the translation of a single Japanese poem on each of the ten pictures, which are as follows:

The first picture, called 'the Searching of the Cow,' represents the cowherd wandering in the wilderness with a vague hope of finding his lost cow that is running wild out of his sight. The reader will notice that the cow is likened to the mind of the student and the cowherd to the student himself.

"I do not see my cow,
But trees and grass,
And hear the empty cries
Of cicadas."

The second picture, called 'the Finding of the Cow's Tracks,' represents the cowherd tracing the cow with the sure hope of restoring her, having found her tracks on the ground.

"The grove is deep, and so
Is my desire.
How glad I am, O lo!
I see her tracks."

---

[275] The pictures were drawn by Kwoh Ngan (Kaku-an), a Chinese Zenist. For the details, see Zen-gaku-ho-ten.

The third picture, called 'the Finding out of the Cow,' represents the cowherd slowly approaching the cow from a distance.

"Her loud and wild mooing
Has led me here;
I see her form afar,
Like a dark shadow."

The fourth 'picture, called 'the Catching of the Cow,' represents the cowherd catching hold of the cow, who struggles to break loose from him.

"Alas! it's hard to keep
The cow I caught.
She tries to run and leap
And snap the cord."

The fifth picture, called 'the Taming of the Cow,' represents the cowherd pacifying the cow, giving her grass and water.

"I'm glad the cow so wild
Is tamed and mild.
She follows me, as if
She were my shadow."

The sixth picture, called 'the Going Home Riding on the Cow,' represents the cowherd playing on a flute, riding on the cow.

"Slowly the clouds return
To their own hill,
Floating along the skies
So calm and still.

The seventh picture, called 'the Forgetting of the Cow and the Remembering of the Man,' represents the cowherd looking at the beautiful scenery surrounding his cottage.

"The cow goes out by day
And comes by night.
I care for her in no way,
But all is right."

The eighth picture, called 'the Forgetting of the Cow and of the Man,' represents a large empty circle.

"There's no cowherd nor cow
Within the pen;
No moon of truth nor clouds
Of doubt in men."

The ninth picture, called 'the Returning to the Root and Source,' represents a beautiful landscape full of lovely trees in full blossom.
"There is no dyer of hills,
Yet they are green;
So flowers smile, and titter rills
At their own wills."

The tenth picture, called 'the Going into the City with Open Hands,' represents a smiling monk, gourd in hand, talking with a man who looks like a pedlar.
"The cares for body make
That body pine;
Let go of cares and thoughts,
O child of mine!"

These Ten Pictures of the Cowherd correspond in meaning to the Five Ranks of Merit above stated, even if there is a slight difference, as is shown in the following table:

THE FIVE RANKS.—-THE TEN PICTURES.

1. The Rank of Turning—	1. The Searching of the Cow.
	2. The Finding of the Cow's Tracks.
2. The Rank of Service—	3. The Finding of the Cow.
	4. The Catching of the Cow.

3. The Rank of Merit—- 5. The Taming of the Cow.
6. The Going Home, Riding on the Cow.

4. The Rank of Co-operative Merit
—-9. The Returning to the Root and Source.
10. The Going into the City with Open Hands.

5. The Rank of Merit-over-Merit
—-7. The Forgetting of the Cow and the Remembering of the Man.
8. The Forgetting of the Cow and of the Man.

Zen and Nirvana

The beatitude of Zen is Nirvana, not in the Hinayanistic sense of the term, but in the sense peculiar to the faith. Nirvana literally means extinction or annihilation; hence the extinction of life or the annihilation of individuality. To Zen, however, it means the state of extinction of pain and the annihilation of sin. Zen never looks for the realization of its beatitude in a place like heaven, nor believes in the realm of Reality transcendental of the phenomenal universe, nor gives countenance to the superstition of Immortality, nor does it hold the world is the best of all possible worlds, nor conceives life simply as blessing. It is in this life, full of shortcomings, misery, and sufferings, that Zen hopes to realize its beatitude. It is in this world, imperfect, changing, and moving, that Zen finds the Divine Light it worships. It is in this phenomenal universe of limitation and relativity that Zen aims to attain to highest Nirvana. "We speak," says the author of Vimalakirtti-nirdeca-sutra, "of the transitoriness of body, but not of the desire of the Nirvana or destruction of it." "Paranirvana," according to the author of Lankavatarasutra, "is neither death nor destruction, but bliss, freedom, and purity." "Nirvana," says Kiai Hwan,[276] "means the extinction of pain or the crossing over of the sea of life and death. It denotes the real permanent state of spiritual attainment. It does not signify destruction or

[276] A commentator of Saddharma-pundarika-sutra.

annihilation. It denotes the belief in the great root of life and spirit." It is Nirvana of Zen to enjoy bliss for all sufferings of life. It is Nirvana of Zen to be serene in mind for all disturbances of actual existence. It is Nirvana of Zen to be in the conscious union with Universal Life or Buddha through Enlightenment.

Nature and her Lesson

Nature offers us nectar and ambrosia every day, and everywhere we go the rose and lily await us. "Spring visits us men," says Gu-do,[277] "her mercy is great. Every blossom holds out the image of Tathagata." "What is the spiritual body of Buddha who is immortal and divine?" asked a man to Ta Lun (Dai-ryu), who instantly replied: "The flowers cover the mountain with golden brocade. The waters tinge the rivulets with heavenly blue." "Universe is the whole body of Tathagata; observed Do-gen. "The worlds in ten directions, the earth, grass, trees, walls, fences, tiles, pebbles-in a word, all the animated and inanimate objects partake of the Buddha-nature. Thereby, those who partake in the benefit of the Wind and Water that rise out of them are, all of them, helped by the mysterious influence of Buddha, and show forth Enlightenment."[278]

Thus you can attain to highest bliss through your conscious union with Buddha. Nothing can disturb your peace, when you can enjoy peace in the midst of disturbances; nothing can cause you to suffer, when you welcome misfortunes and hardships in order to train and strengthen your character; nothing can tempt you to commit sin, when you are constantly ready to listen to the sermon given by everything around you; nothing can distress you, when you make the world the holy temple of Buddha. This is the state of Nirvana which everyone believing in Buddha may secure.

---

[277] One of the distinguished Zenists in the Tokugawa period, who died in 1661.

[278] Sho-bo gen-zo.

The Beatitude of Zen

We are far from denying, as already shown in the foregoing chapters, the existence of troubles, pains, diseases, sorrows, deaths in life. Our bliss consists in seeing the fragrant rose of Divine mercy among the thorns of worldly trouble, in finding the fair oasis of Buddha's wisdom in the desert of misfortunes, in getting the wholesome balm of His love in the seeming poison of pain, in gathering the sweet honey of His spirit even in the sting of horrible death.

History testifies to the truth that it is misery that teaches men more than happiness, that it is poverty that strengthens them more than wealth, that it is adversity that moulds character more than prosperity, that it is disease and death that call forth the inner life more than health and long life. At least, no one can be blind to the fact that good and evil have an equal share in forming the character and working out the destiny of man. Even such a great pessimist as Schopenhauer says: "As our bodily frame would burst asunder if the pressure of atmosphere were removed, so if the lives of men were relieved of all need, hardship, and adversity, if everything they took in hand were successful, they would be so swollen with arrogance . . . that they would present the spectacle of unbridled folly. A ship without ballast is unstable, and will not go straight." Therefore let us make our ship of life go straight with its ballast of miseries and hardships, over which we gain control.

The believer in Buddha is thankful to him, not only for the sunshine of life, but also for its wind, rain, snow, thunder, and lightning, because He gives us nothing in vain. Hisa-nobu (Ko-yama) was, perhaps, one of the happiest persons that Japan ever produced, simply because he was ever thankful to the Merciful One. One day he went out without an umbrella and met with a shower. Hurrying up to go home, he stumbled and fell, wounding both his legs. As he rose up, he was overheard to say: "Thank heaven." And being asked why he was so thankful, replied: "I got both my legs hurt, but, thank heaven, they were not broken." On another occasion he lost consciousness, having been kicked violently by a wild horse. When he came to himself, he exclaimed: "Thank heaven," in hearty joy. Being asked the reason why he was so joyful, he answered: "I have really given up my ghost, but, thank heaven, I have escaped death after all."[279] A person in such a state of mind can do anything with heart and might. Whatever he does is an act of thanks for the grace of Buddha, and he does it, not as his duty, but as the overflowing of his gratitude which lie himself cannot check. Here exists the formation of character. Here exist real happiness and joy. Here exists the realization of Nirvana.

Most people regard death as the greatest of evils, only because they fear death. They fear death only because they have the instinct of self-preservation. Hereupon pessimistic philosophy and religion propose to attain to Nirvana by the extinction of Will-to-live, or by the total annihilation of life. But this is as much as to propose death as the final cure to a patient. Elie Metchnikoff proposes, in his 'Nature of Man,' another cure, saying: 'If man could only contrive to live long enough—say, for one hundred and forty years—a natural desire for extinction would take the place of the instinct for self-preservation, and the call of death would then harmoniously satisfy his legitimate craving of a ripe old age.' Why, we must ask, do you trouble yourself so much about death? Is there any instance of an individual who escaped it in the whole history of mankind? If there be no way of escape, why do you trouble yourself about it? Can you cause things to fall off the earth against the law of gravitation? Is there any example of an individual object that escaped the government of that law in the whole history of the world? Why, then, do you trouble yourself about it? It is no less silly to trouble yourself about death than you do about gravitation. Can you realize that death, which you have yet no immediate experience of, is the greatest of evil? We dare to declare death to be one of the blessings which we have to be thankful for. Death is the scavenger of the world; it sweeps away all uselessness, staleness, and corruption from the world, and keeps life clean and ever now. When you are of no use for the world it comes upon you, removes you to oblivion in order to relieve life of useless encumbrance. The stream of existence should be kept running, otherwise it would become putrid. If old lives were to stop the running stream it would stand still, and consequently become filthy, poisoned, and worthless. Suppose there were only births and no deaths. The earth has to be packed with men and women, who are doomed to live to all eternity,

[279] Ki-jin-den.

jostling, colliding, bumping, trampling each other, and vainly struggling to get out of the Black Hole of the earth. Thanks to death we are not in the Black Hole!

Only birth and no death is far worse than only death and no birth. "The dead," says Chwang Tsz, "have no tyrannical king about, no slavish subject to meet; no change of seasons overtakes them. The heaven and the earth take the places of Spring and Autumn. The king or emperor of a great nation cannot be happier than they." How would you be if death should never overtake you when ugly decrepitude makes you blind and deaf, bodily and mentally, and deprives you of all possible pleasures? How would you be if you should not die when your body is broken to pieces or terribly burned by an accident—say, by a violent earthquake followed by a great conflagration? Just imagine Satan, immortal Satan, thrown down by the ire of God into Hell's fiery gulf, rolling himself in dreadful torture to the end of time. You cannot but conclude that it is only death which relieves you of extreme sufferings, incurable diseases, and it is one of the blessings you ought to be thankful for.

The believer of Buddha is thankful even for death itself, the which is the sole means of conquering death. If he be thankful even for death, how much more for the rest of things! He can find a meaning in every form of life. He can perceive a blessing in every change of fortune. He can acknowledge a mission for every individual. He can live in contentment and joy under any conditions. Therefore Lin Tsi (Rin-zai) says: "All the Buddhas might appear before me and I would not be glad. All the Three Regions[280] and Hells might suddenly present themselves before me, and I would not fear. . . . He (an Enlightened person) might get into the fire, and it would not burn him. He might get into water, and it would not drown him. He might be born in Hell, and he would be happy as if he were in a fair garden. He might be born among Pretas and beasts, and he would not suffer from pain. How can he be so? Because he can enjoy everything.'[281]

---

[280] (1) Naraka, or Hell; (2) Pretas, or hungry demons; (3) beasts.

[281] Lin Tsi Luk (Rin-zai-roku).

APPENDIX

ORIGIN OF MAN
(GEN-NIN-RON)
BY
KWEI FUNG TSUNG MIH
THE SEVENTH PATRIARCH OF THE KEGON SECT

TRANSLATED BY KAITEN NUKARIYA

PREFACE

Tsung Mih (Shu-Mitsu, A.D. 774-841), the author of Yuen Jan Lun ('Origin of Man'), one of the greatest scholars that China ever produced, was born in a Confucianist family of the State of Kwo Cheu. Having been converted by Tao Yuen (Do-yen), a noted priest of the Zen Sect, he was known at the age of twenty-nine as a prominent member of that sect, and became the Eleventh Patriarch after Bodhidharma, the First Patriarch of the sect, who had come over to China from India about A.D. 520. Some years after he studied under Chino, Kwan (Cho-kwan) the philosophical doctrine of the Avatamsaka School, now known in Japan as the Kegon Sect, and distinguished himself as the Seventh Patriarch of that school. In A.D. 835 he was received in audience by the Emperor Wan Tsung, who questioned him in a general way about the Buddhist doctrines, and bestowed upon him the honourable title of Great Virtuous Teacher, together with abundant gifts. The author produced over ninety volumes of books, which include a commentary on Avatamsaka-sutra, one on Purnabuddha-sutra-prasannartha-sutra, and many others. Yuen Jan Lun is one of the shortest of his essays, but it contains all the essential doctrines, respecting the origin of life and of the universe, which are found in Taoism, Confucianism, Hinayanism, and Mahayanism. How important a position it holds among the Buddhist books can be well imagined from the fact that over twenty commentaries were written on it both by the Chinese and the Japanese Buddhist scholars. It is said that a short essay under the same title by a

noted contemporary Confucianist scholar, Han Tui Chi (Kan-tai-shi, who flourished 803-823), suggested to him to write a book in order to make clear to the public the Buddhist view on the same subject. Thus be entitled the book 'Origin of Man,' in spite of his treating of the origin of life and of the universe. Throughout the whole book occur coupled sentences, consisting mostly of the same number of Chinese characters, and consequently while one sentence is too laconic, the other is overladen with superfluous words, put in to make the right number in the balanced group of characters. In addition to this, the text is full of too concise phrases, and often of ambiguous ones, as it is intended to state as briefly as possible all the important doctrines of the Buddhist as well as of the outside schools. On this account the author himself wrote a few notes on the passages that lie thought it necessary to explain. The reader will find these notes beginning with 'A' put by the translator to distinguish them from his own.
K. N.

ORIGIN OF MAN[282]

INTRODUCTION

All animated beings that live (under the sun) have an origin, while each of inanimate things, countless in number, owes its existence to some source.[283] There can never be (any being nor) any thing that has (no origin, as there can be no) branch which has no root. How could man, the most spiritual of the Three Powers[284] exist without an origin?

(It is said),[285] moreover, that that which knows others is intellect, and that that which knows itself is wisdom. Now if I, being born among men, know not whence I came (into this life), how could I know whither I am going in the after-life? How could I understand all human affairs, ancient and modern, in the world? So, for some scores of years I learned under many different tutors, and read extensively (not only) the Buddhist (but also) outside books. By that means I tried to trace my Self, and never stopped my research till I attained, as I had expected, to its origin.

Confucianists and Taoists of our age, nevertheless, merely know that our nearest origin is the father or the grandfather, as we are descended from them, and they from their fathers in succession. (They say) that the remotest (origin) is the undefinable (primordial) Gas[286] in the state of

---

282 The author treats the origin of life and of the universe, but the book was entitled as we have seen in the preface.

283 The same idea and expression are found in Tao Teh King (Do-toku-kyo), by Lao Tsz (Ro-shi, 604-522 B.C.).

284 The Three Powers are-(1) Heaven, that has the power of revolution; (2) Earth, that has the power of production; and (3) Man, that has the power of thought.

285 The sentence is a direct quotation of Tao Teh King.

286 Such a statement concerning the creation of the universe as the one here given is found in I King (Eeki-kyo). The primordial substance is not exactly 'gas,' but we may conceive it as being something like a nebula.

chaos; that it split itself into the two (different) principles of the Positive and the Negative; that the two brought forth the Three Powers of Heaven, Earth, and Man, which (in their turn) produced all other things; that man as well as other things originated in the Gas.

(Some)[287] Buddhists, (however), maintain simply that the nearest (origin) is Karma,[288] as we were born among men as the results of the Karma that we had produced in the past existences; and that the remotest (origin) is the Alaya-vijnyana,[289] (because) our Karma is brought forth by illusion, and (illusion by attachment), and so forth, in one word, the Alaya is the origin of life. Although all of (these scholars) claim that they have already grasped the ultimate truth, yet not in fact.

Confucius, Lao Tsz, and Shakya, however, were all the wisest of sages. Each of them gave his teachings in a way different from the other two, that they might meet the spiritual needs of his time and fit to the capacities of men. (So that) the Buddhist and the outside doctrines, each supplementing the other, have done good to the multitude. They were all (intended) to encourage thousands of virtuous acts by explaining the whole chain of causality. They were (also intended) to investigate thousands of things, and throw light on the beginning and on the end of their evolution. Although all these doctrines (might) answer the purpose of the sages, yet there must be some teachings that would be temporary,[290] while others would be eternal. The first two faiths are merely temporary, while Buddhism includes both the temporary and the eternal. We may act according to the precepts of these three faiths, which aim at the peace and welfare (of man), in so far

---

[287] Not all Buddhists, but some of them, are meant here-that is, Hinayanists and Dharma-laksanists.

[288] According to Hinayanists, Karma (action) is that moral germ which survives death and continues in transmigration. It may be conceived as something like an energy, by the influence of which beings undergo metempsychosis.

[289] According to the Dharma-laksana Sect, Alaya-vijnyana (receptacle-knowledge) is the spiritual Substance which holds the 'seeds' or potentialities of all things.

[290] The temporary doctrine means the teaching preached by Shakya Muni to meet the temporary needs of the hearers. The term is always used in contrast with the real or eternal doctrine.

as they encourage thousands of virtuous acts by giving warning against evil and recommending good. (But) Buddhism (alone) is altogether perfect and best of all, in investigating thousands of things and in tracing them back to their first cause, in order to acquire thorough understanding of the natures of things and to attain to the ultimate truth.

Each of our contemporary scholars, nevertheless, adheres to one school of the (above mentioned) teachings. And there are some (even) among the Buddhists who mistake the temporary for the eternal doctrine. In consequence they are never successful in tracing Heaven, Earth, Man, and other things back to their First Cause. But I am now (going to show how) to infer an Ultimate Cause for thousands of things, not only from the Buddhist, but from outsiders' teachings. First I shall treat of the superficial doctrines, and then of the profound, (in order to) free the followers of the temporary faiths from those (prejudices that prove to be) obstructions in their way to the truth, and enable them to attain to the Ultimate Reality. Afterwards I shall point out, according to the perfect doctrine, how things evolved themselves through one stage after another out of the First Cause (in order to) make the incomplete doctrines fuse into the complete one, and to enable the followers to explain the phenomenal universe.[291]

---

[291] A. 'That is, Heaven, Earth, Man, and other things.'

This essay is entitled 'Origin of Man,' and it consists of the (following) four chapters: (1) Refutation of Delusive and Prejudiced (Doctrine); (2) Refutation of Incomplete and Superficial (Doctrine); (3) Direct Explanation of the Real Origin; (4) Reconciliation of the Temporary with the Eternal Doctrine.

CHAPTER I

REFUTATION OF DELUSIVE AND PREJUDICED (DOCTRINE)[292]

According to Confucianism[293] and Taoism all sorts of beings, such as men and beasts, were born out of and brought up by the (so-called) Great Path of Emptiness.[294] That is to say, the Path by the operation of its own law gave rise naturally to the primordial Gas, and that Gas produced Heaven and Earth, which (in their turn) brought forth thousands of things. Accordingly the wise and the unwise, the high and the low, the rich and the poor, the happy and the miserable, are predestined to be so by the heavenly flat, and are at the mercy of Time and Providence. Therefore they (must) come back after death to Heaven and Earth, from which (in turn) they return to the (Path) of Emptiness. The main purpose of these[295] (two) outside teachings is simply to establish morals with regard to bodily actions, but not to trace life to its First Cause. They tell of nothing beyond the phenomenal universe in their explanation of thousands of things. Though they point out the Great Path as the origin, yet they never explain in detail (what is) the direct, and (what) the indirect cause of the phenomenal universe, or how it was created, or how it will be destroyed, how life came forth, whither it will go, (what is) good, (what) evil. Therefore the followers

292 A. 'Those of Confucianists and Taoists.'

293 Confucianists are not of exactly the same opinion as Taoists respecting the creation. The Great Path here mentioned refers exclusively to Taoism.

294 The Great Path of Emptiness, Hu Wu Ta Tao, is the technical name for the Taoist conception of the Absolute. It is something existent in an undeveloped state before the creation of the phenomenal universe. According to Tao Teh King, it is 'self-existent, unchangeable, all-pervading, and the mother of all things. It is unnamable, but it is sometimes called the Path or the Great.' It is also called the Emptiness, as it is entirely devoid of relative activities.

295 Confucianism mainly treats of ethical problems, but Taoism is noted for its metaphysical speculation.

of these doctrines adhere to them as the perfect teachings without knowing that they are merely temporary.

Now I (shall) raise, in brief, a few questions to point out their weaknesses. If everything in the universe, as they say, came out of the Great Path of Emptiness, that Great Path itself should be the cause of (not only) of wisdom, (but) of folly, (not only) of life, (but) of death. It ought to be the source of prosperity (as well as) of adversity, of fortune (as well as) of misfortune. If this origin exist (as it is supposed) to all eternity, it must be possible neither to remove follies, villainies, calamities, and wars, nor to promote wisdom, good, happiness, and welfare. Of what use (then) are the teachings of Lao Tsz and Chwang Tsz?[296] The Path, besides, should have reared the tiger and the wolf, given birth to Kieh[297] and Cheu,[298] caused the premature deaths of Yen[299] and Jan,[300] and placed I[301] and Tsi[302] in their most lamentable condition. How could it be called a noble (path)?

Again, if, as they say, thousands of things could come naturally into existence without direct or indirect causes, they should come forth in all places where there are neither direct nor indirect causes. For instance, a stone would bring forth grass, while grass would give birth to man, and man would beget beasts, etc. In addition to this they would come out all at the same time, nothing being produced before or after the others. They

---

296 One of the greatest Taoist philosophers, and the author of the book entitled after his name. He flourished 339-327 B.C.

297 The last Emperor of the Hia dynasty, notorious for his vices. His reign was 1818-1767 B.C.

298 The last Emperor of the Yin dynasty, one of the worst despots. His reign was 1154-1122 B.C.

299 Yen Hwui (Gan-kai, 541-483 B.C.), a most beloved disciple of Confucius, known as a wise and virtuous scholar.

300 Jan Poh Niu (Zen-pak-giu, 521- . . . B.C.), a prominent disciple, of Confucius, distinguished for his virtues.

301 Poh I (Haku-i), the elder brother of Tsi, who distinguished himself by his faith and wisdom at the downfall of the Yin dynasty.

302 Shuh Tsi (Shiku Sei), the brother of I, with whom he shared the same fate.

would come into existence all at the same moment, nothing being produced sooner or later than the others. Peace and welfare might be secured without the help of the wise and the good. Humanity and righteousness might be acquired without instruction and study. One might even become an immortal genius[303] without taking the miraculous medicine. Why did Lao Tsz, Chwang Tsz, Cheu Kung[304] and Confucius do such a useless task as to found their doctrines and lay down the precepts for men?

Again, if all things, as they say, were made of the primordial Gas (which has no feeling nor will), how could an infant, just born of the Gas, who had never learned to think, or love, or hate, or to be naughty, or wilful (even begin to think or feel)? If, as they may answer, the infant as soon as it was born could quite naturally love or hate, etc., as it wished, it could (as well) gain the Five Virtues[305] and the Six Acquirements,[306]as it wished. Why does it wait for some direct or indirect causes (to gain its knowledge), and to acquire them through study and instruction?

Again, they might say life suddenly came into existence, it being formed of the Gas, and suddenly goes to naught (at death), the Gas being dispersed. What, then, are the spirits of the dead (which they believe in)? Besides, there are in history some instances of persons[307] who could see through

---

303 Degenerated Taoists maintained that they could prepare a certain miraculous draught, by the taking of which one could become immortal.

304 Cheu Kung (Shu-ko), a most noted statesman and scholar, the younger brother of the Emperor Wu (1122-1116 B.C.), the founder of the Chen dynasty.

305 (1) Humanity, (2) Uprightness, (3) Propriety, (4) Wisdom, (5) Sincerity.

306 (1) Reading, (2) Arithmetic, (3) Etiquette, (4) Archery, (5) Horsemanship, (6) Music.

307 According to Tsin Shu, a man, Pao Tsing by name, told his parents, when he was five years, that he had been in the previous life a son to Li, an inhabitant of Kuh Yang, and that he had fallen into the well and died. Thereupon the parents called on Li, and found, to their astonishment, that the boy's statement was actually coincident with the fact.

previous existences, or of persons[[308]who recollected the events in their past lives. Therefore we know that the present is the continuation of the past life, and that it did not come into existence on a sudden by the formation of a Gas. Again, there are some historical facts[309]proving that the supernatural powers of spirits will not be lost. Thus we know that life is not to be suddenly reduced to naught after death by the dispersion of the Gas. Therefore (matters concerning) sacrifices, services, and supplications (to the spirits) are mentioned in the sacred books.[310] Even more than that! Are there not some instances, ancient and modern, of persons who revived after death to tell the matters concerning the unseen world, or who[311] appeared to move the hearts of their wives and children a while after death, or who[312] took vengeance (on the enemy), or who[313] returned favours (to their friends)?

The outside scholars might ask, by way of objection, if one live as a spirit after death, the spirits of the past would fill up streets and roads, and be seen by men; and why are there no eye-witnesses? I say in reply that (as) there are the Six Worlds[314] for the dead, they do not necessarily live in the world of spirits. (Even as spirits) they must die and be born again among men or other beings. How can the spirits of the past always live in a crowd? Moreover, if (as you say) man was born of (primordial) Gas which gave rise

---

308 Yan Hu, a native of Tsin Chen, recollected, at the age of five, that he had been a son to the next-door neighbour, and that he had left his ring under a mulberry-tree close by the fence of the house. Thereupon he went with his nurse and successfully restored it, to the astonishment of the whole family.

309 All the ancient sages of China believed in spirits, and propitiated them by sacrifices.

310 The sacred books of Confucianism, Shu King and Li Ki.

311 Pang Shang, the Prince of Tsi, is said to have appeared after his death.

312 Poh Yiu, of Ching, is said to have become an epidemic spirit to take vengeance on his enemies.

313 According to Tso Chwen (Sa-den), when Wei Wu, a General of Tsin, fought with Tu Hwui, the dead father of his concubine appeared, and prevented the march of the enemy in order to return favours done to him.

314 (1) The heaven, or the world for Devas; (2) the earth, or the world for men; (3) the world for Asuras; (4) the world for Petras; (5) the world for beasts; (6) hell.

to Heaven and Earth, and which was unconscious from the very beginning, how could he be conscious all on a sudden after his birth? Why are trees and grass which were also formed of the same Gas unconscious? Again, if, (as you say), the rich and the poor, the high and the low, the wise and the unwise, the good and the bad, the happy and the unhappy, the lucky and the unlucky, are predestinated alike by heavenly decree, why are so many destined by heaven to be poor and so few to be rich? Why so many to be low and so few to be high? In short, why are so many destined to be unlucky and so few to be lucky?

If it be the will of Heaven to bless so limited a number of persons at all, and to curse so many, why is Heaven so partial? Even more than that! Are there not many who hold a high position without any meritorious conduct, while some are placed in a low one in spite of their keeping to (the rules of) conduct? Are there not many who are rich without any virtues, while some are poor in spite of their virtues? Are there not the unjust who are fortunate, while the just are unfortunate? Are there not the humane, who die young, while the inhuman enjoy long lives? In short, the righteous (are doomed) to perish, while the unrighteous prosper! Thus (we must infer) that all this depends on the heavenly will, which causes the unrighteous to prosper and the righteous to perish. How can there be reward for the good (as it is taught in your sacred books),[[315] that Heaven blesses the good and shows grace to the humble? How can there be punishment for the bad (as it is taught in your holy books),[316] that Heaven curses the evil and inflicts punishment on the proud?

Again, if even all such evils as wars, treacheries, and rebellions depend on the heavenly will, those Sages would be in the wrong who, in the statement of their teaching, censure or chastise men, but not Heaven or the heavenly will. Therefore, even if Shi[317] is full of reproofs against maladministration, while Shu[318] of eulogies for the reigns of the wisest monarchs-even if

---

[315] Shu King and I King.

[316] Ibid.

[317] Shu King, a famous book of odes.

[318] Shu King, the records of the administrations of the wisest monarchs of old.

Propriety[319] is recommended as a most effectual means of creating peace between the governors and the governed, while Music[320] (is recommended as a means of) ameliorating the customs and manners of the people—still, they can hardly be said to realize the Will on High or to conform to the wishes of the Creator. Hence you must acknowledge that those who devote themselves to the study of these doctrines are not able to trace man to his origin.

---

319 Li Ki, the book on proprieties and etiquette.

320 It is said in Hiao King that music is the best means to improve customs and manners.

CHAPTER II

REFUTATION OF INCOMPLETE AND SUPERFICIAL (DOCTRINE)[321]

There are in the Buddhist doctrines, to state briefly, the five grades (of development), beginning with the most superficial, and ending with the most profound teachings. (They are as follows:) (1) The Doctrine for Men and Devas; (2) the Doctrine of the Hinayanists; (3) the Mahayana Doctrine of Dharma-laksana; (4) the Mahayana Doctrine of the Nihilists[322]; (5) the Ekaydna Doctrine that teaches the Ultimate Reality.[323]

The Doctrine for Men and Devas

The Buddha, to meet temporarily the spiritual needs of the uninitiated, preached a doctrine concerning good or bad Karma as the cause, and its retribution as the effect, in the three existences (of the past, the present, and the future). That is, one who commits the tenfold sin[324] must be reborn after death in hell, when these sins are of the highest grade;[325] among Pretas,[326] when of the middle grade; and among animals, when of the lowest grade.

---

[321] A. 'The imperfect doctrines taught by the Buddha.'

[322] A. 'These first four doctrines are treated of in this chapter.'

[323] A. 'This is mentioned in the third chapter.'

[324] (1) Taking life, (2) theft, (3) adultery, (4) lying, (5) exaggeration, (6) abuse, (7) ambiguous talk, (8) coveting, (9) malice, (10) unbelief.

[325] There are three grades in each of the tenfold sin. For instance, the taking of the life of a Buddha, or of a sage, or of a parent, etc., is of the highest grade; while to kill fellow-men is of the middle; and to kill beasts and birds, etc., is of the lowest. Again, to kill any being with pleasure is of the highest grade; while to repent after killing is of the middle; and killing by mistake is of the lowest.

[326] Hungry spirits.

Therefore the Buddha for a temporary purpose made these (uninitiated) observe the Five Precepts similar to the Five Virtues[327] of the outside doctrine, in order to enable them to escape the three (worst) States[328] of Existence, and to be reborn among men. (He also taught that) those who cultivate[329] the tenfold virtue[330] of the highest grade, and who give alms, and keep the precepts, and so forth, are to be born in the Six Celestial Realms of Kama[331] while those who practise the Four[332] Dhyanas, the

---

[327] The five cardinal virtues of Confucianism are quite similar to the five precepts of Buddhism, as we see by this table:

VIRTUES.—-PRECEPTS.

1. Humanity.—-1. Not to take life. 2. Uprightness.—-2. Not to steal. 3. Propriety.—-3. Not to be adulterous. 4. Wisdom.—-4. Not to get drunk. 5. Sincerity.—-5. Not to lie.

[328] (1) Hell, (2) Pretas, (3) Beasts.

[329] A. 'The Buddhist precepts are different from the Confucian teachings in the form of expression, but they agree in their warning against the evil and in encouraging the good. The moral conduct of the Buddhist can be secured by the cultivation of the five virtues of humanity, uprightness, etc., as though people in this country hold up their hands joined in the respectable salutation, while the same object is attained by those of The Fan, who stand with their bands hanging down. Not to kill is humanity. Not to steal is uprightness. Not to be adulterous is propriety. Not to lie is sincerity. Not to drink spirits nor eat meat is to increase wisdom, keeping mind pure.'

[330] (1) Not to take life, (2) not to steal, (3) not to be adulterous, (4) not to lie, (5) not to exaggerate, (6) not to abuse, (7) not to talk ambiguously, (8) not to covet, (9) not to be malicious, (10) not to unbelieve.

[331] Kama-loka, the world of desire, is the first of the Three Worlds. It consists of the earth and the six heavenly worlds, all the inhabitants of which are subject to sensual desires.

[332] The Buddhists taught the four Dhyanas, or the four different degrees of abstract contemplation, by which the mind could free itself from all subjective and objective trammels, until it reached a state of absolute absence of unconcentrated thought. The practiser of the four Dhyanas would be born in the four regions of the Rupa-lokas in accordance with his spiritual state.

Eight Samadhis,[333] are to be reborn in the heavenly worlds of Rupa[334] and Arupa. For this reason this doctrine is called the doctrine for men and Devas. According to this doctrine Karma is the origin of life.[335]

Arupa-loka, the world of formlessness, is the third of the Three Worlds. It consists of four heavens. The first is called 'the heaven of unlimited space,' the second 'the heaven of unlimited knowledge,' the third 'the heaven of absolute non-existence,' the fourth 'the heaven of neither consciousness nor unconsciousness.'

A. 'None of heavens, or of hells, or of the worlds of spirits, is mentioned in the title of this book, because these worlds are entirely different from ours, and absolutely beyond the sight and hearing. Ordinary people know not even the phenomena actually occurring before them; how could they understand the unseen? So I entitled it simply, "The Origin of Man " in agreement with the worldly teachings. Now that I treat, however, of the Buddhist doctrine, it is reasonable to enumerate these worlds in full.'

Now let me raise some questions by way of objection. Granting that one has to be born in the Five States of Existences[336] by virtue of Karma produced (in previous lives), is it not doubtful who is the author of Karma, and who the recipient of its consequences? If it might be said that the eyes, ears, hands, and feet produce Karma, then the eyes, ears, hands, and feet of a newly-dead person are still as they were. So why do they not see and hear

---

333 Namely, the above-mentioned four degrees of contemplation, and other four deeper ecstatic meditations. The practiser of the latter would be born in the four spiritual regions of Arupa-loka in accordance with his state of abstraction.

334 Rupa-loka, the world of form, is the second of the Three Worlds. It consists of eighteen heavens, which were divided into four regions. The first Dhyana region comprised the first three of the eighteen heavens, the second Dhyana region the next three, the third Dhyana region the following three, and the fourth Dhyana region the remaining nine.

335 A. 'But there are three sorts of Karmas: (1) The bad, (2) the good, (3) the immovable. There are the three periods for retribution: (1) In this life, (2) in the next life, (3) in some remote future life.'

336 The states of—(1) heavenly beings, (2) men, (3) beings in hell, (4) hungry spirits, (5) beasts.

and thus produce Karma?

If it be said that it is the mind that produces Karma (I ask), what is the mind? If you mean the heart, the heart is a material thing, and is located within the body. How can it, by coming quickly into the eyes and ears, distinguish the pleasing from the disgusting in external objects? If there be no distinction between the pleasing and the disgusting, why does it accept the one or reject the other?

Besides, the heart is as much material and impenetrable as the eyes, ears, hands, and feet. How, then, can the heart within freely pass to the organs of sense without? How can this one put the others in motion, or communicate with them, in order to co-operate in producing Karma? If it be said that only such passions as joy, anger, love, and hatred act through the body and the mouth and enable them to produce Karma, (I should say) those passions—joy, anger, and the rest—are too transitory, and come and go in a moment. They have no Substance (behind their appearances). What, then, is the chief agent that produces Karma?

It might be said that we should not seek after (the author of Karma) by taking mind and body separately (as we have just done), because body and mind, as a whole, conjointly produce Karma. Who, then, after the destruction of body by death, would receive the retribution (in the form) of pain or of pleasure?

If it be assumed that another body is to come into existence after death, then the body and mind of the present life, committing sins or cultivating virtues, would cause another body and mind in the future which would suffer from the pains or enjoy the pleasures. Accordingly, those who cultivate virtues would be extremely unlucky, while those who commit sins very lucky. How can the divine law of causality be so unreasonable? Therefore we (must) acknowledge that those who merely follow this doctrine are far from a thorough understanding of the origin of life, though they believe in the theory of Karma.

The Doctrine of the Hinayanists

This doctrine tells us that (both) the body, that is formed of matter, and the mind, that thinks and reflects, continually exist from eternity to eternity, being destroyed and recreated by means of direct or indirect causes, just as the water of a river glides continually, or the flame of a lamp keeps burning constantly. Mind and body unite themselves temporarily, and seem to be one and changeless. The common people, ignorant of all this, are attached to (the two combined) as being Atman.[337]

For the sake of this Atman, which they hold to be the most precious thing (in the world), they are subject to the Three Poisons Of lust,[338] anger,[339] and folly,[340] which (in their turn) give impulse to the will and bring forth Karma of all kinds through speech and action. Karma being thus produced, no one can evade its effects. Consequently all must be born[341] in the Five States of Existence either to suffer pain or to enjoy pleasure; some are born in the higher places, while others in the lower of the Three Worlds.[342]

When born (in the future lives) they are attached again to the body (and mind) as Atman, and become subject to lust and the other two passions. Karma is again produced by them, and they have to receive its inevitable results. (Thus) body undergoes birth, old age, disease, death, and is reborn after death; while the world passes through the stages of formation, existence, destruction, and emptiness, and is re-formed again after

---

337 Atman means ego, or self, on which individuality is based.

338 A. 'The passion that covets fame and gain to keep oneself in prosperity.'

339 A. 'The passion against disagreeable things, for fear of their inflicting injuries on oneself.'

340 A. 'Wrong thoughts and inferences.'

341 A. 'Different sorts of beings are born by virtue of the individualizing Karma.'

342 A. 'Worlds are produced by virtue of the Karma common to all beings that live in them.'

emptiness. Kalpa after Kalpa[343] (passes by), life after life (comes on), and the circle of continuous rebirths knows no beginning nor end, and resembles the pulley for drawing water from the well.[344]

A. "The following verses describe how the world was first created in the period of emptiness: A strong wind began to blow through empty space. Its length and breadth were infinite. It was 16 lakhs thick, and so strong that it could not be cut even with a diamond. Its name was the world-supporting-wind. The golden clouds of Abhasvara heaven (the sixth of eighteen heavens of the Rupa-loka) covered all the skies of the Three Thousand Worlds. Down came the heavy rain, each drop being as large as the axle of a waggon. The water stood on the wind that checked its running down. It was 11 lakhs deep. The first layer was made of adamant (by the congealing water). Gradually the cloud poured down the rain and filled it. First the Brahma-raja worlds, next the Yama-heaven (the third of six heavens of the Kama loka), were made. The pure water rose up, driven by the wind, and Sumeru, (the central mountain, or axis of the universe) and the seven concentric circles of mountains, and so on, were formed. Out of dirty sediments the mountains, the four continents, the hells, oceans, and outer ring of mountains, were made. This is called the formation of the universe. The time of one Increase and one Decrease (human life is increased from 10 to 84,000 years, increasing by one year at every one hundred years; then it is decreased from 84,000 to 10 years, decreasing by one year at every one hundred years) elapsed. In short, those beings in the second region of Rupa-loka, whose good Karma had spent its force, came down on the earth. At first there were the 'earth bread' and the wild vine for them. Afterwards they could not completely digest rice, and began to excrete and to urinate. Thus men were differentiated from women. They divided the cultivated land among them. Chiefs were elected; assistants and subjects

---

343 Kalpa, a mundane cycle, is not reckoned by months and years. It is a period during which a physical universe is formed to the moment when another is put into its place.

344 A. 'Taoists merely know that there was one Kalpa of Emptiness before the formation of this present universe, and point out the Emptiness, the Chaos, the primordial Gas, and the rest, naming them as the first or the beginningless. But they do not know that the universe had already gone through myriads of cycles of Kalpas of formation, existence, destruction, and emptiness. Thus even the most superficial of the Hinayana doctrines far excels the most profound of the outside doctrines.'

were sought out; hence different classes of people. A period of nineteen Increases and Decreases elapsed. Added to the above-mentioned period, it amounted to twenty Increases and Decreases. This is called the Kalpa of the formation of the universe.

"Now let us discuss this point. The Kalpa of Emptiness is what the Taoist calls the Path of Emptiness. The Path or the Reality, however, is not empty, but bright, transcendental, spiritual, and omnipresent. Lao Tsz, led by his mistaken idea, called the Kalpa of Emptiness the Path; otherwise he did so for the temporary purpose of denouncing worldly desires. The wind in the empty space is what the Taoist calls the undefinable Gas in the state of Chaos. Therefore Lao Tsz said, 'The Path brings forth one.' The golden clouds, the first of all physical objects, is (what the Confucianist calls) the First Principle. The rain-water standing (on the wind) is the production of the Negative Principle. The Positive, united with the Negative, brought forth the phenomenal universe. The Brahma-raja-loka, the Sumeru, and others, are what they call the Heaven. The dirty waters and sediment are the Earth. So Lao Tsz said, 'One produces two.' Those in the second region of the Rupra-loka, whose good Karma had spent its force, came down upon the earth and became human beings. Therefore Lao Tsz said, 'The two produce three.' Thus the Three Powers were completed. The earth-bread and different classes of people, and so on, are the so-called 'production of thousands of things by the Three.' This was the time when people lived in eaves or wandered in the wilderness, and knew not the use of fire. As it belongs to the remote past of the prehistoric age, previous to the reigns of the first three Emperors, the traditions handed down to us are neither clear nor certain. Many errors crept into them one generation after another, and consequently no one of the statements given in the various works of scholars agrees with another. Besides, when the Buddhist books explain the formation of the Three Thousand Worlds, they do not confine themselves merely within the limits of this country. Hence their records are entirely different from those of the outsiders (which are confined to China).

"'Existence' means the Kalpa of Existence that lasts twenty Increases and Decreases. 'Destruction' means the Kalpa of Destruction that lasts also twenty Increases and Decreases. During the first nineteen Increases and Decreases living beings are destroyed; while in the last worlds are demolished through the three periods of distress (1) the period of water,

(2) the period of fire, (3) the period of wind. 'Emptiness' means the Kalpa of Emptiness, during which no beings nor worlds exist. This Kalpa also lasts twenty Increases and Decreases."

All this is due to Ignorance which does not understand that no bodily existence, by its very nature, can be Atman. The reason why it is not Atman is this, that its formation is, after all, due to the union of matter and mind. Now (let us) examine and analyze (mind and body). Matter consists of the four elements of earth, water, fire, and wind, while mind consists of the four aggregates of perception,[345] consciousness,[346] conception,[347] and knowledge.[348]

If all (these elements) be taken as Atman, there must be eight Atmans (for each person). More than that! There are many different things, even in the element of earth. Now, there are three hundred and sixty bones, each one distinct from the other. No one is the same as any other, either of the skin, hair, muscles, the liver, the heart, the spleen, and the kidneys. Furthermore, there are a great many mental qualities each different from the others. Sight is different from hearing. Joy is not the same as anger. If we enumerate them, in short, one after another, there are eighty thousand passions.[349]

As things are thus so innumerable, none can tell which of these (without mistake) is to be taken as the Atman. In case all be taken as the Atman, there must be hundreds and thousands of Atmans, among which there would be as many conflicts and disturbances as there are masters living in the one (house of) body. As there exists no body nor mind separated from these things, one can never find the Atman, even if he seeks for it over and

---

345 A. 'It receives both the agreeable and the disagreeable impressions from without.' It is Yedana, the second of the five Skandhas, or aggregates.

346 A. 'It perceives the forms of external objects.' It is Samjnya, name, the third of the five aggregates.

347 A. 'It acts, one idea changing after another.' It is Samskara, the fourth of the five aggregates.

348 A. 'It recognizes.' It is Vijnyana, the last of the five aggregates.

349 Eighty thousand simply means a great many.

over again.

Hereupon anyone understands that this life (of ours) is no more than the temporary union of numerous elements (mental and physical). Originally there is no Atman to distinguish one being from another. For whose sake, then, should he be lustful or angry? For whose sake should he take life,[350] or commit theft, or give alms, or keep precepts? (Thus thinking) at length he sets his mind free from the virtues and vices subjected to the passions[351] of the Three Worlds, and abides in the discriminative insight into (the nature of) the Anatman[352] only. By means of that discriminative insight he makes himself pure from lust, and the other (two passions) puts an end to various sorts of Karma, and realizes the Bhutatathata[353] of Anatman. In brief, he attains to the State of Arhat,[354] has his body reduced to ashes, his intelligence annihilated, and entirely gets rid of sufferings.

According to the doctrine of this school the two aggregates, material and spiritual, together with lust, anger, and folly, are the origin of ourselves and of the world in which we live. There exists nothing else, either in the past or in the future, that can be regarded as the origin.

---

350 A. 'He understands the truth of misery.' The truth of Duhkha, or misery, is the first of the four Noble Satyas, or Truths, that ought to be realized by the Hinayanists. According to the Hinayana doctrine, misery is a necessary concomitant of sentient life.'

351 A. 'He destroys Samudaya.' The truth of Samudaya, or accumulation, the second of the four Satyas, means that misery is accumulated or produced by passions. This truth should be realized by the removal of passions.

352 A. 'This is the truth of Marga.' The truth of Marga, or Path, is the fourth of the four Satyas. There are the eight right Paths that lead to the extinction of passions; (1) Right view (to discern truth), (2) right thought (or purity of will and thought), (3) right speech (free from nonsense and errors), (4) right action, (5) right diligence, (6) right meditation, (7) right memory, (8) right livelihood.

353 A. 'This is the truth of Nirodha.' Nirodha, or destruction, the third of the four Satyas, means the extinction of passions. Bhutatathati of Anatman means the truth of the non existence of Atma or soul, and is the aim and end of the Hinayanist philosophy.

354 Arhat, the Killer of thieves (i.e., passions), means one who conquered his passions. It means, secondly, one who is exempted from birth, or one who is free from transmigration. Thirdly, it means one deserving worship. So the Arhat is the highest sage who has attained to Nirvana by the destruction of all passions.

Now let us say (a few words) by way of refutation. That which (always) stands as the origin of life, birth after birth, generation after generation, should exist by itself without cessation. Yet the Five Vijnyanas[355] cease to perform their functions when they lack proper conditions, (while) the Mano-vijnyana[356] is lost at times (in unconsciousness). There are none of those four (material) elements in the heavenly worlds of Arupa. How, then, is life sustained there and kept up in continuous birth after birth? Therefore we know that those who devote themselves to the study of this doctrine also cannot trace life to its origin.

The Mahayana Doctrine of Dharmalaksana[357]

This doctrine tells us that from time immemorial all sentient beings naturally have eight different Vijnyanas[358] and the eighth, Alaya-vijnyana,[359]

---

355 A. 'The conditions are the Indriyas and the Visayas, etc.' Indriyas are organs of sense, and Visayas are objects on which the sense acts. Five Vijnyanas are—(1) The sense of sight, (2) the sense of hearing, (3) the sense of smell, (4) the sense of taste, (5) the sense of touch.

356 Mano-vijnyana is the mind itself, and the last of the six Vijnyanas of the Hinayana doctrine. A. '(For instance), in a state of trance, in deep slumber, in Nirodha-samapatti (where no thought exists), in Asamjnyi-samapatti (in which no consciousness exists), and in Avrhaloka (the thirteenth of Brahmalokas).

357 This school studies in the main the nature of things (Dharma), and was so named. The doctrine is based on Avatamsaka-sutra and Samdhi-nirmocana-sutra, and was systematized by Asamga and Vasu-bandhu. The latter's book, Vidyamatra-siddhi-castra-karika, is held to be the best authoritative work of the school.

358 (1) The sense of sight; (2) the sense of hearing; (3) the sense of smell; (4) the sense of taste; (5) the sense of touch; (6) Mano-vijnyana (lit., mind-knowledge), or the perceptive faculty; (7) Klista-mano-vijnyana (lit., soiled-mind-knowledge), or an introspective faculty; (8) Alaya-vijnyana (lit., receptacle-knowledge), or ultimate-mind-substance.

359 The first seven Vijnyanas depend on the Alaya, which is said to hold all the 'seeds' of physical and mental objects.

is the origin of them. (That is), the Alaya suddenly brings forth the 'seeds'[360] of living beings and of the world in which they live, and through transformation gives rise to the seven Vijnyanas. Each of them causes external objects on which it acts to take form and appear. In reality there is nothing externally existent. How, then, does Alaya give rise to them through transformation? Because, as this doctrine tells us, we habitually form the erroneous idea that Atman and external objects exist in reality, and it acts upon Alaya and leaves its impressions[361] there. Consequently, when Vijnyanas are awakened, these impressions (or the seed-ideas) transform and present themselves (before the mind's eye) Atman and external objects.

Then the sixth and the seventh[362] Vijnyana veiled with Avidya, dwelling on them, mistake them for real Atman and the real external objects. This (error) may be compared with one diseased[363] in the eye, who imagines that he sees various things (floating in the air) on account of his illness; or with a dreamer[364] whose fanciful thoughts assume various forms of external objects, and present themselves before him. While in the dream he fancies that there exist external objects in reality, but on awakening he finds that they are nothing other than the transformation of his dreaming thoughts.
So are our lives. They are no other than the transformation of the Vijnyanas; but in consequence of illusion, we take them for the Atman and

---

360 This school is an extreme form of Idealism, and maintains that nothing separated from the Alaya can exist externally. The mind-substance, from the first, holds the seed ideas of everything, and they seem to the non-enlightened mind to be the external universe, but are no other than the transformation of the seed-ideas. The five senses, and the Mano-vijnyana acting on them, take them for external objects really existent, while the seventh Vijnyana mistakes the eighth for Atman.

361 The non-enlightened mind, habitually thinking that Atman and external objects exist, leaves the impression of the seed-ideas on its own Alaya.

362 Avidya, or ignorance, which mistakes the illusory phenomena for realities.

363 A. 'A person with a serious disease sees the vision of strange colours, men, and things in his trance.'

364 A. 'That a dreamer fancies he sees things is well known to everybody.'

external objects existing in reality. From these erroneous ideas arise delusive thoughts that lead to the production of Karma; hence the round-of rebirth to time without end.[365] When we understand these reasons, we can realize the fact that our lives are nothing but transformations of the Vijnyanas, and that the (eighth) Vijnyana is the origin.[366]

Mahayana Doctrine of the Nihilists

This doctrine disproves (both) the Mahayana and the Hinayana doctrines above mentioned that adhere to Dharma-laksana, and suggestively discloses the truth of Transcendental Reality which is to be treated later.[367] Let me state, first of all, what it would say in the refutation of Dharma-laksana.
If the external objects which are transformed are unreal, how can the Vijnyana, the transformer, be real? If you say the latter is really existent, but not the former,[368] then (you assume that) the dreaming mind (which is compared with Alaya-vijnyana) is entirely different from the objects seen in the dream (which are compared with external objects). If they are entirely

---

365 A. 'As it was detailed above.'

366 A. 'An imperfect doctrine, which is refuted later.'

367 A. "The nihilistic doctrine is stated not only in the various Prajnya-sutras (the books having Prajnya-paramita in their titles), but also in almost all Mahayana sutras. The above-mentioned three doctrines were preached (by the Buddha) in the three successive periods. But this doctrine was not preached at any particular period; it was intended to destroy at any time the attachment to the phenomenal objects. Therefore Nagarjuna tells us that there are two sorts of Prajnyas, the Common and the Special. The Çravakas (lit., hearers) and the Pratyekabuddhas (lit., singly enlightened ones), or the Hinayanists, could hear and believe in, with the Bodhisattvas or the Mahayanists, the Common Prajnya, as it was intended to destroy their attachment to the external objects. Bodhisattvas alone could understand the Special Prajnya, as it secretly revealed the Buddha nature, or the Absolute. Each of the two great Indian teachers, Çilabhadra and Jnyanaprabha, divided the whole teachings of the Buddha into three periods. (According to Çilabhadra, A.D. 625, teacher of Hiuen Tsang, the Buddha first preached the doctrine of 'existence' to the effect that every living being is unreal, but things are real. All the Hinayana sutras belong to this period. Next the Buddha preached the doctrine of the middle path, in Samdhi-nirmocana-sutra and others, to the effect that all the phenomenal universe is unreal, but that the mental substance is real. According to Jnyanaprabha, the Buddha first preached the doctrine of existence, next that of the existence of mental substance, and lastly that of unreality.) One says the doctrine of unreality was preached before that of Dharma-laksana, while the others say it was preached after. Here I adopt the latters' opinion."

368 A. 'In the following sentences I refute it, making use of the simile of the dream.'

different, you ought not to identify the dream with the things dreamed, nor to identify the things dreamed with the dream itself. In other words, they ought to have separate existences. (And) when you awake your dream may disappear, but the things dreamed would remain.

Again, if (you say) that the things dreamed are not identical with the dream, then they would be really existent things. If the dream is not the same as the things dreamed, in what other form does it appear to you? Therefore you must acknowledge that there is every reason to believe that both the dreaming mind and the things dreamed are equally unreal, and that nothing exists in reality, though it seems to you as if there were a seer, and a seen, in a dream.

Thus those Vijnyanas also would be unreal, because all of them are not self-existent realities, their existence being temporary, and dependent upon various conditions.

"There is nothing," (the author of) Madhyamika-castra[369] says, "that ever came into existence without direct and indirect causes. Therefore there is anything that is not unreal in the world." He says again: "Things produced through direct and indirect causes I declare to be the very things which are unreal." (The author of) Craddhotdada-castra[370] says: "All things in the universe present themselves in different forms only on account of false ideas. If separated from the (false) ideas and thoughts, no forms of those external objects exist." "All the physical forms (ascribed to Buddha)," says (the author of) a sutra,[371] "are false and unreal. The beings that transcend all forms are called Buddhas."[372] Consequently you must acknowledge that mind as well as external objects are unreal. This is the eternal truth of the Mahayana doctrine. We are driven to the conclusion that unreality is the origin of life, if we trace it back according to this doctrine.

---

[369] The principal textbook of the Madhyamika School, by Nagarjuna and Nilanetra, translated into Chinese (A.D. 409) by Kumarajiva.

[370] A well-known Mahayana book ascribed to Acvaghosa, translated into Chinese by Paramartha. There exists an English translation by D. Suzuki.

[371] Vajracchedha-prajnya-paramita-sutra, of which there exist three Chinese translations.

[372] A. 'Similar passages are found in every book of the Mahayana Tripitaka.'

Now let us say (a few words) to refute this doctrine also. If mind as well as external objects be unreal, who is it that knows they are so? Again, if there be nothing real in the universe, what is it that causes unreal objects to appear? We stand witness to the fact there is no one of the unreal things on earth that is not made to appear by something real. If there be no water of unchanging fluidity,[373] how can there be the unreal and temporary forms of waves? If there be no unchanging mirror, bright and clean, how can there be various images, unreal and temporary, reflected in it? It is true in sooth that the dreaming mind as well as the things dreamed, as said above, are equally unreal, but does not that unreal dream necessarily presuppose the existence of some (real) sleepers?

Now, if both mind and external objects, as declared above, be nothing at all, no- one can tell what it is that causes these unreal appearances. Therefore this doctrine, we know, simply serves to refute the erroneous theory held by those who are passionately attached to Dharma-laksana, but never clearly discloses spiritual Reality. So that Mahabheri-harakaparivarta-sutra[374] says as follows: "All the sutras that teach the unreality of things belong to an imperfect doctrine (of the Buddha). Mahaprajnya-paramita-sutra[375] says: "The doctrine of unreality is the first entrance-gate to Mahayanism."

When the above-mentioned four doctrines are compared with one another in the order of succession, each is more profound than the preceding. They are called the superficial, provided that the follower, learning them a short while, knows them by himself to be imperfect; (but) if he adheres to them as perfect, these same (doctrines) are called incomplete. They are (thus) said to be superficial and incomplete with regard to the follower.

---

[373] The Absolute is compared with the ocean, and the phenomenal universe with the waves.

[374] The book was translated into Chinese by Gunabhadra, A.D. 420-479.

[375] This is not the direct quotation from the sutra translated by Hiuen Tsang. The words are found in Mahaprajnya-paramita-sutra, the commentary on the sutra by Nagarjuna.

CHAPTER III

THE DIRECT EXPLANATION OF THE REAL ORIGIN[376]

The Ekayana Doctrine that Teaches the Ultimate Reality

This doctrine teaches us that all sentient beings have the Real Spirit[377] of Original Enlightenment (within themselves). From time immemorial it is unchanging and pure. It is eternally bright, and clear, and conscious. It is also named the Buddha-nature, or Tathagata-garbha.[378] As it is, however, veiled by illusion from time without beginning, (sentient beings) are not conscious of its existence, and think that the nature within themselves are degenerated. Consequently they are given to bodily pleasures, and producing Karma, suffer from birth and death. The great Enlightened One, having compassion on them, taught that everything in the universe is unreal. He pointed out that the Real Spirit of Mysterious Enlightenment (within them) is pure and exactly the same as that of Buddha. Therefore he says in Avatamsaka-sutra[379]: "There are no sentient beings, the children of Buddha, who are not endowed with wisdom of Tathagata;[380] but they cannot attain to Enlightenment simply because of illusion and attachment. When they are free from illusion, the Universal Intelligence,[381] the Natural

---

[376] A. 'The perfect doctrine, in which eternal truth is taught by the Buddha.'

[377] The ultimate reality is conceived by the Mahayanist as an entity self-existent, omnipresent, spiritual, impersonal, free from all illusions. It may be regarded as something like the universal and enlightened soul.

[378] Tathagata's womb, Tathagata being another name for Buddha.

[379] The book was translated into Chinese by Buddhabhadra, A.D. 418-420.

[380] The highest epithet of the Buddha, meaning one who comes into the world like the coming of his predecessors.

[381] The all-knowing wisdom that is acquired by Enlightenment.

Intelligence,[382] the Unimpeded Intelligence,[383] will be disclosed (in their minds)."

Then he tells a parable of a single grain of minute dust[384] containing large volumes of Sutra, equal in dimension of the Great Chiliocosmos.[385] The grain is compared with a sentient being, and the Sutra with the wisdom of Buddha. Again he says later:[386] "Once Tathagata, having observed every sort of sentient beings all over the universe, said as follows: 'Wonderful, how wonderful! That these various sentient beings, endowed with the wisdom of Tathagata, are not conscious of it because of their errors and illusions! I shall teach them the sacred truth and make them free from illusion for ever. I shall (thus) enable them to find by themselves the Great Wisdom of Tathagatha within them and make them equal to Buddha.'

Let me say (a few words) about this doctrine by way of criticism. So many Kalpas we spent never meeting with this true doctrine, and knew not how to trace our life back to its origin. Having been attached to nothing but the unreal outward forms, we willingly acknowledged ourselves to be a common herd of lowly beings. Some regarded themselves as beasts, (while) others as men.

But now, tracing life to its origin according to the highest doctrine, we have fully understood that we ourselves were originally Buddhas. Therefore we should act in conformity to Buddha's (action), and keep our mind in harmony with his. Lot us betake ourselves once more to the source of Enlightened Spirit, restoring ourselves to the original Buddhahood. Let us

---

[382] The inborn wisdom of the Original Enlightenment.

[383] The wisdom that is acquired by the union of Enlightenment with the Original Enlightenment.

[384] One of the famous parables in the sutra.

[385] According to the Buddhist literature, one universe comprises one sun, one moon, one central mountain or Sumeru, four continents, etc. One thousand of these universes form the Small Thousand Worlds; one thousand of the Small Thousand Worlds form the Middle Thousand Worlds; and the Great Thousand Worlds, or Great Chiliocosmos, comprises one thousand of the Middle Thousand Worlds.

[386] This is not an exact quotation of the sutra.

cut off the bond of attachment, and remove the illusion that common people are habitually given to.

Illusion being destroyed,[387] the will to destroy it is also removed, and at last there remains nothing to be done (except complete peace and joy). This naturally results in Enlightenment, whose practical uses are as innumerable as the grains of sand in the Ganges. This state is called Buddhahood. We should know that the illusory as well as the Enlightened are originally of one and the same Real Spirit. How great, how excellent, is the doctrine that traces man to such an origin![388]

'If there is a person of the highest grade of understanding, he may first of all learn the most profound, next the less profound, and, lastly, the most superficial doctrine-that is, he may at the outset come "Suddenly" to the understanding of the One Reality of True Spirit, as it is taught in the fifth doctrine. When the Spiritual Reality is disclosed before his mind's eye, he may naturally see that it originally transcends all appearances which are unreal, and that unrealities appear on account of illusion, their existence depending on Reality. Then he must give up evil, practise good, put away unrealities by the wisdom of Enlightenment, and reduce them to Reality. When unrealities are all gone, and Reality alone remains complete, he is called the Dharma-kaya-Buddha.'

---

387 The passage occurs in Tao Teh King.

388 A. 'Although all of the above-mentioned five doctrines were preached by the Buddha Himself, yet there are some that belong to the Sudden, while others to the Gradual, Teachings. If there were persons of the middle or the lowest grade of understanding, He first taught the most superficial doctrine, then the less superficial, and "Gradually" led them up to the profound. At the outset of His career as a teacher He preached the first doctrine to enable them to give up evil and abide by good; next He preached the second and the third doctrine that they might remove the Pollution and attain to the Purity; and, lastly, He preached the fourth and the fifth doctrine to destroy their attachment to unreal forms, and to show the Ultimate Reality. (Thus) He reduced (all) the temporary doctrines into the eternal one, and taught them how to practise the Law according to the eternal and attain to Buddhahood.

CHAPTER IV

RECONCILIATION OF THE TEMPORARY WITH THE REAL DOCTRINE[389]

EVEN if Reality is the origin of life, there must be in all probability some causes for its coming into existence, as it cannot suddenly assume the form of body by accident. In the preceding chapters I have refuted the first four doctrines, merely because they are imperfect, and in this chapter I shall reconcile the temporary with the eternal doctrine. In short, I shall show that even Confucianism is in the right.[390] That is to say, from the beginning there exists Reality (within all beings), which is one and spiritual. It can never be created nor destroyed. It does not increase nor decrease itself. It is subject to neither change nor decay. Sentient beings, slumbering in (the night of) illusion from time immemorial, are not conscious of its existence. As it is hidden and veiled, it is named Tathagata-garbha.[391] On this Tathagata-garbha the mental phenomena that are subject to growth and decay depend. Real Spirit, as is stated (in the Acvaghosa's Çastra), that transcends creation and destruction, is united with illusion, which is subject to creation and destruction; and the one is not absolutely the same as nor different from the other. This union (with illusion) has the two sides of enlightenment and non -enlightenment,' and is called Alaya-vijnyana. Because of non-enlightenment,[392] it first arouses itself, and forms some ideas. This activity

---

[389] A. 'The doctrines refuted above are reconciled with the real doctrine in this chapter. They are all in the right in their pointing to the true origin.'

[390] A. 'The first section states the fifth doctrine that reveals the Reality, and the statements in the following sections are the same as the other doctrines, as shown in the notes.'

[391] A. 'The following statement is similar to the fourth doctrine explained above in the refutation of the phenomenal existence subject to growth and decay.' Compare Çraddhotpada-castra.

[392] A. 'The following statement is similar to the doctrine of Dharma-laksana.'

of the Vijnyana is named 'the state of Karma.[393] Furthermore, since one does not understand that these ideas are unreal from the beginning, they transform themselves into the subject (within) and the object (without), into the seer and the seen. One is at a loss how to understand that these external objects are no more than the creation of his own delusive mind, and believes them to be really existent. This is called the erroneous belief in the existence of external objects.[394] In consequence of these erroneous beliefs, he distinguishes Self and non-self, and at last forms the erroneous belief of Atman. Since he is attached to the form of the Self, he yearns after various objects agreeable to the sense for the sake of the good of his Self. He is offended, (however), with various disagreeable objects, and is afraid of the injuries and troubles which they bring on him. (Thus) his foolish passions[395] are strengthened step by step.

Thus (on one hand) the souls of those who committed the crimes of killing, stealing, and so on, are born, by the influence of the bad Karma, in hell, or among Pretas, or among beasts, or elsewhere. On the other hand, the souls of those who, being afraid of such sufferings, or being good-natured, gave alms, kept precepts, and so on, undergo Antarabhava[396] by the influence of the good Kharma, enter into the womb of their mothers.[397]

There they are endowed with the (so-called) Gas, or material (for body).[398] The Gas first consists of four elements[399] and it gradually forms various

[393] Here Karma simply means an active state; it should be distinguished from Karma, produced by actions.

[394] A. 'The following statement is similar to the second doctrine, or Hinayanism.'

[395] A. 'The following statement is similar to the first doctrine for men and Devas.'

[396] The spiritual existence between this and another life.

[397] A. 'The following statement is similar to Confucianism and Taoism.'

[398] A. 'This harmonizes with the outside opinion that Gas is the origin.'

[399] (1) Earth, (2) water, (3) fire, (4) air.

sense-organs. The mind first consists of the four aggregates,[400] and it gradually forms various Vijnyanas. After the whole course of ten months they are born and called men. These are our present bodies and minds. Therefore we must know that body and mind has each its own origin, and that the two, being united, form one human being. They are born among Devas and Asuras, and so on in a manner almost similar to this.

Though we are born among men by virtue of 'the generalizing Karma,'[401] yet, by the influence of 'the particularizing Karma,'[402] some are placed in a high rank, while others in a low; some are poor, while others rich; some enjoy a long life, while others die in youth; some are sickly, while others healthy; some are rising, while others are falling; some suffer from pains, while others enjoy pleasures. For instance, reverence or indolence in the previous existence, working as the cause, brings forth high birth or low in the present as the effect. So also benevolence in the past results in long life in the present; the taking of life, a short life; the giving of alms, richness, miserliness, Poverty. There are so many particular cases of retribution that cannot be mentioned in detail. Hence there are some who happen to be unfortunate, doing no evil, while others fortunate, doing no good in the present life. So also some enjoy a long life, in spite of their inhuman conduct; while others die young, in spite of their taking no life, and so forth. As all this is predestinated by 'the particularizing Karma' produced in the past, it would seem to occur naturally, quite independent of one's actions in the present life. Outside scholars ignorant of the previous existences, relying simply on their observations, believe it to be nothing more than natural.

Besides, there are some who cultivated virtues in the earlier, and committed crimes in the later, stages of their past existences; while others were vicious in youth, and virtuous in old age. In consequence, some are happy in youth, being rich and noble, but unhappy in old age, being poor and low in the

---

400 (1) Perception, (2) consciousness, (3) conception, (4) knowledge.

401 The Karma that determines different classes of beings, such as men, beasts, Pretas, etc.

402 The Karma that determines the particular state of an individual in the world.

present life; while others lead poor and miserable lives when young, but grow rich and noble when old, and so on. Hence outside scholars come to believe that one's prosperity or adversity merely depends on a heavenly decree.[403]

The body with which man is endowed, when traced step by step to its origin, proves to be nothing but one primordial Gas in its undeveloped state. And the mind with which man thinks, when traced step by step to its source, proves to be nothing but the One Real Spirit. To tell the truth, there exists nothing outside of Spirit, and even the Primordial Gas is also a mode of it, for it is one of the external objects projected by the above-stated Vijnyanas, and is one of the mental images of Alaya, out of whose idea, when it is in the state of Karma, come both the subject and the object. As the subject developed itself, the feebler ideas grow stronger step by step, and form erroneous beliefs that end in the production of Karma.[404] Similarly, the object increases in size, the finer objects grow gradually grosser, and gives rise to unreal things that end in the formation[405] of Heaven and Earth. When Karma is ripe enough, one is endowed by father and mother with sperm and ovum, which, united with his consciousness under the influence of Karma, completes a human form.

According to this view (of Dharmalaksana), things brought forth through the transformations of Alaya and the other Vijnyanas are divided into two parts; one part (remaining), united with Alaya and the other Vijnyanas, becomes man, while the other, becoming separated from them, becomes Heaven, Earth, mountains, rivers, countries, and towns. (Thus) man is the outcome of the union of the two; this is the reason why he alone of the

---

403 A. 'This harmonizes with the outside opinion that everything depends on providence.'

404 A. 'As above stated.'

405 A. "In the beginning, according to the outside school, there was 'the great changeableness,' which underwent fivefold evolutions, and brought out the Five Principles. Out of that Principle, which they call the Great Path of Nature, came the two subordinate principles of the Positive and the Negative. They seem to explain the Ultimate Reality, but the Path, in fact, no more than the 'perceiving division' of the Alaya. The so-called primordial Gas seems to be the first idea in the awakening Alaya, but it is a mere external object."

Three Powers is spiritual. This was taught by the Buddha[406] himself when he stated that there existed two different kinds of the four elements—the internal and the external.[407]

[406] Ratnakuta-sutra (?), translated into Chinese by Jnyanagupta.

Alas! O ye half-educated scholars who adhere to imperfect doctrines, each of which conflicts with another! Ye that seek after truth, if ye would attain to Buddhahood, clearly understand which is the subtler and which is the grosser (form of illusive ideas), which is the originator and which is the originated. (Then) give ye up the originated and return ye to the originator, and to reflect on the Spirit, the Source (of all). When the grosser is exterminated and the subtler removed, the wonderful wisdom of spirit is disclosed, and nothing is beyond its understanding. This is called the Dharma-sambhoga-kaya. It can of itself transform itself and appear among men in numberless ways. This is called the Nirmana-kaya of Buddha.

[407] Every Buddha has three bodies: (1) Dharma-kaya, or spiritual body; (2) Sambhoga-kaya, or the body of compensation; (3) Nirmana-kaya, or the body capable of transformation.

Printed in Great Britain
by Amazon

26640082R10132

Printed in Great Britain
by Amazon

26640082R10132